Praise for Talk Matters!

"A lifelong student of change and conflict, two of the big challenges of our times, Mary Gelinas has provided us with a comprehensive treatment of how to navigate these challenges with wisdom and grace. Drawing from a lifetime of experience, her book does an excellent job of integrating brain science, various wisdom traditions, and the latest and best practices from the social and behavioral sciences. I recommend it highly to anyone who works with groups, organizations, or other human systems."

—Susan Campbell, Ph.D., author of *Getting Real: 10 Truth Skills You Need to Live an Authentic Life, Beyond the Power Struggle,* and *Five-Minute Relationship Repair*

"Mary brings insight to an extremely complex issue — how we communicate — and raises it to a level of simplicity that I can use in my day to day communications with communities, companies and even in my own family."

—Kit Cole, President-elect, International Association for Public Participation USA

"Leaders, managers, and public officials, activists, and organizers: Heed the lessons of this inspiring book! Many of our organizations and institutions are stuck in old paradigms and destructive communication patterns. Mary Gelinas invites us to imagine institutions built on the value of 'we are in this together.' Drawing on new brain science and organizational development insights, Gelinas offers us the tools to transform ourselves and our institutions."

—Chuck Collins, Senior Scholar at Institute for Policy Studies and author of *99 to 1: How Wealth Inequality Is Wrecking the World and What We Can Do about It*

"Mary's gift is breaking through the noise, cutting to the quick, and doing it all with grace and care for the overall mission of the organization, the people we serve, and those of us that work to manifest a complicated vision. When we take the time to bring these three together, thoughtfully, the results are undeniable."

—Amanda Eichel, Special Advisor to Michael R. Bloomberg, UN Secretary-General's Special Envoy for Cities and Climate Change and former COO for the C40 Cities Climate Leadership Group

"This is an important and timely book. At this time in our collective evolution, I cannot think of a more important and less-developed skill than communicating effectively with each other. Mary Gelinas has summarized years of devoted study of this subject in a book that is both deep and accessible. Simply put, through words we create our relationships to the world, for good or ill. Becoming more effective in how we talk with one another will literally change our world. I highly recommend this book for the blossoming of your personal and professional relationships."

—Russell Delman, Founder, The Embodied Life School

"Mary teaches us to hear the poetry between the lines. With deep listening, careful observations, and discernment, we guide ourselves, our businesses, and communities to reach sustainable decisions that ultimately make us all stronger. In *Talk Matters!* we learn how our brains support or inhibit our ability to learn and think together so that we make wise choices. Time is precious. Relationships are our most precious possessions. Mary's research and insight help us protect these valuable parts of life."

—Julie Fulkerson, entrepreneur, facilitator, and musician who has served
Humboldt County, California, as an elected official for 32 years

"*Talk Matters!* is an invaluable contribution to public engagement practices. It provides us with the process savvy to increase our ability to work together across partisan, ethnic, and other divides to address today's toughest problems. Gelinas's work gives us the essential individual and collective keys to being more effective participants in and leaders of our democratic processes."

—Sandy Heierbacher, Director, National Coalition for Dialogue
& Deliberation

"This book is an exquisite operator's manual for anyone who wants to bridge the differences between themselves and others so they can reach across the divides that keep us from thinking really well together. It is like a warm hand on your back, guiding you to develop the kind of mastery our world so sorely needs."

—Dawna Markova, Ph.D., co-author of *Collaborative Intelligence* and
author of *I Will Not Die an Unlived Life: Reclaiming Purpose and Passion*

"*Talk Matters!* fulfills its promise and bridges the exciting new brain science with highly effective conflict management strategies. This extraordinary book provides the tools to resolve seemingly irresolvable challenges. A liberating perspective for turning stumbling blocks into stepping stones."

—Robert Maurer, Ph.D., staff member of University of Washington School of Medicine and Santa Monica UCLA Medical Center and author of *One Small Step Can Change Your Life* and *The Spirit of Kaizen*

"*Talk Matters!* brings to the world the best of what Mary Gelinas has been bringing to my company for decades: increased ability for leaders to have honest, frank conversations that result in stronger relationships and good decisions. I know firsthand how the practices in this book help companies and individuals communicate more effectively up, down, and sideways. She brings us behind the sciences into what is happening in our brains and minds when we talk so that each of us can bring out the innate leadership abilities of ourselves and others."

—Steve O'Meara, President and Founder, Kōkatat

"I have been fortunate to watch Mary Gelinas produce her magic with groups of people in a number of instances, some of which are the subject of examples in this book. Mary's deep listening, compassion, effective tools, and mental clarity free participants to relax with them themselves and understand others, to see new possibilities and create more productive outcomes in ways that are regularly transformative. This book captures her extraordinary gifts in ways that are beautiful, compelling, and made accessible to the rest of us. I did not think it could be done."

—Peter H. Pennekamp, Senior Fellow and Operations Manager of the Community Democracy Workshop, a national program of Philanthropy Northwest; Emeritus Executive Director of Humboldt

"If you have issues in your community that seem to cause a divide that cannot be bridged, then you should read this book and take the insights on conflict resolution to heart. As a director of our special district, I have seen firsthand how the skills and perspectives proposed in Mary's book have been put to work with great success. The result has been better governance and broad support with real trust. This is how government of the people should work."

—Bruce Rupp, Director, Humboldt Bay Municipal Water District

"Dr. Mary Gelinas does an outstanding job of integrating multiple viewpoints about the questions of how we can all communicate, work, and solve problems together. She writes from experience, and she draws upon psychology, physiology, brain science, and common sense in making her case. This book will be valuable to anyone who wants stronger results from meetings, conversations, and any interactions with other people. He goal is nothing less than to save the world!"

—Lisa Rossbacher, Ph.D., President of Humboldt State University and
President Emerita of Southern Polytechnic State University

"Mary Gelinas has written a very important and useful book on how to create more effective conversations and meetings using principles of cutting-edge neuroscience and the timeless wisdom of mindfulness. Essential reading for anyone concerned with building bridges across differences to find better solutions for us all."

—M. J. Ryan, author of *This Year I Will . . .*
and *How to Survive Change . . . You Didn't Ask For*

"*Talk Matters!* What we say and how we say it (and how we indeed 'think' about it and understand how our brains listen and interpret our environment) is critical to the health of our future relationships. Mary's intentionality and attention to the careful design and detail of our human interactions is like a classically trained pianist who plays every note and movement; but then like a jazz pianist, she can throw the written music away and let the people and the moment rise organically to achieve what the group needs to achieve together in that musical moment. Read it. Ingest it. And be thankful for its existence because it will help you and the things you care about communicate better."

—Terry Supahan, Karuk Tribal Member, Executive Director of True North Organizing Network and Senior Fellow with the Community Democracy Workshop, a national program of Philanthropy Northwest

TALK MATTERS!

Saving the World One Word at a Time
Solving Complex Issues Through Brain Science,
Mindful Awareness and Effective Process

by Mary V. Gelinas
with forewords by Julie O'Mara and Pete N. Peterson

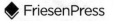 FriesenPress

Suite 300 - 990 Fort St
Victoria, BC, V8V 3K2
Canada

www.friesenpress.com

ISBN
978-1-4602-8632-6 (Hardcover)
978-1-4602-8633-3 (Paperback)
978-1-4602-8634-0 (eBook)

1. SELF-HELP, COMMUNICATION & SOCIAL SKILLS

Distributed to the trade by The Ingram Book Company

Table of Contents

For my best friend and beloved husband, Roger G. James

In honor of my parents, Mary Lonergan Gelinas
and Ulric J. Gelinas, Sr.

Acknowledgments

Every day I'm grateful for the wit, wisdom, and kindness of my husband and business partner, Roger James. I couldn't have written this book without his counsel, reviews, and support. He's a generous and insightful thinking partner. In over 25 years of working together, we have developed the theory and practices that are the foundation of this book.

I've been graced with two great teachers in my life. Angeles Arrien believed in me and in this book for many years. She was scheduled to write the Foreword for it but died in 2014 before its completion. I remain honored that she wanted to. Russell Delman's teachings helped me create the awareness and focus on which this book rests. I'm a more effective and compassionate consultant, facilitator, writer, and human being because of what I've learned from him.

Nancy Dye, good friend and editor extraordinaire, made invaluable suggestions that improved the clarity of the writing and helped emphasize key ideas. Her insights inspired me. Melanie

Bettenhausen's comments and edits were spot-on and encouraging. Lori James helped me avoid errors with brain science. I'm grateful to all three and, of course, am responsible for any lack of clarity or misunderstandings about the science.

I'm thankful for Heather Equinoss's drawings along with her noteworthy facilitation and visual recording abilities. In many meetings, I would have been lost without her.

Dawna Markova consistently encouraged me to "write the book only I could write." I've done my best to do just that. Denise Vanden Bos and Julie Fulkerson provided steadying and generous friendship throughout.

For inspiration, encouragement, friendship, and camaraderie while writing this book, I wholeheartedly appreciate Sue and Bill Agnew, Heidi Bourne, Karen Buckley, Susan Stuart Clark, Kit Cole, Tina Dawson, Brenda Donahoe, Nancy French, Elysia Frink, Joe Gelinas, Michael and Georgene Gelinas, Alicia Hamann, Amy Jester, Marshall Kaufman, Carolyn Lukensmeyer, Lee Leer, Joe Mark, Peggy Mark, Robert Maurer, Julie O'Mara, Peter Pennekamp, Pete N. Peterson, Brenda Rasch, Kristy Regan, Jen Rice, Roxanne Suprina, Simeon Tauber, and Marion Vittitow.

For courage and foresight, I applaud the Board of Directors and staff of the Humboldt Bay Municipal Water District as well as members of the Advisory Group of its Water Resource Planning Process. They demonstrated what is possible and set the gold standard for public process in northern California. I'm grateful to directors Barbara Hecathorn, Aldaron Laird, J. Bruce Rupp, Kaitlin Sopoci-Belknap, and Sheri Woo as well as staff member Sherrie Sobol and former general manager Carol Rische. In addition to Rupp and Sopoci-Belknap, Advisory Group members included

Jacqueline Debets, Verne R. Frost, Michelle Fuller, Jana Ganion, David Lindberg, Dennis Mayo, Dennis Mullins, Pete Nichols, Jim Smith, William Thorington, Dave Varshok, and Mark Wheetley.

I still lean on what I learned in the early days from friends and colleagues in and around Interaction Associates, Inc.: Geoff Ball, Cathy DeForest, Michael Donahoe, Michael Doyle, Peter Gibb, Rae Levine, Sharon Jeffrey Lehrer, George Long, Vic Ortiz, Barry Rosen, Leslie Salmon-Zhu, William Spencer, and David Straus. And for those who guided me even before the early days, I bow in gratitude to Pete Abrahams, Juanita Brown, Mary Curran, Richard Keyes, and Jean M. Westcott.

Foreword

The time has come for us to get serious about the way we talk with each other. All of us. All around the world.

I am writing this foreword as 2015 draws to a close and as fear of "the other" seems to be gaining over understanding of different viewpoints and respect. It is a sad, concerning state we are in. And it is very clear that how we talk matters.

Some of the fear is fueled by politicians with big egos and groups banded by ethnocentric points of view—some are well-meaning fundamentalists, some are members of longstanding religious and secular institutions, and some are terrorists. It seems that what they share is anxiety, fear, and anger blamed on "the other." Many don't want to or don't know how to talk about something that seems to be—and may be—a vehement disagreement. The only solution appears to be taking sides and fighting.

Mary's book brings us hope. Hope in the form of practical, well-researched, thoughtful behaviors and skills that we can all put into practice.

Here are two of the book's key messages I'd like to emphasize.

First, it's brilliant to identify and elevate the importance of eight essential practices that enable us to engage constructively with people who differ from us in order to tackle the complex issues facing us locally, nationally, and globally at work and in our communities. All the practices are within our capability because we don't have to wait for anyone else to do anything. We can just change our behavior. No waiting. No whining.

Second, one of the practices is especially meaningful to me: "listening attentively to understand what others are saying and feeling —why what they are saying is important to them." It reminds me of the words of a colleague: "Listen to others as if they are wise." Reflect on that for a moment. It doesn't presume that you agree with the other, but it does ask for listening first. Too often we go into interactions with the intention of disagreement.

One of the first thoughts I had when reading Mary's manuscript was how easy, comforting, intriguing and informative her writing is. Her book is consistent with her message of helping us all find a way to bridge the divides we have in our lives, organizations, and communities. I could read her book again and again. It inspires me to do this work.

I once told a colleague that Mary was the "real thing." What I mean by that is that in her consulting, facilitating, and teaching, she embodies what she writes about. This book is yet another example of her sincerity and congruence.

I'm glad Mary had the courage to put "save the world" in the title. What a bold statement. This book has already changed one of my behaviors. I've tended to brush off "save the world" in a humorous put-down way. When people ask me what I'm doing now (some think I'm retired), I say, "Well, I'm still trying to save the world." I'm going to stop joking about that. The world needs saving.

Publishers are keen to put books into categories, usually to position them in catalogues or on a shelf . . . but finding the right category for Mary's book is tough. I, of course, see it as a diversity and inclusion book. And it is also a management and leadership book for business, nonprofits, and government; an organizational development book; a self-help/personal growth book; a parenting book; a current affairs book; and, well, too many categories. But that's a good thing, as there are a lot of ways to get the key points of the book into the hands, hearts, and minds of those who might most benefit.

Talk Matters! needs to be read by those who might not find it. So that is the job of you, the reader. First read it, and then use the vehicles and platforms you have to spread the word. There are hundreds of tweetable statements and passages that can go into blogs, articles, book chapters, presentations, and speeches. Spread the word and give the book to others.

Julie O'Mara

Co-author of *Global Diversity and Inclusion Benchmarks: Standards for Organizations Around the World* and *Managing Workforce 2000*

Member, Board of Directors, Berrett-Koehler Publishers, Inc.

In 2015, named to *The Economist's* Global Diversity List of Top 50 Diversity Professionals in Industry with co-author Alan Richter and honored as the Diversity Legacy Leader by the Forum for Workplace Inclusion

Foreword

A recent survey of California public sector officials' views of public engagement yielded several disturbing results. The project, titled "Testing the Waters: California's Local Officials Experiment with New Ways to Engage the Public," interviewed 900 elected and administrative municipal government leaders across a variety of entities (city, county, special district). Importantly, these officials had served an average term of 22 years in public service.

Several data points leap out from the dozens of questions asked. First, 76 percent of those surveyed believed their public meetings are "typically dominated by people with narrow agendas." Related, 69 percent of these experienced public servants felt that "community members have become much angrier and mistrustful of public officials in recent years." And 69 percent believed that "a lack of resources and staff could stand in the way of a deliberative public engagement approach."

Taken together, these three results form what I call the "Trilemma of Public Engagement in the Public Sector": 1) Officials know they have to engage their residents; 2) They often dislike the residents they have to engage; and 3) They wonder whether they have the skills or resources on staff to more effectively involve their publics.

This Trilemma is on display in so many efforts to engage citizens in the hard work of solving fundamental policy challenges on issues ranging from the services our governments offer to the design of the places we live to the ways in which we educate our next generation of citizens and so much more.

In an era of declining trust in our governing institutions and decreasing levels of civic participation, if and how we can resolve this Trilemma may be the most crucial question facing American democracy.

Years of training and consulting with public sector officials in how to improve their public participation efforts have taught me a simple but profound truth: Often, the problem that ticks at the heart of our Trilemma is not the public, and it's not our public leaders; it is the process by which government generally engages us. The tragic irony is that what passes for public engagement in most American cities—usually called "public comment"—is often the least inclusive, least informative, and least collaborative way for any bureaucracy to listen to its constituents.

The hallowed American tradition of the town hall meeting has degenerated into a place of confrontation where the "three minutes at a microphone" format precludes the exchange of information between public agency and public and prevents any engagement *between* members of the public. And this is part of the dynamic that we rarely consider—that for many of our most contentious public challenges, our standard public meeting doesn't even allow us to talk to one another, to work with government to discover what has been known as a "common sense"—a sense of what we agree on in common.

I have sketched the outlines of what is nothing less than a broken relationship between government and citizens. I have described what is dysfunctional but have not gone further. We did not get here overnight, and the reasons behind this current state of affairs run deeper than simply fixing our public hearing procedures. But it does include that.

What excites me most about Mary Gelinas's work and the pages you're about to read is that for the first time, the connection is made between how we engage one another and why it's not working. She compares the regular public processes and the latest in brain research to reach a provocative conclusion: Many of the ways government agencies engage the public in creating policy actually trigger defensiveness, a lack of deliberative thought, and an inability to consider multiple perspectives.

Mary brings a uniquely important background to this project. An expert facilitator, she understands the importance of process design and creating environments that promise the best opportunities for collaborative decision-making. But as a student of the brain and its role in interpersonal communications, she is able to take us into the inner workings of our minds, to show what happens when the wrong process decisions are made or the wrong types of questions are asked.

The public leader will find an "a-ha moment" on almost every page. As the earlier referenced survey data notes, most experienced public sector officials know their public processes are counterproductive, and this book provides answers you can apply to your next staff meeting and your next council meeting.

This book could not come at a more important time. The scale and scope of our public policy challenges—from the local to the national levels—has never been greater. On issues ranging from budgets and land use to public safety and environmental regulations, it's no wonder that Bob O'Neill—the head of the International City/County Management Association—recently dubbed this time as an "era of creative destruction in government."

In an essay listing some of the reasons behind this destructive environment—from fiscal challenges to demographic changes to technological impacts—O'Neill calls for a "new brand of leadership" by which problems are solved more collaboratively and transparently.

So in very real ways, what Mary Gelinas has given us here with *Talk Matters!* is not so much a book about communications and public decision-making as a book to prepare public leaders for the 21st century. For this, we as citizens and leaders, should all be thankful.

Pete N. Peterson

Dean, Pepperdine School of Public Policy

Former Executive Director,
Davenport Institute for Public Engagement & Civic Leadership

TALK MATTERS!

Introduction

Now, if you ask me, what's going on is that we're all up to here in it, and probably the most important thing is that we not yell at one another.

—Anne Lamott

We *are* all up to here in serious issues, and it seems that more often than not, we *are* yelling at one another.

The need for us to work together has never been greater. As the problems facing us get more numerous and serious, we're less able to deal with them. As members of work teams and communities, and as citizens of this country and the world, we all can point to the complex issues we face, like access to clean air and water, terrorism, healthcare, climate change, education, inequality, safety, and security. The best that most of our leaders seem to be able to do these days, especially in political arenas, is frighten and divide us. This creates a sense of "us" and "them." But there is *only* an "us." There is only you and me and all the other *you*s and *me*s on the planet to figure out the perfect storm of issues in which we swim.

This is why I want to talk with you about how we talk with one another. It matters more than you might think. It matters because we shape the present and future every day in our interactions. How we speak, listen, and ask questions affects the quality of our understanding and thinking and therefore the quality of our decisions. It also significantly affects how we feel about one another. Are we friends or foes?

We all have different degrees of concern about different issues. Perhaps the notion of "enlightened self-interest" might inspire us to interact more effectively across the boundaries that interfere with our working together to tackle tough, interconnected issues. What I mean by *enlightened self-interest* is that we simultaneously look out for ourselves while looking out for others. We do this because we understand that getting what we need means we must consider what all of us need in the short and long term. For example, multiple studies indicate that the crime rate increases when unemployment increases and the crime rate declines when the unemployment rate declines. If we care about safety and security, we also need to care about unemployment.

So how might we get better at working together in our interactions at home, at work, and in our communities and legislative bodies? How might we learn to listen and speak across and through that which divides us so that *together* we can take on the challenges we face in multiple and overlapping arenas?

My quest to answer these questions began over 40 years ago in a dorm room at a university on Long Island, New York. I was a 22-year-old student at Northeastern University in Boston working as an intern at what was then the U.S. Office of Education. In 1970, I was writing a piece for *American Education* magazine about four federally funded drug education training centers. My first stop was at Adelphi University.

Picture a circle of 12 students, teachers, administrators, and school board members sitting on the floor listening to Sam, a slender 16-year-old whose face was hidden behind a curtain of hair. This high school sophomore was explaining why he smoked dope every morning on the way to school. I was leaning against a wall outside the circle, listening to the group discuss how to approach this challenge.

It was difficult to distinguish teachers and administrators from students; most had long hair and were wearing cut-offs and tie-dyed t-shirts on that warm afternoon. Sam was looking down at the carpet on which he sat cross-legged as he haltingly described how "cool" being stoned made him feel and how it earned him inclusion in the "in" group. As he flicked the ashes off his cigarette and pulled the hair out of his eyes, he exclaimed, "It's the only way I can get through the day at school. It's so boring."

One of the teachers leaned back, folded his arms, and sighed. "I am so frustrated," he said. "You don't understand how all of this affects your health, education, and really your whole future."

Sam slowly nodded his head and whispered, "Maybe."

The conversation continued as the afternoon wore on and the temperature dropped. People listened intently, asked tough questions, and spoke passionately. At times they disagreed vociferously, just managing to avoid yelling at one another. It was a life-changing surprise for me: a heartfelt, intimate, honest, respectful, and productive conversation among people of different ages and points of view. They closed with an understanding that belied their differences in age, gender, race, culture, and political leanings. Although they did not all assent to the dangers of drugs, they did agree that they wanted to work together to create more meaningful and engaging activities for kids in their community.

That afternoon, I fell in love with the breathtaking possibilities of conversations about things that matter. To this very moment, I remain passionately intrigued with what happens when we work hard to understand others' points of view and how they arrived at them; when we communicate a perspective that differs from that of others as simply a different outlook rather than the irrefutable truth; when we talk about what is really important to us and why; when we're open to new ways of thinking; and when we seek outcomes that benefit not just one or a few of us but all of us.

I've facilitated thousands of conversations in organizations and communities large and small since that afternoon, in a blur of various settings around the world as well as in my own community. In that time, I have seen miracles: A traditionally polarized community agreed on how it wanted to protect and use its water; thousands of doctors and staff in a teaching hospital came together to transform how they work to better serve patients and cut costs; and a manufacturing company changed its culture from top-down command and control to collaboration.

Now, as a business leader, community member, consultant, educator, process designer, and facilitator, I have a more nuanced understanding of how deceptively simple yet truly difficult it is to converse effectively across the boundaries of age and ethnicity, experience and titles, class and ideology. Still, I continue to be amazed at the potential of good conversation and at the significant difference individual skill and good process design make in coming to well-considered decisions.

In my quest to help people have productive conversations about things that matter, I've been investigating the elements that effective approaches to human interactions have in common. As I've been busy doing this, scientists have been diligently probing the workings of the human brain, including the impact of mindfulness practices on it. Although the research, like much of brain science, is still in its infancy, results increasingly indicate that we can, by practicing mindful awareness, learn to manage the primitive survival habits of the brain. Through the miracle of neuroplasticity, we can change our brains. This is key to being more constructive in our interactions, especially when we're polarized around difficult issues. Because of the fruits of brain research and decades of experimentation with processes to improve human interaction, we know how to design, conduct, and participate in processes that result in good, even wise decisions.

For the first time in human history, we know enough about the human brain as well as about effective communication strategies and meeting design to help us (a) manage the more primitive parts of the brain, (b) interact constructively, and (c) design and conduct productive collaborative problem-solving sessions with groups of 2 to 200 or more. Given this knowledge, we can use what we know to help us work across ideological, professional, cultural, racial, economic, and social differences.

Imagine the impact of millions of constructive conversations occurring every day at work and in our communities. Envision the creative solutions that might emerge. When we apply what we now know about ourselves and effective interactions, we come upon a well of universal compassion and aspiration in which our divisiveness seems foolish and unnecessary. Such experiences help us know, down to the marrow in our bones, that we are in this together.

Regardless of whether you're a leader or a participant in interactions at work, in your community, or in a legislative body, you can make a positive and consequential difference to the quality of any interaction and therefore to the quality of what comes out of it. This book will help you do the following:

- understand essential information about the brain and the impact of emotions on it;
- learn how to calm and manage its reactive survival instincts;
- communicate in ways that build relationships and move a conversation forward; and
- custom-design conversational or meeting processes that help participants understand complex issues and work together to solve them.

If you want to create effective, even transformative, conversations with colleagues, with leaders at work or in your community, or with neighbors and family members, this book is for you.

Section One: Why and How Talk Matters makes the case for why talking better together has never been more important, describes the forces that are creating a perfectly human conversational storm, and introduces the propositions underlying the eight practices that are the focus of this book. This section provides pertinent information about the human brain and explains what emotions are, how they impact us, and why they get evoked when we interact in groups. Finally, this part of the book lays the conceptual and scientific foundation for the eight practices that are the focus of the remaining three sections.

Section Two: Managing Our Survival Instincts elucidates three practices that help us manage the survival instincts in the brain, with information on what mindful awareness is, how to develop it, and the impact of mindfulness meditation on the structure and functioning of the brain. This section describes how defining intentions for interactions can guide our conduct when we're interacting with others. It also explains how mindful awareness and intentions can help us take advantage of the brain's ability to change itself through neuroplasticity by making conscious choices and being open to change.

Section Three: Interacting Constructively focuses on three practices that are instrumental to our ability to interact effectively. It describes how compassion helps us interact capably with others, especially those who differ from us. The section considers why it can be challenging to talk with those who differ from us and elucidates the six essential communication skills that are critical to interacting constructively.

Section Four: Designing Productive Conversational Processes explains how to design individual meetings and processes involving multiple meetings. It provides tips and tools on how to plan and conduct effective meetings that build collaboration. It also explains how to design process architecture to help stakeholder groups collaboratively investigate and solve complex issues over time.

While writing this book, I had a dream. In it, hundreds of people stand in rows in a large field of knee-high, yellow-green grass swaying in the sun. Each of us holds multicolor filaments of light and color looped around our fingers, and our arms are spread as far apart as they can go. We spin these luminescent threads in front of our hearts in wide, arcing circles like a human loom, singing with the world. This book is one of those threads. What you say in your next conversation is another. Together we weave a new story of light and sound for our world.

Section One:
Why Talk Matters

Chapter 1:
Navigating a Perfectly Human Storm

We obviously cannot confront this tangled world alone. . . . It takes no great insight to realize that we have no choice but to think together, ponder together, in groups and communities.

—Jacob Needleman

I love the wild, titillating summer storms in the Berkshire Mountains of western Massachusetts. As a child, I spun around on the grass and shouted with joy at the first scent of impending rain as rolling thunder approached and gusts of wind exposed the silver underbellies of maple leaves. I didn't understand how dangerous these storms could be. "Nor'easters" are as perilous as the perfectly human storms we create in our meetings.

Every day, we meet with co-workers on the job, talk with neighbors in our communities, or speak at public hearings in towns and cities. But we have a problem—a potentially disastrous one. The way we talk with one another and try to solve problems is, for the most part, not working. Too often we get immobilized by not being able to understand or relate across different points of view. As the problems facing us become more numerous and serious, we're becoming less able to deal with them.

A sea of difficult issues are colliding with three additional forces and creating a perfect storm that is undermining our ability to create a desirable future. These forces are the survival instincts of the human brain, ineffective or destructive communication, and archaic meeting processes.

The grave problems facing our organizations and communities are urgent. We no longer have time for truculent and unproductive discussions that lead to stalemate, destructive compromises, and downright bad decisions. Although such interactions might allow us to feel temporarily satisfied when we express righteous indignation at the wrongheadedness of others, we diminish our ability and desire to learn and think effectively with them.

Of course, there are conversational bright spots here and there at work and in our communities. We just need to ignite a lot more of them, particularly around the issues that are threatening the quality of our lives and the life of the planet as a whole. Three largely untapped resources can help us do this. First, brain research is accumulating evidence that when we meditate mindfully, we quiet the amygdala, the alarm bell in the brain, making it less likely that we'll feel threatened and be triggered emotionally. Practicing mindfulness strengthens the connections between the newer and older parts of the brain, enabling us to make conscious choices about how we want to respond to difficult situations in which we find ourselves instead of reacting in self-protective ways like fighting, fleeing, or freezing. This form of mental training also strengthens the sense of compassion we feel for others so that it doesn't get drowned out by the warning signals coming from the midbrain.

Second, we know from research and experience that certain behaviors promote effective communication and engender a sense of safety and inclusion. These help us avoid derailment of meetings or the damage to relationships that occurs when we speak out of fear or anger. It is harder to use skills like listening, asking good questions, or speaking in inclusive (versus authoritarian) ways when we become reactive and are driven by the defensive maneuvers of the older areas of the brain.

Third, innovative and effective conversational processes (e.g., Dialogue, Future Search conferences, Open Space Technology, and World Cafés) continue to emerge and transform conversations in our organizations and communities. The burgeoning knowledge about the human brain allows us to custom-design and conduct meetings more productively than many of us of have been able to do previously. Do not underestimate the positive difference that an effective process can make in empowering people to work together to solve problems. The future is not a place we're being driven to; it's a place we have the opportunity to create through our interactions.

Three Bodies of Knowledge

Brain science & mindfulness

Effective
communication skills

Innovative
conversational forms

When we weave together what we know about the human brain with behaviors that promote effective communication, along with the best elements of effective approaches to conversational processes, we come to a set of universal practices that help us work better together to understand and make headway with the complex and difficult issues facing us. I call them "practices" because there seems to be no end to learning how to use them ever more skillfully. When applied with good intentions, these practices increase the likelihood that any approach to solving problems, developing policies, or making decisions will achieve the desired results. These eight practices are

- making conscious choices;
- defining intentions;
- opening to change;
- being compassionate;
- engaging with people who differ from us;

- using six indispensable communication skills;
- creating collaboration in meetings; and
- tackling complex issues together.

Before describing the practices, let's take a closer look at why they're needed now more than ever before: the four colliding forces that create this perfectly human storm.

Four Forces Creating a Perfectly Human Storm

Destructive communication

Brain's Survival instincts

Archaic Processes

Complex issues & people

Force One: Complexity of Issues and People

The issues facing us are complex because they are interconnected and have diverse, interdependent elements that can't be understood or solved by tackling any single element. They're also complex because we need to work with others across multiple perspectives to solve them. Regardless of whether we're working in an organization or working on a local, regional, national, or global level, we need to engage effectively with diverse stakeholders. We cannot understand, let alone solve, complex issues by working in ideological, organizational, or professional bubbles.

For instance, drought-prone California grants water rights to licensed agencies. In one municipal water district that provided water to several cities and towns, the water-guzzling pulp mills that had largely underwritten the cost of the district's infrastructure and domestic water had closed. If the district didn't find new uses for the water, it would lose the rights to it; the state could then grant those rights to someone else.

The district decided to create a collaborative process that engaged multiple stakeholders, including environmentalists, business and union leaders, economic development specialists, and content experts, to help them figure out what to do. They found out that if they sold water to drier regions, they would need to consider the impact of less water on the watershed, the fish, the estuary, and the fishermen, farmers, and ranchers who depended on it, along with the financial and environmental costs of moving the water via pipes. They also needed to make this decision in a volatile political environment in a region that lived in the shadow of the painful legacy of the "timber wars" of the '90s. Memories of these battles tended to keep the fires of different political camps burning.

Complex Issues. The water district's challenge was local. However, it's similar to many others that we face regionally, nationally, and globally in that it was complex and required engaging productively with people who differ from one another. Other complex issues include wealth inequality, poverty, and homelessness; lack of access to good air, water, healthcare, and education; environmental degradation and climate change; political turmoil, violence, and refugees fleeing both; and access to weapons large and small. The labels for these issues belie the individual and collective human suffering that each of these words represents.

Such issues are daunting. Whether you focus on their global, national, or local manifestation, it's hard to wrap your head or heart around any one of them. In the face of complexity, we can feel a sense of helplessness that pushes us into two different reactions: stay below deck where it feels safer or blame anyone we think might be in a position to do something useful. Blame seems to be the modus operandi in the political arena and can often be found at work—we criticize colleagues in another department or political camp, censure the mayor, blame the boss, or conduct recall elections.

Blaming enemies "out there" distracts us from the fear and anger many of us feel "in here" that might motivate us to get involved to tackle these issues. Blaming also evokes defensiveness and escalates conflict. It focuses on the past when we need to be looking toward the future. I understand how tempting it can be to just yell at someone, anyone. However, if we continue to blame other individuals, organizations, or political parties, we just make our perfectly human storm worse.

Diverse Stakeholders. To understand and solve complex issues, we need to work with people with different backgrounds and points of view. This includes those who make decisions and those who are affected by them.

Consider any single public meeting in your city or town. Who shows up? Women and men; old, young, and middle-aged; conservatives, liberals, and middle-of-the-roaders; the rich, the poor, and the middle class; the educated and the not-so-educated; those who speak English and those who don't; people of different races, ethnicities, and sexual orientations; and people who are accustomed to meetings or speaking in public and those for whom it's an alien and frightening prospect. Meetings at work also include co-workers with different jobs, professional expertise, and experience; various levels of formal decision-making authority; and different styles of leadership. Given all these differences and dynamics, each time a group of people successfully works together to solve a problem, we should all leap up and applaud.

An Invitation from the Universe. The combination of dealing with complex issues and diverse stakeholders can intimidate even the strongest of hearts. It's tempting to tell ourselves, "I'm only one person, without power in the world. Surely I can't make a difference." Each of us is a kind of Jonah standing before God, crying, "God, you can't mean me!"

There are some who say, "Why bother?" or who discount those of us who continue to be hopeful for the good that might still be accomplished. Their cynicism enjoins us to believe that (a) most issues are too big, too complex, or simply intractable and (b) it's impossible to bridge the great divides among us.

We can't afford the comfort of cynicism or hunkering down in our foxholes, hoping that somehow things will work out by themselves. Our quality of life and perhaps even life itself is at stake. As Dag Hammarskjöld, second Secretary-General of the United Nations, stated in 1958,

> I cannot belong to or join those who believe in our movement toward catastrophe. I believe in growth, a growth to which we have a responsibility to add our few fractions of an inch. [This] is not the facile faith of generations before us, who thought that everything was arranged for the best in the best of worlds. . . . It is in a sense a much harder belief—the belief and faith that the future will be all right because there will always be enough people to fight for a decent future. (Lipsey, 2010, p. 29)

What if you were to view this sea of complexity as an earnest invitation from the universe to radically reshape how you manage yourself in interactions and reconsider your role in shaping the future for good?

Force Two: Self-Protective Habits of the Brain

Because the human brain developed to keep us alive, it constantly scans the environment for anything that might harm us. Although day-to-day interactions involve far fewer real threats than we might imagine, the habits of the brain remain steadfast and incline us to notice what might harm us more than we notice what might help us. It has what psychologist Rick Hanson calls a "negativity bias."

Because the brain is focused on our survival, it loves certainty and abhors unpredictability. Thus, we can feel threatened when working on complex issues for which there are usually no known answers. Wading into a myriad of interconnected issues with too much, too little, or conflicting information tends to evoke anxiety at the very least and anger at most. This is one reason it's so tempting for people to fall back onto preconceived beliefs or positions. They feel safer with what they think they know.

In addition to the unnerving experience of dealing with complex issues, engaging with diverse groups can be frightening because we feel safer talking with people who are like us or who think as we do. In the face of difference, especially when the issues at hand are important to us, we can become anxious, even angry, as the more primitive parts of the brain take charge and drive us to do combat, flee the scene, or play possum. Although we might appear okay on the surface, underneath we've lost access to the newer brain circuits' executive functions, including understanding new ideas, making conscious decisions, and managing our social behavior. In order to solve tough problems with others, we need to have access to the whole brain. We have that only when we feel safe.

Force Three: Communicating Ineffectively or Destructively

Your brain reacts swiftly and strongly when it perceives, rightly or wrongly, a threat to your safety. So although there are probably no lions, tigers, or bears in your meetings, the brain can perceive ineffective or destructive communication as threatening.

Interactions can be perceived as threatening when we
- don't listen;
- interrupt one another;
- criticize others' ideas or one another as human beings;

- speak as if our opinions are the truth, the only truth;
- ask false questions like "Don't you think that . . . ?" (these are simply sneaky ways for us to say what we think); or
- hold fixed and critical views of others, even if they're unstated.

Think about when you've been at the receiving end of any of these and its impact on your emotions, thoughts, and motivation to contribute constructively to a conversation.

These behaviors can feel like a threat because they challenge basic human needs that are inexorably linked to our sense of safety. I've already noted the need for certainty. Our other needs are to (a) maintain a sense of position or status (i.e., a sense of identity); (b) have choice, retain a sense of autonomy; (c) experience a connection with others; and finally, (d) perceive a conversational process as fair (Rock, 2009, pp. 195–197).

When any one of these needs is menaced, we can easily begin to see the person who, for example, interrupts us or criticizes our ideas as an object to be interrupted or criticized in turn. We can easily lose a sense of others' humanity and, as a result, also lose our ability to talk respectfully with them. Is it any wonder how quickly interactions can become destructive and unproductive? As soon as people start interrupting one another, criticizing others' ideas, or talking as if they're the only ones who have the right answers, others follow suit. At times, we're more adept at creating circular firing squads than we are at engaging one another in constructive and meaningful ways.

Force Four: Archaic and Unproductive Processes

We create our own headwinds when we try to navigate this roiling sea of complexity with inadequate, outdated, and ineffective processes that don't take advantage of what we know about effective human interactions and the brain. Just when our meetings need to generate new possibilities, archaic processes seem to narrow the solution space into *either/or* thinking and polarize people into warring camps.

Processes can be inadequate or downright destructive in several ways.

1) Excluding Voices. First, processes are inadequate when leaders assume a complex issue can be solved by a select group of decision-makers who are heads of an organization, a small group of elected government officials, or hand-picked players—in other words, when processes are exclusive. When a process excludes those who have the most direct knowledge or have the most at stake in the issues at hand, it guarantees that the issue will not be solved for two reasons:

- **Those closest to the issue usually have the best ideas for solving it.** In communities, these people could be the residents who are most affected by plans for rerouting public transportation. In organizations, they could be those who perform the work or are closest to the customers or clients.
- **People who have the most at stake in the issue are the ones who will be most committed to implementing solutions or supporting those responsible for implementation.** If stakeholders aren't involved in the process in some way, they won't willingly support executing solutions unless they're forced to.

This is particularly true in organizations. Solutions implemented with compliance instead of commitment rarely have the desired effect. In public processes when the stakes are high and people are excluded from the decision-making process, their sense of fairness can seem so endangered that they sue an agency or organization to prevent a solution from being carried out.

2) Reducing a Problem to Its Parts. Processes fall short when they reduce complex issues to their components. It's easier to develop solutions to discrete elements of a problem, and these solutions can evoke a sense that at least something is being accomplished. But they'll likely be ineffective because the connections among the issues and the underlying causes aren't addressed. For example, a lack of access to healthy food can't be solved without looking at a community's transportation system, the locations of markets and their offerings, and people's financial resources and buying habits. When the process steps don't invite people to investigate root causes or how a problem interacts with other issues, individuals tend to focus exclusively on the part of the issue that most concerns them. This narrowed focus can quickly divide a group into competing camps, and the solutions rarely last.

3) Limiting Systemic Thinking. When the process prevents people from understanding the causes and interconnections of the issue at hand, they're less able to think systemically. In organizations divided into functional areas, people get used to thinking of a problem from their particular vantage point—for example, from research and development, marketing and sales, or production. It's usually only when an organization-wide project arises, like changing an information technology platform, that they're asked to work across functions and think about the organization as a whole. In governmental organizations, it's a rare chief administrative officer or city manager who would ask, for example, the departments responsible for public health, childcare, public transportation, and economic development to work with the business community to create jobs. Also, activists tend to advocate for their issues or solutions separately from others. For example, at public hearings, elected bodies listen to the testimony of those pushing for more childcare facilities separately from those advocating for a more business-friendly environment.

4) Polarizing Groups. The fourth way archaic or unproductive processes add to the perfect storm might be the most destructive. Ineffective processes tend to exacerbate the divisions among people who work in different organizational units or who affiliate with community members who have similar political perspectives. At their worst, they harden people's points of view into positions, separate them into opposing camps, and corrode a sense of connection or community. People can be more polarized at the end of an interaction than they were at the beginning.

When the process doesn't explicitly invite people to understand the points of view of others, all they can hear is their own position and those who support it. Ultimately, this instigates people to vilify one another either during or outside of meetings and makes it that much harder for people to interact constructively in the future.

5) Establishing Status with Room Arrangements. The fifth and final aspect of process that is often overlooked—and whose impact is underestimated—is how you arrange a room for a meeting or conversation. Room arrangements can, by themselves, make people anxious and undermine their ability to speak and think rationally.

Consider the impact on individuals unused to speaking in public or into a microphone when they have to stand in line to talk to an elected body sitting above them on a dais. When residents sit in rows facing elevated decision-makers, it sends a message: We decision-makers will decide whose view is important. Such room arrangements encourage people to talk *at* one another, not with one another.

The processes of businesses and other organizations are similarly ineffective but in different ways. More often than not, employees sit around a large, rectangular table with the boss at its head. When asked to say something, people either remain silent or respond tentatively, testing the waters for how forthright they can be.

In either setting, the sense of not being seen or heard or of being treated as "less than" generates an anxiety or anger that can impair people's ability to think and communicate their thoughts clearly and constructively. This is a sad waste of human talent and doesn't help us create solutions for the complex issues so in need of our considered attention.

Certainly, many successful organizations and communities conduct meetings more effectively than this. We can make this more the norm than the exception. What might be possible in our communities and organizations if every one of us were to believe that *how* we talk with one another is as important as what we talk about?

Consider what we might be able to accomplish together if, instead of interrupting one another and making authoritative pronouncements, we each listened attentively to others and shared our perspectives as just that: one person's point of view. What new possibilities might open up if we were to make the conscious and courageous choice to work hard to understand the points of view of others and how they came to have them, especially of those who differ from us?

Propositions Underlying the Practices

During my college years, I questioned everything. My father wisely understood the rebellious context of the '60s and early '70s in which I was thrashing about. His counsel was "I don't care what you believe in, as long as you believe in something." And so I do. I believe in the good we can do when we interact in ways that encourage us to bring the best of who we are to bear on difficult issues. I believe in our individual and collective ability to create a desirable future together. In fact, working together is the *only* way we can create it.

Here is what I've learned from designing, facilitating, and participating in thousands of meetings; investigating relevant research about the brain; and practicing mindfulness. These propositions are the reasons I believe the eight practices described in this book are critical to the effectiveness of our conversations, especially about consequential issues.

Our Survival Depends on Our Ability to Talk Better Together. Our ability to bridge differences and converse constructively is essential to the survival of our organizations and communities, our democracy, and, most likely, the world as we know it. By "constructive," I mean conversing in ways that strengthen and further collaboration.

This means managing the harmful effects of the self-protective habits in the brain; using foundational communication skills adeptly; and designing and conducting fruitful interactions (meetings, conversations, public hearings, and informal gatherings). We can no longer ignore the impact of mindless participation, destructive communication, and inadequate processes on our ability to understand difficult issues and develop promising solutions. In fact, I believe we need to advocate for mindful participation, constructive communication skills, and adroitly designed and conducted meetings.

We Need All of Us to Get to Where We Want to Go. There are possibilities that can be found or created only when diverse individuals and groups think and learn in concert. You might miss what others see or know. They might miss the same in you. Every person has something of value from which we can learn or that will help move the cause forward (understand and solve the problem, achieve the goal). In the web of relationships that gets woven in interactions, an intelligence or wisdom grows that differs from and is more than what resides in any individual.

Process Matters. *How* we interact with one another affects the quality of our listening, understanding, learning, thinking, speaking, and decision-making. Interactions have an impact far beyond individual events. Process affects not only the quality of our interactions (meetings, conversations, gab fests) but also the quality of the decisions and actions that come out of them. The past becomes the future through each moment of an interaction, and process significantly affects what occurs in each moment.

We Need to Ask Really Big Questions. It's difficult to adequately respond to pressing questions at work or tackle issues in our communities because we try to do so without having considered the bigger questions and issues underlying them. For example,

What are the fundamental principles of human rights and well-being that we want to guide every decision we make in our institutions (public, private, or nonprofit)?

How do we balance current priorities with the desire to pass on a healthy and peaceful world to our children?

What is the Common Good, or the Greatest Good for the Greatest Number? And who cares?

How do we expand our sense of time and space so that we think in terms of whole, living systems, not just the symptomatic issues that rear their heads or grab the day's headlines?

How do we evolve our individual and collective process intelligence so we can understand and solve complex issues in concert with others?

Emotions, Thoughts, and Actions Have Consequences. Simultaneously, our emotions affect our thinking and behavior, our thinking affects our emotions and behavior, and our behavior affects our thinking and emotions. These three also influence the emotions, thinking, and behavior of others, for good or ill. *Behavior* includes what we say along with how and when we say it. Because of this, to improve how we talk with one another, we need to be able to observe and make conscious choices about our emotions, thoughts, and actions.

We Can Train Our Minds to Manage Our Brains. A growing body of research indicates that when we train the mind to be more aware of what is going on inside and around us moment to moment, we're less likely to have knee-jerk, defensive reactions to situations. We're more able to respond skillfully by making conscious choices about what to do or say.

Winning Usually Means Losing. When one of us or a group of us is intent on winning, pushing our agenda, beating the opposition, or silencing or intimidating those with whom we disagree, we all lose. This could be a whole organization, a community, or simply a larger group of which we're a part. We lose because a solution or decision that comes out of a win/lose process doesn't get us to where we want to go.

There are several reasons for this. The results of win/lose interactions are usually piecemeal solutions that

- don't touch the real issue;
- don't have the benefit of everyone's best thinking;
- will be implemented slowly, begrudgingly, or not at all;
- can easily become the target of litigation by those who "lost"; and
- deepen the divides among people.

The need to win or get our way in interactions means we lose the opportunity to learn, solve problems, and create a sense of community that can help all of us win in the long run.

People Want to Contribute. Organizations and communities underutilize the gifts and talents of their employees and residents. Interactions—meetings or gatherings of all kinds—are venues in which people can contribute to the health and well-being of their communities and places of work.

We Can Create Constructive Conversations. Each of us is responsible for the quality of our interactions and the quality of the outcomes that ensue. The eight practices described in this book help us create the conversations that many of us hope for and all of us need to have. This is hard work, and it takes practice.

Many people underestimate the power of constructive conversations to bridge differences so that we can create a desired future. The opportunity we have to create such a future is here, now. It's questionable how much longer we'll have it. Every day, decisions are being made that open or close our opportunities to influence our future.

Key Points

- We're in the midst of a perfect human storm in our communities and places of work in which complex issues are colliding with the self-protective habits of the brain, ineffective or harmful ways of communicating, and outdated and unproductive interactive processes.
- The best approaches to interactive processes have many elements in common. When we weave them together with what we know about the human brain, about the impact of mindfulness practice on our perceptions and responses, and about effective human interactions, we come to a set of eight universal practices.
- These practices, described in the following chapters, can make any approach to problem-solving, decision-making, collective learning, or policy-making be constructive and productive.

Questions for Reflection

Which of the four forces seem the most problematic or difficult for you to deal with at work or in your communities: complexity of issues or dealing with diverse groups, the self-protective habits of the brain, ineffective or harmful patterns of communication, or poorly planned or conducted meeting process?

Which of the propositions make the most sense to you? Why?

With which of the propositions do you disagree? Why?

Chapter 2:
The Brain's
Competing Instincts

The amazing fact is that through mental activity alone
we can intentionally change our own brains.

—Richard J. Davidson

It was 1995, and I had just started a new book. The longer I read, the more excited I became. Here in this book was a missing link for bringing meetings to the next level—for helping them move beyond rambling, endless discussions that too often led nowhere and toward meetings in which people could find ways to work together and solve tough issues. Here, I thought, was the essential ingredient to help people understand the impact of their "bad behavior" in conversations: not listening, interrupting, dominating the discussion, arguing ad hominem, adamantly defending positions at all costs, and even ignoring facts in order to win.

I was perusing Daniel Goleman's groundbreaking book *Emotional Intelligence*. The missing link was and is brain science. In a blinding flash of the obvious (or a "BFO," as a former colleague dubbed it), I realized that not only does brain science help explain why the elements that many of us already include in meetings are effective—icebreakers, agendas with clear desired outcomes, and ground rules—but it also helps explain why sometimes these elements aren't enough to help participants bring the best of who they are and what they know to the table. Brain science helps us understand what people need in order to be able to do this—for example, they need to feel safe or at least "safe enough" that the self-protective mechanisms in the brain are quiet. It also provides information that enables us to be even more adept at designing and conducting productive processes that build a sense of community and result in good solutions.

I saw the possibility of how each of us can learn to use the newer part of the brain—the neocortex—to help consciously manage the older, sometimes destructive parts—the limbic system and brain stem. Goleman describes these parts of the brain as "two minds" (1995, pp. 8–9). I've come to see them as two competing instincts: to defend ourselves and to connect with and care for others. To balance these ostensibly competing instincts—to protect or connect—we need to be able to observe them and their effects on us. Based on a nonjudgmental and compassionate awareness, we can make conscious and beneficial choices about which instinct we want to drive our behavior.

To understand how you might go about balancing these instincts, it's helpful to understand the brain areas from which these instincts operate. In the following sections, I offer an introductory tour. (Before we begin, I offer a caveat: Despite the great advances in technology that allow us to study the brain in ever-greater detail, brain science is still in its infancy. In this and ensuing chapters, I provide pertinent information about the human brain so that you understand how the practices described are based in part on growing albeit incomplete knowledge. I do this with circumspection because the current popularity of neuroscience can lead one to make facile and simplistic claims about what we know from brain science and its relationship to complex human behaviors. There is much yet to understand.)

The Brain

The most complex organ in the human body is the brain: approximately 3.3 pounds of tissue, nerves, and fluid. Although the brain is only 2 percent of the body's weight, it uses 20 to 25 percent of the body's oxygen and glucose. While we live, it is "on" 24 hours a day, seven days a week, 365 days a year.

The primary functional units of the brain and the rest of the nervous system are neurons. More than 100 billion of them, each with an average of 10,000 connections, generate and pass on electrical impulses many times a second via chemical signals to other neurons. This means there are hundreds of trillions of connections through which energy and information flow in an intricate, spider web–like network throughout your brain and body. There are more connections in a cubic centimeter of the brain than there are stars in the Milky Way galaxy. And they are fast. Neurons communicate with other neurons in less than a thousandth of a second through neurotransmitters.

The brain is the main organ of the nervous system. As such, it serves as the decision-making and communication center of this system. It coordinates all the functions of the body. Essentially, it's a system of interconnected parts that evolved over millions of years to keep us alive. Because of this, it constantly scans the world around and within us, assessing whether anything is a threat to our survival. It seems to pay less attention to that which supports our well-being. I'll say more about this imbalance later, because it ends up being an important aspect of improving how we talk with one another.

To understand how the brain works, first look at its major regions and their primary functions.

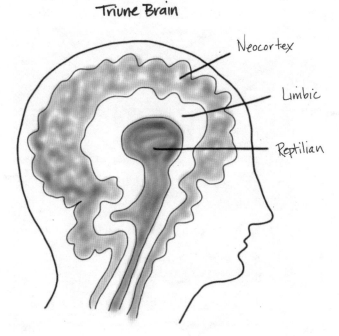

In 1967, Paul MacLean suggested that the human brain functions as three brains, each of which represents a stage in evolutionary development (Sweeney, 2009, p. 69). This is what's commonly referred to as the *triune brain*. The three parts nest inside one another like Russian dolls, with the more primitive or older areas lying under the more recently developed layers. The three brains, or areas of the brain, are the brain stem, or reptilian brain; the mammalian brain, or midbrain; and the cerebral cortex.

Because the cortex is the most recently developed part of the brain, it's tempting to think of it as the most advanced or in charge of the rest. We do so to our peril, because it leads us to underestimate the significance of the interconnections among all parts of the brain. As Lewis, Amini, and Lannon noted, "Because people are most aware of the verbal, rational part of their brains, they assume that every part of their mind should be amenable to the pressure of argument and will. Not so. Words, good ideas, and logic mean nothing to at least two brains out of three. Much of one's mind does not take orders" (2000, p. 33). This in part explains why people often are not convinced by other people's "logical" arguments for or against a particular point of view.

So much of what occurs in human interaction depends on how congruent these three parts or brains are with one another. When they're integrated, the brain is marvelous, and we have access to three ways of understanding what we and others are thinking, feeling, and experiencing.

To help you understand these three parts or brains, I borrow a "hand model" of the brain from Daniel J. Siegel (2011, pp. 14–15). Hold up one of your hands with the palm open and facing toward you. Place your thumb in the middle of your palm and tuck your fingers over the thumb. Imagine that the front of your knuckles is the face and that the back of the hand is the back of the head. In this model, the wrist and arm are the spinal column, and the palm is the brain stem, or reptilian brain. The thumb represents the mid-brain, or limbic area, and the fingers folded over your thumb and the back of your hand symbolize the cortex. (This would be more accurate if you could fold two thumbs into your palm to represent the limbic area, but that would be awkward, so one thumb represents both sides of it.)

Hand Model of the Brain

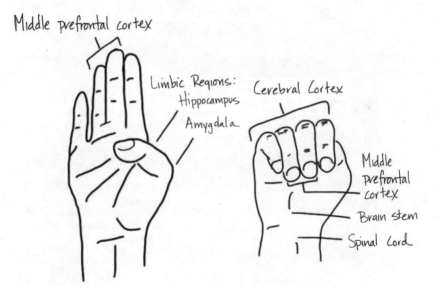

The Reptilian Brain

The reptilian brain, or brain stem, regulates our physiology. It's an area of neural tissue at the base of the brain where the spinal cord enters the skull. It developed hundreds of millions of years ago, and it's called *reptilian* because it resembles the simple brains of reptiles.

You might think of the reptilian brain as the automatic survival center. It regulates many of our most basic functions. Take a moment to notice your breathing and periodic swallowing. Can you hear or feel your heart beating? How about your body temperature—are you feeling too cold, too hot, or just right? Are you hungry or satiated? Alert or sleepy? How's your blood pressure? All of these are regulated for the most part outside your conscious awareness by the reptilian brain.

This part of the brain is asocial, but in humans, it works in concert with the limbic area in the midbrain and the higher regions of the cortex to keep us alive. When we face real danger or think that we do, the brain stem is the source of fight, flee, or freeze behaviors.

The Mammalian Brain

When a squat, spiny creature waddled into the bushes on the southeast coast of Australia, startling my vacationing husband and me, we didn't appreciate the significance of this echidna: It was a biological bridge between the brains of reptiles and those of mammals (Lewis, Amini, & Lannon, 2000, p. 51).

Although the echidna is technically classified as a mammal, it's somewhat of a reptilian one. It lays a leathery, reptilian-like egg and moves like a lizard with an oscillating gait. It's a solitary creature that comes into contact with another echidna only to mate. However, the echidna is mammalian in that the female carries an egg in two folds of her body: a kind of primitive, external uterus. She digs a burrow in which she hatches a puggle, and she returns there regularly for seven months in order to nurse her newborn. Compare this nurturing behavior to the indifference that characterizes the parenting of typical reptiles: They lay their eggs, and without so much as a friendly pat or a scratch, they walk or slither away.

Like the reptilian brain, the mammalian part is deep within the brain, approximately where your thumb rests in your closed hand. The mammalian brain, or midbrain, is often referred to as the *limbic area* because this part of the brain grew on the margin of the reptilian brain. *Limbus* is Latin for "margin" or "border."

The development of the mammalian brain brought a revolutionary change: Our ancestors became social beings who related to and connected with one another. These long-ago ancestors began to take care of their offspring; live in close-knit, mutually nurturing groups; and protect their children and mates. In other words, as Daniel Goleman describes it, we became "wired to connect" (2006). From our earliest moments, these connections help us survive. When we're newborns, we learn to regulate our physiological functions through a reciprocal and simultaneous synchronization with the limbic areas of our parents or caretakers. The limbic region is instrumental in how we form relationships, connect, and care for others. It orients us to be loyal, concerned, affectionate, and compassionate.

In addition to the instinct to connect and care, the limbic system monitors and appraises external and internal variables (in the environment and in our viscera) to decipher their meaning: Is the situation safe, dangerous, or life-threatening? Stephen Porges refers to this function as "neuroception" (2011, p. 57). The limbic area generates emotions depending on whether the limbic region perceives the circumstance as safe or threatening. This evaluation and the emotions it triggers happen outside of our awareness. Emotions like joy, fear, sadness, or anger begin before we're conscious of them. This helps explain why sometimes we say or do things that we often later regret (i.e., have knee-jerk reactions).

When the limbic area perceives a threat from outside the body—colleagues not making eye contact or disagreeing adamantly with our ideas—the amygdala, or the "alarm bell of the brain" in the limbic area, snaps to attention and instructs the brain stem to send the signal to fight, flee, or freeze. "Threat" hormones—adrenaline, noradrenaline, and cortisol—flood the body, preparing it to protect itself. The heart rate increases, and muscles tighten. This occurs automatically, initially outside our awareness. (Although the brain has two amygdalae within the temporal lobes on each side of the brain, I use the singular, *amygdala,* to refer to both.)

A sense of threat can also come from your perceptions or interpretations of what is going on around you. For example, you might be thinking, "Sue is looking out the window because she's bored and wants me to stop talking" or "Tom is disagreeing with me because I'm a woman." In others words, you threaten yourself with your own thinking, making up stories about why people aren't making eye contact or are ignoring your comments.

Two seemingly competing survival instincts—to protect and connect—are located in the same region of the brain that is part of the limbic area. Think of it as two doors in a game show: Will I protect myself in the instinctive way of fighting, fleeing, or freezing? Or will I protect myself by reaching out and connecting with others?

This book is about creating a third door, one in which you notice and acknowledge the survival instincts in the brain before they take over and drive behavior outside of your conscious awareness—and in which you make conscious choices about what you want to do or say to connect with others and move things forward in a positive way. The cortex is the key player in creating a third door.

The Cortex

Let's return to the hand model of the brain. Once again, hold your hand up with the palm facing you. Tuck your thumb into the palm and curl your fingers over the thumb. Previously, you learned that the back of your hand and the fingers folded over the thumb in your palm represent the cortex, the newest part of the brain. This part is about a tenth of an inch thick, and it wraps around the limbic area and the brain stem. *Cortex* comes from the Latin word for "rind" or "bark."

The cortex is the source of intellectual activities. It's often described as the thinking part of the brain, where we initiate speaking, writing, planning, and reasoning. It enables us to think and imagine, hold memories, and plan for the future. Perhaps one of the greatest gifts of the cortex is its ability to create symbolic representations—that is, spoken and written language, art, and music. It's also where we are aware of our senses and wield conscious control over our actions. The cortex is the biological seat of the functions that, if we choose, enable us to meet and converse constructively. Through the functions of the cortex, we can solve problems, envision possible futures, and strategize how to create them.

The Prefrontal Cortex

A particular part of the cortex is instrumental in managing emotions. In the hand model of the brain, look at the area from the first knuckles to your fingertips. This represents the part of the cortex known as the *prefrontal cortex*. It sits just behind the forehead in the anterior frontal lobe. This part of the cortex is a key player in conversations. It's sometimes called the "fourth brain" in that it notices and moderates the actions of the other three: cortex, midbrain, and brain stem. It enables us to be conscious or mindful of the inner workings of the brain itself.

According to David Rock (2009, p. 8), the prefrontal cortex helps us do five things:

- understand new ideas and how they connect to what we already know;
- make decisions or make value judgments;
- recall what we already know, bring up memories;
- memorize information and ideas (in concert with the hippocampus in the limbic system); and
- inhibit impulses or reactions (such as yelling at a colleague in a meeting when he interrupts us).

All of these enable us to talk and think things through, define and solve problems, set goals, think creatively, visualize things we've never seen before, and remain civil.

The prefrontal cortex helps us do these things by orchestrating billions of neurological circuits. You could think of this part of the brain as its integrator or executive. And—this is noteworthy—according to Rock, the prefrontal cortex prefers to perform these five functions one at a time. In other words, it isn't designed to multi-task. Many of us try to perform all five functions simultaneously in our meetings. Not only is this ineffective, but it also taxes the energy-hungry prefrontal cortex and puts the limbic system on alert.

The Neuroplastic Brain

In addition to being the most complex organ in the human body, the brain is the only one capable of changing its own structure and function through the thoughts we think and the experiences we have. This remarkable ability, called *neuroplasticity*, isn't without its challenges. While neuroplasticity enables us to be resourceful, it also renders the brain vulnerable to influences outside of itself. Norman Doidge calls this "the plastic paradox" (2007, p. xx). After a neural pathway—such as a bad habit—develops in the brain, it can be hard to change (Doidge, 2016, p. 8). This is in part why awareness, choice, and the functions of the prefrontal cortex are key to choosing which pathways, or habits, we want to develop or maintain. As Doidge asserted, "Mental activity is not only the product of the brain but also the shaper of it" (2016, p. xiv).

Let's pause and consider the opportunity and responsibility that this power presents. We can change our brains through our thoughts and intentions and what or who we allow to influence us. In describing neuroplasticity, psychiatrist and psychologist Richard J. Davidson wrote,

> These changes include altering the function of brain regions, expanding or contracting the amount of neural territory devoted to particular tasks, strengthening or weakening connections between different brain regions, increasing

or decreasing the level of activity in specific brain circuits, and modulating the neurochemical messenger service that continuously courses through the brain. (2012, p. 9–10)

This unique ability of the human brain means that we can choose to make a change in how we interact with others and in our ability to collaborate to solve problems for the greatest common good. We can consciously choose to create or strengthen pathways in the brain that help us engage with others effectively by shifting our attention from unhelpful thoughts to helpful ones. We can develop our ability to notice and manage difficult emotions like fear or anger before they hijack us and drive us to do destructive things. We can make a conscious choice to interact in constructive ways. How will we choose to use this remarkable ability?

I'll end this brief brain tour with a reminder that the three brains, or areas of one brain, do not function separately or independently of one another. It's more accurate to think of the three parts as a dance trio with each member taking turns as the lead. Under alert, the brain stem leads. When you're connecting with a close friend or lover, the limbic system leads. And if you're analyzing a problem, the cortex leads. In meetings, the part of the brain that leads frequently shifts, depending on what's occurring. When you're presenting your ideas to your colleagues, your cortex and limbic region might be leading. If your ideas are challenged, the limbic area and brain stem might go on alert. If you continue to be criticized, your brain stem might take over and drown out messages from the limbic area and cortex.

We can, through the brain's ability to change itself, learn to observe and make conscious choices about which part or parts of the brain will lead.

In the next chapter, you explore emotions: what they are, how they get evoked, and what role they play in the brain and in our meetings.

Key Points

- Although the brain is highly interconnected, we can increase our understanding of it by understanding the three regions that developed as it evolved: the reptilian brain, or brain stem; the mammalian brain, or midbrain; and the cortex.

- At the risk of oversimplifying, you can think of the brain stem as the survival center, the midbrain as the emotional center, and the cortex as the creative and civilizing center.

- The prefrontal cortex directs particular functions that are key to how we talk with one another. These include understanding new ideas and connecting them to what we already know; making decisions or value judgments; recalling what we already know, bringing up memories; memorizing information and ideas; and inhibiting impulses or reactions.

- The brain changes in response to thoughts and experiences. This means we can intentionally change the brain by directing our mental activity and selecting experiences and how we want them to influence us. This neuroplastic quality of the brain is a gift and a responsibility.

Questions for Reflection

How might understanding more about the human brain help you improve how you interact at meetings at work or in your community?

How do you respond to the idea that you can change your brain? How is the ability of the brain to change itself both a gift and a responsibility?

Chapter 3:
Emotions: The Bane or Boon of Our Interactions

Every interaction has an emotional subtext.

—Daniel Goleman

The executive team of a utility company kicked off a retreat by collaboratively creating a history of their organization on an 8-foot-long and 4-foot-high timeline taped to a wall of a meeting room. As one of the managers started to share a story about when he had joined the firm and a graphic recorder took notes on the timeline, another manager threw a sheaf of papers on the floor and shouted, "Wait a minute! What are you doing? I thought I was supposed to present the history. Don't tell me I wasted my time researching the history of this organization!" He had apparently misunderstood the preparation that had been requested and believed he was individually responsible for chronicling the company's past. He didn't understand that the intention was to build the history as a team. His outburst infected others with anxiety. This lingered, dampening the team's enthusiasm for what was meant to be an engaging and informative opening to a two-day team-building and planning session. Such is the power of one team member hijacked by anger.

Contrast this with a meeting of 50 physician leaders and hospital administrators gathered to kick off a comprehensive change effort in a teaching hospital. As the CEO and his direct reports made their case for change, expressions ranged from cynical eye-rolling to enthusiastic head-nodding. After a lackluster period of Q&A, one of the well-respected physicians, his voice cracking with emotion, beseeched the group. "As you all know," he said, "this is an extremely challenging time in healthcare. The success of this project is crucial to the survival of this institution, to the health of our patients, and the skills of the doctors and nurses we train. This is why I so strongly believe in this project. I want us to find new ways to work together to make it an absolute success." As his voice reverberated in the wood-paneled room, people leaned forward in their seats. They began to talk about what the project could mean for the future and how they needed to work more effectively across departmental boundaries. Such is the power of emotion intentionally and skillfully expressed.

Emotions are a powerful force in our interactions. They wield more influence over the quality of our meetings than any other variable. They can turn a conversation among colleagues or neighbors into a snarling, polarizing, and enervating event or a high-fiving, bonding, and renewing one. When emotions are a bane, they disturb people's equilibrium and activate the more primitive parts of the brain. For example, anger creates a sense of isolation that in turn generates fear and more anger. Because these two emotions in particular are highly contagious (Goleman, 2006, pp. 14–20), they're the usual culprits in instigating destructive and unproductive conversations. However, emotions can be a boon when they connect us with one another and create a sense of trust. Although not as contagious as fear or anger, joy and camaraderie are also infectious. They increase the levels of oxytocin in our bodies. This neurotransmitter, which promotes a sense of relatedness that generates trust, is known as the "cuddle" or "love" hormone.

Some people attempt to repress or deny emotions in the hope that an interaction will be purely rational. This is neither possible nor healthy. There's an emotional subtext in every meeting. Emotions are "integral to the process of reasoning," wrote psychiatrist John J. Ratey. "We are learning that emotions are the result of multiple brain and body systems that are distributed over the whole person. We cannot separate emotion from cognition or cognition from the body" (2002, p. 223). This happens in part because the amygdala, in concert with memories and outside of our conscious awareness, assigns emotional meanings to every stimulus, or bit of incoming information. Because the brain filters everything through the sieve of protecting our well-being, we're constantly judging and reacting to the world. Either we like what we're seeing or experiencing and want more of it, or we don't like it and try push it away or get rid of it. It's challenging for us to simply see things clearly, without tainting what we see, hear, or experience with memory, reaction, and judgment. One way to help us see more clearly is to look at how emotions shape our perceptions.

For us to be able to talk effectively together and take on the issues we want to tackle, we need to understand what emotions are and how to notice, manage, and use them in constructive ways. In particular, we need to learn to notice fear or anger *before* it overwhelms us so we can pause, explore what's stimulating the emotion, and figure out what we want to do with it. One option is to let our emotions mobilize us to speak but not destructively. Just like the physician, we can describe them with intention and skill.

Too often, we express emotions in ways that damage relationships and undermine the clarity of people's thinking, like the manager at the planning retreat mentioned earlier. When the self-appointed chronologist threw paper in the air and yelled, he had gone on automatic, propelled by anger. Fear likely preceded this: fear of embarrassment that he had misunderstood the assignment and would appear foolish or incompetent to his peers and boss. The primitive parts of the brain—the brain stem and limbic system—propelled his behavior outside of his awareness. You might think that this manager should have been more able to control his emotions. But when we get unpleasantly surprised in front of others, as he did, it can be extremely difficult to manage ourselves because our emotions are so interconnected with the self-protective mechanisms in the brain.

What Emotions Are and How They Work

Psychologist Paul Ekman defines emotion as "a process, a particular kind of automatic appraisal influenced by our evolutionary and personal past, in which we sense that something important to our welfare is occurring, and a set of physiological changes and emotional behaviors begins to deal with the situation" (Ekman, 2003, p. 13). The "automatic appraisal" Ekman refers to is the brain's vigilant and constant scanning of any situation to assess its potential impact on our well-being.

"Evolutionary and personal past" pertains to the fact that the human brain evolved to keep us alive and that memories of events that threatened our survival in the past can get cued up by similar events today. If you felt humiliated as a child in a public setting such as a classroom, any hint or threat of this in a meeting can evoke shame today. Or suppose that last week, you proposed a new idea about improving customer service to your colleagues at work, and no one acknowledged you or responded. And then, 15 minutes later, someone suggested the same idea, but this time people greeted it with great enthusiasm. You might be frustrated, angry, or sad and far less motivated to propose new ideas in a meeting.

Although survival is rarely at stake in a meeting, it can feel as if it is. Seemingly innocuous and all-too-familiar behaviors like interruptions or criticisms of ideas can evoke hurt, fear, or anger and self-protective behaviors in any of us. When the brain perceives that something might harm us, emotions arise. They start with automatic physiological changes that occur outside of our awareness, preparing us to deal with the situation that the brain believes is a threat. In other words, the body gets ready to argue, placate, or get tongue-tied.

Women tend to have other options because they have higher levels of oxytocin in their bodies than males. Because of this, they're more able to reach out to others for support, or "tend and befriend" (Taylor et al., 2000). However, we aren't limited by our biology. Men can be aware of the impulse to fight, flee, or freeze and make a conscious choice to reach out to others instead.

Please note that we become aware of emotions *after* the body has already begun to react to a threatening situation. The amygdala receives input from the senses directly before information gets fully registered by the neocortex. The brain developed this way for a reason. We react to danger almost instantaneously—swerving away from an oncoming car, for example, or applying the brakes when a child's ball rolls into the street in front of us—without taking time to think about out what to do. If the brain hadn't developed this way, then by the time we would have figured out what to do cognitively, we would already have crashed or hurt a child chasing after the errant ball.

Because we become conscious of emotions *after* they begin, it can seem as if we don't have a choice about what we feel. I imagine this is what the manager at the retreat thought. As you'll discover in the next chapter, this isn't the whole story.

Because emotions play such an important role in our meetings, it's necessary to understand more about them and their impact on us:

- **Unless we have some sort of damage to the brain, we all experience emotions to a greater or lesser degree.** It's part of being human. Every person on the planet at one time or another feels glad, sad, mad, or afraid.

Emotions

Happy   Angry   Sad   Scared

- **We all express emotions in common ways.** Wherever you are—touring the bush of Borneo, leading a meeting at work, talking with your neighbors, or traveling in Europe—it's possible to recognize emotions on people's faces.

- **Every one of us communicates emotions even when we aren't conscious of them or want to hide them.** It's impossible to fully control facial muscles and the tone of your voice, because the brain stem governs these outside of your awareness. A slight change in a minor muscle or a crack in your voice communicates what you're feeling. Although others might not be aware of what they're picking up, their limbic systems read what's going on inside you.

- **Emotions, especially anger, are contagious.** Like a grass fire on a hot and windy day, anger spreads quickly throughout a group via the reactions of the limbic areas and mirror neurons in the brain. *Mirror neurons* are a class of brain cells that track and tend to replicate the emotions, actions, and intentions of the people we're with.

- **Despite what we might want to believe, we can't completely control our emotions.** In fact, trying to control them seems to intensify them. When we try to ignore or repress them, we can end up blurting them out in more vociferous and harmful ways than if we had simply decided whether, how, and when to communicate them when they first arose.

How Emotions Can Be Destructive

Emotions are destructive when they evoke the self-protective mechanisms in the brain so much that we lose access to the important functions of the prefrontal cortex, especially the ability to inhibit impulsive behavior. Such emotions make it difficult, if not impossible, to make conscious and considered choices about what to say and do. When we're in this state, emotions are "disrupting the mind's equilibrium" (Goleman, 2003, p. 157), and we can harm others and ourselves.

Anxiety, fear, and anger are the most destructive emotions. They're the focus of this chapter because they're the ones that most frequently disrupt and derail meetings. However, feelings that you might deem positive, such as joy, enthusiasm, and contentment, can be destructive if they diminish our ability to use the functions of the prefrontal cortex. For example, over-the-top enthusiasm for a particular point of view undermines our equipoise and prevents us from hearing different or conflicting perspectives.

On the other hand, anxiety, fear, and anger aren't always destructive. They can alert us to real dangers in our environment and mobilize us to protect ourselves. They can also clarify our thinking about an issue and motivate us to act on what matters to us. The challenge is to be able to tap the benefits of these emotions without being carried away by them; that way, we do and say things that help move a situation forward for the good without destroying relationships and provoking unhelpful and unnecessary conflict. For me, it's been a life-long lesson to learn how to speak about what matters to me with passion—for example, with enthusiasm or even anger when needed—while maintaining a connection to my whole brain and to the people I'm speaking with. Doing both enables me to speak skillfully and inspire others without alienating or frightening them.

Becoming aware of our emotions and their impact on us gives us the opportunity to make choices about how we want to handle them, especially if they have the potential to be destructive. For example, when an advisory committee of stakeholders in a community started to finalize their recommendations, people started talking faster and interrupting one another in ways they hadn't previously done. They argued over details in uncharacteristic ways. As the facilitator, I wondered aloud, "I notice that you're starting to interrupt one another and seem to be speaking more quickly than usual. Are you aware of this? What do you think is going on?" After a long pause, one of the quieter members of the group responded, "I think we're nervous about making our final recommendations to the Board." Several people nodded their heads in agreement. Now that they knew how they felt and how it was influencing them, they reverted to interacting as effectively as they had in past meetings.

Although most of us have learned to behave as if our emotions were not influencing our words and actions in meetings, they do so routinely. So regardless of how we might appear, emotions, for good or ill, influence our thinking and our behavior. When people aren't aware of their emotions and how those emotions affect them, the impact can be costly. For example, at a planning session of a pharmaceutical company, a small group of scientists reluctantly agreed to proceed with a controversial project because, as they admitted later, they had been afraid of being cast as "bad team players." In subsequent meetings, their objections gradually surfaced. The project was eventually shelved—but only after millions of dollars and several months of work had been wasted.

Tiny tweaks or big threats to people's sense of safety occur in most meetings. When survival systems are aroused a little or a lot, the energy-hungry prefrontal cortex has fewer resources to perform any of the functions that, according to David Rock, are so important to effective interactions. As mentioned earlier, these functions include the following:

- understanding new ideas and how they connect to what we already know;
- making decisions or value judgments;
- recalling what we already know;
- memorizing information and ideas; and
- perhaps most significantly, managing emotions and inhibiting impulsive behavior (Rock, 2009, p. 34)—in other words, when you are about to get emotionally hijacked.

Depending on how quickly and strongly you get hijacked, your ability to access the functions in the prefrontal cortex dwindles. When this occurs, energy and attention shift to protecting or defending yourself and away from achieving the purpose of the meeting. Anxiety, fear, or anger derails meetings when you (a) lose awareness of what is actually going on, (b) go on automatic, (c) cut yourself off from others, and (d) need to take time for your physiology to return to some degree of homeostasis.

Lose Awareness. Interactions are uncertain propositions at best. You think today's staff meeting is to plan next year's budget but find out when you arrive that it's to cut this year's. Yikes! You prepared for the former but not the latter. As the resources (oxygen and glucose) available to the prefrontal cortex decrease (Rock, 2009, p. 108), your awareness of what's going on inside and around you decreases, and you become less able to manage your emotions and direct your thoughts and behaviors.

Because "the prefrontal cortex is the biological seat of your *conscious* interactions with the world" (Rock, 2009, p. 6), when your access to it gets diminished, you also begin to lose awareness of the purpose of the meeting, what you're talking about, and what others are saying. You become less able to observe the expressions of impatience or anxiety on the faces of co-workers as you rail on about how you thought the meeting was about next year's budget. In addition to undermining your ability to be aware of others and the situation, you're less able to notice what's going on inside you. Ironically, self-absorption makes you less self-aware.

Go on Automatic. We're on automatic when emotions have hijacked the brain and our behavior is largely out of our conscious control, driven by the primitive parts of the brain. Going on automatic leads to three unhelpful behaviors.

First, with survival mechanisms on alert, we decrease or lose our ability to inhibit or manage impulsive behavior. The brain looks even more diligently for signs of danger. We react more suspiciously to others than we would if we were functioning with access to the whole brain. It's difficult to stop yourself from saying and doing things that make the situation worse and that you'll likely later regret. Have you ever watched in amazement and horror as hurtful words poured out of your mouth but you didn't seem to be able to stop yourself? These ultimately embarrassing and potentially damaging incidents occur when the "braking system" in the prefrontal cortex (the *ventrolateral prefrontal cortex*) that sits behind the right and left temples runs out of steam to do its job.

Second, our ability to accurately perceive what's going on around us is diminished. We "cannot incorporate information that does not fit, maintain, or justify the emotion we are feeling" (Ekman, 2007, p. 39). On automatic, we miss or misread what people say and have trouble processing it, let alone understanding it. For instance, if you interrupt or disagree with me, I may begin to hear everything you say as just another example of your being "out to get me." The effects of being on automatic can be startling. Have you ever been so angry or scared that you had difficulty hearing what someone was saying, your vision started to narrow, and you interpreted what a person said as the opposite of what she intended? Most of us don't realize how automatic or mindless our interactions can become.

Third, on automatic, our behavior—especially in fight mode—tends to be become either chaotic or rigid. When the manager at the meeting threw his papers up in the air and began sounding off, his reaction was chaotic. Rigidity is equally unproductive. Years ago, when I was about to facilitate one of my first public meetings for a large community group in southern California, I remember becoming obsessed with exactly how the tables and chairs were arranged, how the paper was hung on the walls, and exactly where the recorder and I should sit. It took me a while to calm down and realize that I was anxious and operating rigidly on automatic. When our behavior becomes chaotic or rigid, it can trigger anxiety and anger in others.

Cut Ourselves Off. When we get hijacked, we also lose a sense of connection to others. We can get so focused on our own needs that we don't notice or even care about the needs of others. Only when we feel safe and when we have access to the whole brain can we pay attention to and be interested in what might be going on with other people.

According to Stephen Porges, "A neuroception of safety is necessary before social engagement behaviors can occur" (2011, p. 17). *Neuroception* is a process through which you *unconsciously* evaluate the risks in a situation by tracking people's facial expressions, voice intonation, gestures, the quality of their gaze, and the feeling in your "gut."

When you feel cut off, it can seem like you're the only player on the world's only stage, trying to survive. A hospital administrator described this as crawling into a "Joe Cave" where he falsely believes that he has to figure everything out by himself and where he "throws logs on the worry fire." In his psychological cave, he becomes unaware of the support around him and loses his ability to connect with others.

Need Time to Calm Down. Reactions to perceived danger happen quickly, are hard to stop, and last much longer than reactions to pleasant events. Think about how your heart races when you swerve away from an oncoming car crossing a lane marker and how long it takes for your pulse to return to normal. The experience is similar in meetings. Imagine the deer-in-the-headlights sensation you might experience if your boss, in front of your peers, said you did a terrible job on a project you thought was a success. Calming down can take five minutes or five hours, depending on what stories or thoughts you spin and on whether those around you have become infected with your emotions, which in turn continue to excite yours (Ekman, 2003, pp. 39–40).

"Threat hormones," like adrenaline, impair memory and our ability to retrieve information stored in the hippocampus—some of the very information we need to calm ourselves down, like the value of pausing to take a conscious breath and staying quiet until we feel calmer and can speak constructively. (The hippocampus is part of the limbic system and plays a central role in memory.)

When asked to contribute to the discussion of the history of the organization, the manager at the planning retreat demurred, indicating he needed to "cool down." This was a smart move on his part. Eventually, he did calm down and began to participate in the meeting. However, it took the better part of the morning before he was able to do so. It takes time for your whole system—brain and body—to get back to homeostasis before you have full access to your whole brain, especially the functions of the prefrontal cortex.

How We Fan the Flames of Fear and Anger

We fan the flames of emotion in these ways, lengthening the time it takes to get back to homeostasis:
- making up stories to validate our emotions;
- replaying or elaborating on the events that evoked the emotions in the first place;
- creating threatening scenarios about the future; and
- not distinguishing between our thoughts about what's occurring from what is actually occurring.

Unfortunately, we usually do these four things unconsciously. Knowing how you might exacerbate your emotions can help you avoid doing so.

Making Up Stories. In the small gap between when emotions get evoked and when we become aware of them, we quickly make up stories to justify them. Unfortunately, too many of these stories relate to previous experiences and emotions that have little to do with what triggered the emotions in the present situation. For example, suppose an older colleague ignores an idea put forward by a younger co-worker, and anger starts to rise in the young man. He gets even angrier as a parade of images flashes through his brain about the previous times his proposals were overlooked by peers older than he is. He starts embellishing his storyline about "older employees," especially the one who just disregarded him.

This happens in part because the stress hormones—adrenaline, noradrenaline, and norepinephrine—prime the brain to implant emotionally charged memories (Goleman, 1994; Hanson, 2013, p. 22). This, combined with the brain's tendency to remember unpleasant experiences more than pleasant ones, gives us easier access to memories of when we felt threatened than when we felt supported. Thus, the stories we make up tend to be more dire interpretations of what is happening than what the present moment usually deserves.

Some good news: The tendency to remember unpleasant experiences and concoct dire interpretations appears to decrease as we age (Charles, Mather, & Carstensen, 2003).

Replaying or Elaborating on Events. When we replay our version of events or elaborate on them, we intensify our emotions. A number of years ago, I spoke to an audience of 750 in an auditorium at the site of my clients. Just as I began to speak, my ears started to ring so loudly I could barely hear myself think. In addition, the person in the sound booth in the back couldn't hear me, so she didn't know when to change the slides. Although I muddled through, I replayed that situation over and over again in my mind for months afterward until my heart ached with embarrassment. Despite the fact that the feedback was positive, I had painted such a horrible picture in my mind's eye that I had convinced myself that people were just being nice to me. The dynamics of our negatively biased brains can be punitive.

Anticipating a Threatening Future. We have an uncanny ability to imagine the future. Unfortunately, this ability is frequently influenced by the imbalance between pleasant and unpleasant memories for the reasons explained earlier.

Let's say you're driving to a city council meeting to testify in favor of a traffic circle at an intersection of a heavily traveled street near your home. Having experienced the bored or distracted faces of the councilors in the past, you feel anxious that you will, once again, feel the pain of perceiving yourself as not heard or downright ignored. Because of this, during the public comment period, you begin your three minutes at the mic expecting the worst. And because of this, you don't speak with the clarity and strength you know you're capable of. Unfortunately, when we create threatening scenarios of the future in our minds, we often then create them in real life. It's a self-fulfilling prophecy.

Being Unable to Distinguish between What We Think Is Occurring and What Is Occurring. Most of us aren't practiced in staying present in the moment. Our brains are often preoccupied with judging the present, rehashing the past, or fantasizing about the future. One study found that people's minds wander 47% of the time during waking hours (Killingsworth & Gilbert, 2010, p. 932). It also found that when people's minds were wandering they were less happy than when they were focused on what they were doing.

Wandering seems to be the brain's default mode until something wakes it up to experiencing the present moment. Because of this, we miss what's happening right now and see current reality through a glass, darkly. And because the limbic brain isn't able to distinguish between what's actually occurring and what we think is occurring (Lewis, Amini, & Lannon, 2000, p. 46), we can experience the present moment as a threat to our safety, whether it is or not. The brain reacts according to our perceptions. It's the old story of seeing a circle of rope on a trail: If we think it's a snake, we jump or cry out.

For instance, think about the last time someone didn't look at you when you spoke at a meeting. What was the storyline in your head? "Susan ignored me at the last meeting. How dare she not pay attention? I have more seniority and experience than she does. Maybe I should just stop coming to these meetings or begin ignoring others when I do. I'll show them!" You can play this story until your brain is on fire. However, Susan might have been listening to what you said and looking away to help her take it in more fully. Sometimes I close my eyes or take notes when I'm trying to better understand what another is saying. What's more painful: the actual event of someone not making eye contact or your thoughts about it?

Unfortunately, when emotions get the better of us, we fan the flames and keep firing the same circuits in the brain, thereby strengthening these unhelpful pathways.

What Threatens Us in Meetings?

Although the sources of threat in meetings differ dramatically from those experienced by our long-ago ancestors, the self-protective mechanisms do not. We are profoundly social beings with a brain and nervous system that is focused on keeping us safe.

You might be surprised at what can undermine a sense of safety when you're interacting with others. Some of the unspoken threats from meetings come from issues of inclusion and sense of relationship with others. Our unconscious questions often include "Will I be welcomed?" "Can I say what I really think?" "Will I be liked?" and "Will my ideas and opinions be valued?"

David Rock has identified five types of possible threats that, although they don't threaten our physical safety, still ring the alarm bell in the brain. Threats to one's sense of status, certainty, autonomy, relatedness, or fairness (the acronym is SCARF) can quickly activate the more primitive parts of the brain and push people into some version of fighting, fleeing, freezing, or, less frequently, reaching out to others for support in meetings at work or in their communities (2009, pp. 195–197). As noted earlier, women's instinct to fight or flee gets buffered by increased levels of oxytocin in their systems when they're threatened, so they're more inclined to "tend and befriend" others. Unfortunately, when men are under stress, their testosterone levels increase and reduce the calming effects of oxytocin (Kaplan, 2009).

Threats to Status. We are social beings, concerned with how others perceive and care about us. In other words, we pay attention to our social position or status. Early in my career, I was often the only female in meetings of high-ranking male executives. Although the demographics have changed over the years, when I'm interrupted or when my ideas are ignored today, I sometimes still feel vestiges of the fear and bristling annoyance I experienced then.

When I was part of a consulting team at the design center of one of the world's oldest and most prestigious automobile companies, I remember being surprised by the care in which people protected their sense of status by where they sat in executive meetings. The highest-ranking person sat at the base of a huge, mahogany V-shaped table. The 40 or so other men sat in descending order of position along the sides. This seating order was strictly followed. It was rare for someone at the bottom of the order to speak before those sitting closer to the CEO did. Many organizations still follow this less-than-productive pattern of interacting in ways that maintain or diminish people's sense of status.

Threats to Certainty. The brain craves certainty. However, because the only absolute in life is change, threats to one's sense of certainty are ubiquitous, especially when people converse. Meetings are very uncertain because of (a) the nature of conversation itself, (b) people's different beliefs and opinions, (c) inadequate or ineffective process, and (d) complex issues with no obvious solutions.

The nature of conversation. Interacting with others is as uncertain an experience as there is. The only thing that is certain is that you can't predict what people will say and do. Because the default process for most meetings is discussion, interactions can be chaotic as people's thoughts and feelings ricochet around the room. Here's what a threat to certainty might sound like inside your head during a discussion: "What are we talking about now? What does this have to do with anything? What are we trying to get done? How do I get a word in edgewise? There are many ideas on the table—which ones make sense? I don't even remember most of them."

Discussions usually mean there are going to be multiple, diverse, and seemingly unrelated ideas or topics being considered. When this occurs, people get anxious trying to track it all. It drains energy from the cortex and strains its capability. A classic study indicated that the maximum number of items a person can hold in mind at a time is seven, plus or minus two. This is why phone numbers have seven digits. More recent studies indicate that the actual number we can hold in working memory—depending on how new, unfamiliar, and complex the items are—is more likely four. The unpredictability of conversations along with the number of ideas expressed can threaten people's sense of certainty and evoke anxiety.

Different beliefs and opinions. Unless you're meeting with your clones, someone is going to say something that calls your beliefs or opinions into question. Because of this, conversations often create *cognitive dissonance,* or the discomfort of holding two or more conflicting ideas simultaneously. For example, suppose you believe there's scientific evidence that proves that human actions are the primary cause of climate change, and others do not. Both can't be true, can they? To reduce the discomfort of this dissonance, you need to make others or yourself wrong. Guess whom you're going to pick. The need for certainty and the desire to reduce the discomfort of dissonance is in part responsible for people getting trapped in *either/or* thinking and clinging to beliefs even in the face of evidence that they're wrong.

Poor process. Inadequate or ineffective process creates anxiety in the steadiest of us. For example, when the purpose, outcomes, ground rules, or length of a meeting is unclear; when people's roles are ambiguous and "real" agendas are hidden; and when decision-making authority isn't disclosed, people's sense of certainty is unnecessarily undermined.

Complex issues. Humans seem to prefer black and white answers: clear lines of sight between problems and solutions. The brain likes to know what's what. This is this, and that is that. Having right answers creates a "cognitive ease" and decreases the "cognitive strain" that decision-making asks of us (Kahneman, 2011, pp. 59–60). In fact, in the face of uncertainty, the brain makes up explanations for why things are the way they are so it can feel safer. As a colleague of mine said, "I am often wrong but never in doubt."

Most of us were educated in institutions where knowing the right answers was how we got rewarded. However, many meetings at work and in our communities involve conversations about complex issues for which there is no one known answer, or at least not one that people agree upon. The comfort of simple issues and clear solutions eludes us, which creates an unnerving sense of uncertainty about what to think or do.

Threats to Autonomy. The third area of potential threat is autonomy: the desire to be self-directing, be self-governing, or have choice. When we feel forced or that we "have to" do something—attend a meeting, listen to long presentations, support a decision we don't agree with—the limbic system lights up, often with some variation of resentment or anger. These are not, one assumes, the emotions we want emanating from people at a meeting.

Threats to autonomy can occur when people don't have a say in the purpose of a meeting or how it will be conducted; when people make authoritative pronouncements, interrupt one another, or dismiss the points of view of others; or when people are excluded from influencing decisions made during the conversation. Usually what upsets people is not what the decision is but rather *how* it was reached. The key question is whether they're included in or excluded from the process.

Threats to Relatedness. Humans are essentially and ultimately social beings. To the human brain, being included and in relationship with others is as important as food or water. Because of the way the brain evolved, this need is intimately interwoven with a sense of safety.

We threaten people's sense of relatedness when we don't listen to or we simply ignore their point of view; when we devalue or criticize what they say or who they are; or when we don't communicate our understanding or appreciation of what they contribute to the meeting. Remember that the opposite of love is not hate; it's indifference, or not paying attention. When people perceive themselves to be ignored, isolated, or estranged, they get can get anxious, sad, sarcastic, or angry.

Meeting process can unintentionally undermine people's sense of relatedness. At public meetings, people sit "theatre style," in long rows in large, sometimes darkened rooms, staring across a spatial chasm at, for example, a city council or planning commission seated above them on a dais under bright lights. One at a time, people walk to a microphone to speak to bodies of decision-makers. This corrodes a sense of connection among people and triggers the need to protect oneself. This, at least in part, explains the frequent less-than-civil behavior in public meetings.

In organizations, a sense of relatedness gets undermined by seating arrangements, as in the case of the automobile manufacturer's large, V-shaped table or when a manager sits at the head of any table and talks at people and discourages conversation among them.

Threats to Fairness. Fear and anger can be sparked by doubts about the fairness of a process. Even when people agree with the results, they often contest the results if they believe that the process through which they were achieved was unfair. For example, a group of lab technicians in a pharmaceutical company fought tooth and nail to keep their lab open. Although the decision to close the lab made sense to them—the product for which they ran tests had been mothballed—they didn't like how they were being treated during the decision-making process. They thought their concerns weren't heard or considered. In this instance, both their sense of fairness and their relationships were threatened, because they were going to be assigned to different labs throughout the company and separated from their current co-workers.

Process is usually deemed fair when the following criteria are met (Kim & Mauborgne, 1997):

- People understand what the process is, including who gets to make the final decisions.
- They have an equitable share of airtime and are involved in providing input to or feedback on decisions that affect them.
- Their input and feedback are heard and taken seriously by decision-makers.
- They have a chance to discuss the merits of one another's ideas.
- They understand why decisions are made as they are.
- They're clear about what is expected after the decisions are made.

A Meeting's Context Can Be a Petri Dish for Fear and Anger

The extent to which we react to threats to status, certainty, autonomy, relatedness, or fairness depends a great deal on the context in which we experience them. Context includes the culture of the organization or community we're interacting in, along with the stake we have in the content or outcomes of the interaction.

Our Culture. *Culture* can be loosely defined as "the way we do things around here." It's a combination of people's underlying assumptions, beliefs, and values that shape how they think, feel, and behave. Leaders, both formal and informal, in organizations and communities, are significant players in the creation of a conversational culture. They forge it through verbal expressions—what they say and do at meetings—and what they reinforce through what they recognize, reward, or sanction. For example, when a county supervisor called another supervisor a "bureaucratic whore" at a public meeting, he communicated by example what was acceptable to say in public (this really happened). And when an executive director of a nonprofit unabashedly described his passion for the mission of his organization, he communicated that it's okay to express one's emotions at work.

Conversational cultures include the unwritten rules about how people are supposed to interact, what is and isn't okay to talk about, and what tone is considered "normal." For instance, in the culture of the automobile manufacturer referred to earlier, people did not feel safe. They rarely talked about problems unless it was to criticize another department, blame others for "screw-ups," and see who could be the most lethally sarcastic. In stark contrast was the culture of a Catholic hospital where politeness ruled the day and, for the most part, also stymied honest exchanges. At the manufacturer, only anger, sarcasm, and criticism were allowed; at the hospital, only carefully worded expressions of kindness. Both cultures negated the full spectrum of human emotions and imprisoned the possibilities of human interaction in an unproductive cage.

Over the past few decades, anger and arguing seem to have become more acceptable in interactions. Making public and private displays of anger and attacking the credibility or character of others (versus the merits of a point of view) now appear to be a legitimate and accepted approach to get one's way. Are these the qualities we want to distinguish the conversational cultures in our organizations and communities?

Our Stake. The more important the potential outcomes of a meeting are to us, the more inclined we are to feel threatened and become reactive. At work, for example, a budget discussion can be quite rational until it devolves into specific allocations for individual departments or teams. A meeting can get heated when decisions pertain to *your* resources and staffing. And in communities, the same dynamic applies. When the topic is building low-income housing in someone else's neighborhood, we might be all for it. But when the proposal is to build it in our neighborhood, the fur starts to fly.

Millions of year ago, threats to our physical safety occurred every day. Now, such threats to our physical well-being tend to be rare (depending, of course, on where you live and work). But the survival mechanism in the brain remains vigilant. The amygdala receives direct input from the senses before the prefrontal cortex fully notices them. Because our emotions are "precognitive," we need to train the mind to help us become aware of our emotions *before* we react to perceived threats in our meetings so that we can choose what to say and do. This is why the practice of making conscious choices (described in the next chapter) is essential to constructive and productive interactions. It's up to us to choose to create pathways in the brain that will benefit our interactions and not undermine them.

Key Points

- Emotions—particularly fear and anger—are a physiological process and set of behaviors that prepare us to act so we can stay safe.
- Emotions are a powerful force in interactions. They can frighten and divide us or help us feel connected with one another and able to interact constructively.
- Emotions are destructive when they cause us to lose awareness, drive us to function on automatic, lead us to cut ourselves off from others, or force us to take time to calm down.

- We all experience and communicate emotions whether we want to or not. They start before we're conscious of them, and they can infect others.
- In interactions, we can feel unsafe when we perceive threats to our status, certainty, autonomy, relationship, and fairness (SCARF).
- The intensity with which we react to these threats is influenced by the context: the conversational culture of the organization or the community in which we're interacting, along with what's at stake for us.

Questions for Reflection

What triggers your fear or anger when you're part of a group interaction? What happens when you get triggered?

How would you describe the conversational culture at work or in your community? Which aspects of the culture support constructive interactions, and which generate destructive ones?

What topics are the most emotional ones for you to discuss at work or in your community?

Section Two: Managing Our Survival Instincts

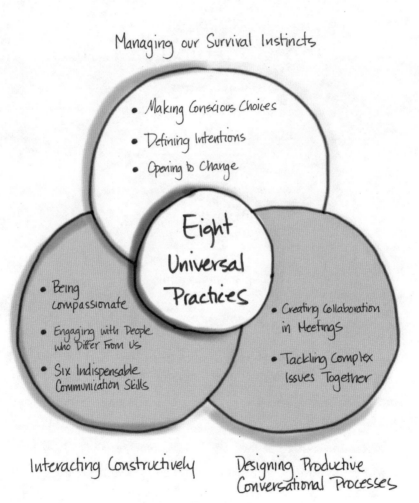

Managing our Survival Instincts

- Making Conscious Choices
- Defining Intentions
- Opening to Change

Eight Universal Practices

- Being Compassionate
- Engaging with People who Differ From Us
- Six Indispensable Communication Skills

- Creating Collaboration in Meetings
- Tackling Complex Issues Together

Interacting Constructively

Designing Productive Conversational Processes

Chapter 4:
Making Conscious Choices

The more mindful we are, the more choices we
have, and the less reactive we become.

—Ellen Langer

As I sat on the edge of a low-standing massage table, Judy, a Feldenkrais practitioner, stood behind me and gently placed her hands on my shoulders. While Judy "listened" to my body, I began to tune in to what was going on "in there." As I became aware of pain in the right side of my neck, opinions started swirling ("I'm so tired of this. This has been going on for . . .") and emotions arose (mostly frustration and fear). I paused, took a breath, and expanded my attention to become aware of Judy's attentive hands, along with the micro sensations that made up this thing I called "pain." I also observed the thoughts and emotions roiling inside. In the slight space that opened in this awareness, I relaxed into the physical sensations, accepted them, and took a nonjudgmental look at the part of me that was judging and resisting this experience. As I did this, thoughts slowed and sensations started changing and softening. Some even disappeared.

I was experiencing kinesthetically the paradoxical nature of awareness and change: When we are aware of and accept what's occurring without opinion (e.g., "This pain is awful.") or criticism (e.g., "So stupid to have sat at the computer so long yesterday.") or the need for it to be different (e.g., "I'm fed up with this. I want this pain to stop right now."), it starts to change. As Carl R. Rogers expressed it, "The curious paradox is that when I accept myself as I am, then I can change" (Rogers, 1961, p. 17). In other words, I can't change myself by judging myself or trying to control my thoughts and feelings. By fully being and accepting who I am, I become something else.

Developing awareness and acceptance of current reality—or *mindfulness*—is a prerequisite for change and for making conscious choices about the direction of that change.

Unfortunately, when we interact with others, we're often unaware of what's going on within and among the people in our immediate environment. From here, especially if we get disturbed, it's easy to start functioning on automatic. This reactive mode doesn't leave room for awareness or conscious choice. Making conscious choices is the first practice in this book because it's the foundation on which we can adopt and use the other seven practices.

Mindfulness

According to Jon Kabat-Zinn, "Mindfulness can be thought of as moment-to-moment, non-judgmental awareness, cultivated by paying attention in a specific way, that is, in the present moment, and as non-reactively, as non-judgmentally and as openheartedly as possible" (2005, p. 108). Mindfulness includes paying attention to your body sensations, emotions, and thoughts along with what's occurring around you. It's being in and with the present moment, just as it is.

Although meditation practice is an effective way to develop mindfulness, developing it without meditating is also possible. My husband grows mindfulness by walking in the forest and playing golf. The key, according to Zen priest Norman Fischer, is "simply doing whatever you are doing with awareness, carefulness, and love. And, when you are not doing this, coming back to it" (2012, p. 68). So when you walk, pay attention to how your feet are touching the ground, the relationship between your pace and the rhythm of your breathing, the sensation of the ground or floor under your feet, the temperature and sensation of the air on your skin.

Psychologist Ellen Langer has provided us a third definition of mindfulness: "Mindfulness is an effortless, simple process that consists of drawing novel distinctions, that is noticing new things. The more we notice, the more we become aware of how things change depending on the context and perspective from which they are viewed." She noted that "mindfulness requires, however, that we give up the fixed ways in which we've learned to look at the world" (Langer, 2005, p. 5). Perhaps most importantly, mindfully noticing new things brings us into the present moment. It also sensitizes us to perspective and context, an important element of interacting effectively with others.

Mindfulness means living as if every moment matters. It is intentionally paying attention to and being non-judgmenally aware of, experience as it occurs. Walk with mindful awareness to your next meeting. When you enter the room, let go of your expectations and bring fresh eyes and ears to your colleagues. As you stroll around your neighborhood, notice new things. When the phone rings, pause, stop what you're doing, and come more fully into the present moment before you say "hello." Wherever you are, take a moment to become aware of your breathing. You can do this while standing in line at the grocery store, waiting for your flight to take off, or being on hold as you wait to talk with a live human being. Every moment is an opportunity to practice being mindfully aware. Notice the length of your exhale and inhale; sense where you feel the breath in your body. Sense your feet on the floor or ground. When I pay attention in this way, my mind calms; I can see and experience my circumstances more clearly, and a wise way forward becomes obvious. In essence, I become more aware of what's going on inside and around me.

Being mindful enables us to notice our opinions about what's occurring and expand our attention so that we can simultaneously be aware of what is actually occurring and our judgments about it. As meditation teacher Heidi Bourne wrote, "Mindfulness asks us to develop awareness based on our direct experience, not the stories we tell ourselves from old conditioned beliefs that may not be accurate or relevant to our present experience" (Bourne, 2014).

Given the brain's negativity bias, our beliefs about what's happening usually exacerbate the very emotions that make it difficult for us be aware of current reality and make conscious choices about how we want to respond to it. Choosing where we want to focus our attention is important because the brain, left to its own devices, tends to notice what we don't like or what appears to threaten us more than it notices what we like or signs that we're safe. As psychologist Rick Hanson wrote, "Your brain is like Velcro for negative experiences but Teflon for positive ones" (2013, p. 27). Practicing mindfulness can help reverse this habit. For example, when someone expresses appreciation for your contributions to a conversation, pay attention to it. Replay it in your mind. Notice the impact on your inner state. This trains the brain to become more like Velcro for the positive.

This kind of mindfulness is essential to being able to interact constructively with others. It enables us to avoid being emotionally hijacked and helps us recover more quickly when we are. This gives us the wherewithal to decide what we want to think, say, do, and even feel in meetings. Noticing and accepting what we're experiencing is the first step to being able to make such choices. If we act before pausing, taking a breath, and noticing what's going on, we're more likely to say or do something that makes the situation worse.

For example, suppose you get frustrated in a community meeting during which John and Patrick are ping-ponging back and forth with critical stories about the city's building permit process. As they try to outdo one another with ain't-it-awful tales, you start silently criticizing them: "This is such a waste of time. I didn't come to this meeting to listen to these two sound off." You feed your upset by developing a story about them: "Who died and left these loudmouths in charge?" You fantasize about how you could tell them off: "Would you two morons please shut up!" By the time you intervene, you're so annoyed that you can't hide your anger, and you say in a hard-edged tone, "Any chance you two talkers would let someone else get a word in edgewise?" Nine times out of ten, when you react to a situation in this way (instead of choosing how to respond to it), you evoke fear and/or anger in others—especially John and Patrick, because they'll feel their sense of status or autonomy is threatened.

Noticing and accepting a situation as it is gives you the opportunity to try to avoid getting reactive so you can change it skillfully. For example, when there's a slight, even infinitesimal pause in the interaction between John and Patrick, you could say, "Please let me interrupt. You two have been going back and forth for a while. I'd like to hear others' perspectives and have a chance to share my own. Is that okay?" If you intervene in as neutral a tone and attitude as possible, people rarely say no. They're often surprised because they weren't aware that they were dominating the meeting. Or, if they were aware, they tend not to get defensive when the situation is described in a calm, impersonal way.

Making conscious choices depends on our ability to pause, become aware of what's going on inside and around us, and discern how to help a conversation move forward in a productive way. This is difficult, if not impossible, to do when we're agitated or overrun by emotion. When the older, more primitive parts of the brain are in charge, we lose the trail of breadcrumbs to the prefrontal cortex and the ability to choose our responses. Most likely, you've said something out of fear or anger that in hindsight you wish you hadn't. You might look back on those moments and not recognize yourself. Who *was* that? That was you reacting while under the control of the older parts of the brain.

I look back on the scared 20-year-old me who once called my boss "stupid" at a staff meeting. I don't recall what provoked me to be so irate and say something so mean. Even as the word spilled out of my mouth, I regretted it. It was as if I were watching the scene, unable to stop myself. Even though I apologized and my boss and I remained friends for years, that moment remains a sobering reminder of the power of the subcortical parts of the brain and the destructive consequences of mindless or automatic behavior—and it shows how quickly any one of us can be hijacked by fear and anger and express it destructively. Mindlessness closes the door to choice.

Of course, the effects of emotions are rarely this severe or dramatic. More frequently, they subtly influence how we think and interact with others. Being able to notice even their faint murmurings and track their influence on our thinking and behavior allows us to make better choices. Even taking three breaths mindfully opens the door to finding good alternatives to knee-jerk reactions. It creates an opening within which you can pause, take a breath, notice what's going on, and consider what, if anything, you want to say or do. In this pause, you can consciously *decide* what you want to do versus what you're unconsciously being driven to do.

Mindfulness is about developing the ability to become aware of body sensations, thoughts, and emotions as soon as possible so you avoid fabricating the thoughts that aggravate emotions; you can thus prevent your behavior from being driven by the habitual self-protective mechanisms in the brain. It's possible and desirable to develop what nature did not give us: the ability to notice emotions before they hijack us.

Meditation

One effective way to develop mindfulness is to meditate. Meditative or contemplative practices have been around for 5,000 years or more. Although most are seen as growing out of the 2,500-year-old Buddhist tradition, these practices have antecedents in multiple religious traditions. There are many forms of meditation. The one I want to focus on is mindfulness meditation.

Mindfulness meditation is a powerful tool that helps us develop the ability to pay attention to present experience, moment to moment, with openness and kindness. It means becoming adept observers of physical, emotional, and mental activities within us without censoring, judging, or getting lost in them. Basically, mindfulness meditation is sitting and noticing what's occurring in each moment. Russell Delman described meditation as "learning to be intimate with our lives. . . . The core practice is wholeheartedly welcoming the moment" and "[resting] in the awareness that notices" (2013).

There are two basic approaches to developing this ability:

- expanding one's field of awareness to notice all the phenomena—the ever-changing parade of physical sensations, emotions, and thoughts—while also being aware of the one who is experiencing the phenomena and awareness itself; and
- focusing one's mind on an object, like one's breath, to which one returns over and over again when the mind inevitably gets lost in thinking

Initially, focusing on an object might sound something like this: "I am noticing the breath raising and lowering my chest . . . the sensation of my buttocks on the chair, more weight on the right . . . wondering what I will have for lunch . . . back to the breath: noticing that the length of the exhale is longer than the inhale . . . worrying about the meeting later today . . . anxious about my presentation . . . sensing a slight raggedness in the inhale . . . noticing butterflies in my belly . . . I need to get groceries on the way home this afternoon . . . oh, I'm lost in thought . . . back to the breath, noticing that it has slowed . . ."

Mindfulness meditation increases awareness of our internal states and bodily processes so we can make conscious choices about how to manage emotions. It also opens the door to our inner wisdom, unclouded by the mindless reactions evoked by the self-protective mechanisms in the brain. Meditating mindfully creates a kind of "mental space" between an emotion like fear or anger, our thoughts about the emotion, and the impulse to react. In this mental space, we can make conscious choices about how best to respond.

Paying attention with openness and kindness is key. *Openness* means that you do the following:

- pay attention to things you wouldn't normally or deliberately pay attention to, like the sensations in your body;
- notice thoughts (opinions, judgments, stories, memories) without getting lost in them; and
- become aware of what might be new—a change in the rhythm of your breathing or a change in the pace of your thinking.

This is not as easy as it sounds. Try it for ten minutes and observe what happens.

During mindfulness meditation, when you get lost in thought (as you're bound to do), notice it and return to the breath. When a judgment arises—"Why can't I do this? What's wrong with me?"— acknowledge it as simply another thought and return your attention to the breath and body sensations. Refraining from judgment is often the biggest challenge. When you're able to observe and accept with kindness what is going on, you'll likely notice that your thoughts and feelings usually change. They get stuck when you judge them or tell yourself stories about why they're there ("I have such a monkey mind. I'll never be able to meditate.").

Given the habits of self-criticism many of us have, kindness is an especially important part of mindfulness meditation. This means having a kind and friendly relationship with ourselves. The kinder we are to ourselves, the kinder we can be to others.

Practicing mindfulness is not a passive activity. It takes energy to continue to draw one's mind back to the present moment when it wanders. You could think of meditation as a practice in returning to the present moment over and over again. Whenever you notice you're lost in thought, you awake to the present moment. As soon as you notice you aren't mindful, you are.

I want to mention two practices that complement mindfulness meditation and that also significantly strengthen and deepen awareness: (a) embodied moving and (b) embodied listening. *Embodied* means that moving and listening, along with our awareness of these activities, occur within the body. As Russell Delman wrote,

> Where do you "have" your experience? Where are your feelings, thoughts, indeed your whole sense of being alive if not organismically known in our bodily experience? We experience life in embodied ways even if our culturally conditioned self-image wants to reduce the non-cognitive to the trivial or the extraneous. (personal communication, Nov. 13, 2015)

Embodied Moving. What does embodied moving involve? When I move my arm, for example, I'm aware of my arm moving, along with the quality of the movement and how this movement affects my breath and other parts of my body. I'm also aware of the temperature and the space as I move my arm through it. Awareness of moving is a constituent part of the moving. The experience and awareness of moving my arm occur within and throughout the body, including but not limited to neural events in the head. (Some refer to this experience as *conscious proprioception.*) Because paying attention to the whole experience of moving my arm slows or stops internal chatter, it brings me fully into the present moment.

Embodied moving is one way to diversify and deepen how we pay attention to what's occurring moment to moment. When we observe the multiple large, small, and subtle body sensations involved in moving, we expand our awareness beyond the more familiar ones of thoughts and emotions. As Russell Delman, founder of the Embodied Life School, described it, "This integration of feeling, thought, intention and action is the hallmark of aware functioning" (2007).

Embodied Listening. Embodied listening means listening to body sensations, emotions, and thoughts in an integrated, holistic way; it's acknowledging that they're all alive and influencing one another. (*Interoception*, or sensing what's going on internally, is an important aspect of embodied listening. Psychiatrist Stephen W. Porges thinks of interoception as the "sixth primary sense" [2011, 76]). As we increase our ability to be aware of fine or delicate body sensations, along with our emotions and thoughts, we bring mind and body together into a congruent, undivided whole. Embodied listening means hearing the "wisdom body," which is "an integration of all ways of knowing" (Russell Delman, personal communication, Nov. 13, 2015).

You increase access to the body's wisdom by pausing and asking, "How is it in there?" or "What wants my attention in there?" You can also ask a specific question, like "How can I help myself stay calm and clear in the midst of this conflict-resolution meeting with my peers?" Then wait for the body to respond. The brain produces thoughts more quickly than the body generates subtle yet discernible sensations. They often start out vague and indescribable, but they become clearer when you acknowledge them with kind attention. Listening attentively and inquiring into the sensations, emotions, thoughts, and images that might all be a part of the "felt sense" often leads to surprising flashes of insight or new understandings of a challenge or situation (Rome, 2014, p. 5). It's usually helpful to acknowledge what you're experiencing by describing your "felt sense," or overall body sense. Here's a truncated description of what an embodied listening experience might be like.

Example of Embodied Listening

I'm about to facilitate an interaction that might be fraught with fear and anger at a time when I'm pressed on all sides with project deadlines. I decide to listen to myself in an embodied way and ask my body to show me how to be calm and clear in the meeting. After sitting quietly and getting grounded in my body and present with myself, I notice a bit of tightness in the lower belly and a sense of pressure on the sternum. I pause to see if these descriptions resonate with those areas. I get a "yes" from the belly but a "no" from the sternum. (It's like the inner felt sense of knowing where you want to go eat or knowing that you don't want a particular food.) Instead of "pressure," I suggest "crowded" for the sternum and get a "yes." I notice thoughts emerging: "I am so tired . . . I can't do this." I also note that part of me feels anxious. I acknowledge all of this with a kind acceptance: "This is my experience right now." As I say this inside, my belly relaxes a bit, and there seems to be more space around the sternum. As I stay with these sensations, more space opens in my torso, and my breath slows and deepens. I ask, "What might you need?" Words come: "Slow down. Stay connected to your body, especially the feeling of your feet on the floor." Until that moment, I hadn't realized how fast my internal pace was. For a few minutes, I sit with this overall sense of a slower pace, noticing my feet on the floor. I end this period of embodied listening with a calm knowing that I'll be able to stay present with whatever occurs in the meeting.

For further instructions, I recommend *Your Body Knows the Answer* by David I. Rome.

When you observe sensations, emotions, or thoughts that are separate or merging into a whole, it's important *not* to equate them with who you are. Your subjective, conscious sensations, thoughts, or emotions—known as *qualia*—differ from the one who is experiencing them (Ramachandran, p. 248). For example, instead of saying, "I'm shaky right now," say, "A part of me feels shaky right now." Or say, "I'm noticing that part of me is getting annoyed." This allows you to acknowledge a sensation or feeling without becoming it. You can then acknowledge that part and ask it what it might need or what it wants to say. You are able to have, be aware of, and reflect on your experience.

For further reading about embodied movement and embodied listening, I recommend the writings of Russell Delman, Moshe Feldenkrais, Eugene Gendlin, and Ann Weiser Cornell.

Misconceptions about Mindfulness Meditation. Common misconceptions about mindfulness meditation are that it helps you get rid of thoughts and emotions, lets you distance yourself from the ups and downs of being alive, creates a stable or fixed mind or brain state, and helps you change your personality or behavior (i.e., become a better person).

All four misunderstandings create a hostile or threatening environment inside you because they all implicitly communicate that you don't accept yourself as you are in this moment. When you threaten yourself with judgments about what you think you're supposed to be, the amygdala goes on alert and you become more vulnerable and reactive to perceived threats from outside. This is the opposite of what one hopes to experience in meditating. Ultimately, one of the most important factors affecting how we talk with one another is our relationship with ourselves, including our thoughts and emotions. The inner conversations trigger our emotional reactions.

It's a deft maneuver to meditate without being attached to what you want to accomplish by meditating. For instance, I continue to meditate and practice embodied moving and listening because they've helped me do the following:

- connect with myself and know what's going on "in there";
- notice before I go on automatic and do or say things that I'll later regret;
- be less likely to get emotionally hijacked and more able to recover quickly when I do;

- have a kinder, more compassionate relationship with myself and others;
- make conscious choices about how to be constructive and helpful in meetings; and
- more frequently and spontaneously "know" what I need to do to be helpful in human interactions.

However, I don't think about any of these benefits when I meditate. They would only get in the way of being present to my current experience. Do they make me a better person? I don't know. Although I started to meditate and practice embodied moving and listening with this intention, this idea no longer makes sense to me. I think of it more now as being present in each moment and choosing to behave as constructively, compassionately, and wisely as I can.

Why Mindful Awareness Matters

To get from where we are to where we want to be in our communities and places of work, we need to be able to learn, think, and interact constructively with one another. A prerequisite is learning to distinguish between what we're actually experiencing and our judgments about what we're experiencing. The former opens the doors to new ways forward in understanding and figuring out solutions to tough problems. The latter foments misunderstanding and conflict.

Developing mindfulness through meditation, embodied movement, and/or embodied listening is essential because it gives us the ability to pause before we react, to consider options, and to choose the most constructive ways to respond to circumstances, even if the best thing to do is simply to be quiet until we can discern the most helpful thing to say or do. Mindfulness also enables us to discern whether what we're about to do or say will harm others or ourselves. We need to make conscious choices that consider the short- and long-term consequences of what we're about to say or do.

Most of the research about the impact of meditation on the brain has been conducted on mindfulness meditation. We now know that it affects and changes us in a number of positive ways, including strengthening the immune system, reducing addictive behaviors, and lessening chronic physical pain. Here, I investigate the three effects that are most relevant to talking better together and finding solutions to tough issues: (a) calming the brain, (b) strengthening the mind, and (c) increasing a sense of interconnectedness and compassion.

Calming and Enhancing the Brain. Mindfulness meditation helps calm the brain in four ways:

- It quiets the amygdala and increases the density of the hippocampus.
- It strengthens the connections between the amygdala and the prefrontal cortex.
- It weakens the chain of associative thoughts that are often negative.
- It improves the tone of the vagus, an influential cranial nerve.

First, when people practice mindfulness meditation, the amygdala (the alarm bell in the brain) quiets, making them less likely to get triggered in interactions that might have seemed threatening in the past. This quieting could be the result of a decrease in the density of the gray matter in the amygdala (Baime, 2011, p. 48) because it's less active.

Mindfulness meditation also activates and strengthens the hippocampus, even "plumping" it up by increasing gray matter density

(Boyce, 2012, p. 43). The hippocampus is part of the limbic system; it plays a central role in learning and in consolidating information from short-term memory into long-term memory.

A quieter amygdala is important for another reason: It decreases the amount of corticosteroids, such as cortisol, in the body. At too high of a level, these chemicals can damage the hippocampus, even causing it to shrink; they also elevate heart rate and blood pressure, creating a spiral of reactivity.

Second, when mindfulness meditation strengthens connections between the amygdala and the prefrontal cortex, the prefrontal cortex is able to inhibit the impulsive actions associated with negative emotions like fear and anger. In other words, we can respond to similar experiences differently.

When the brain is calm, we're more apt to be open and less emotionally reactive to whatever is occurring, even when we dislike it or find it difficult. When we're composed, we have more space in which to notice emotions and thoughts. This allows us to investigate what's evoking them and decide what would be best to do in a particular situation instead of doing what we might previously have been driven to do. If we practice mindfulness, we're more likely to pause, take a breath, notice what's going on, and ask ourselves some useful questions like "What is my intention?" "What might be going on with others?" and "What might I say or do to help us all move forward in a positive way?"

Third, the mental training of mindfulness meditation weakens the chain of associations produced by the highly associative mechanisms in the brain (Davidson, 2012, p. 243). This is helpful because the negative bias of the brain inclines it to remember more negative experiences than positive ones. Thus, the brain has more negative memories or thoughts with which to associate current circumstances. These can keep the amygdala on alert in a whirlpool of emotions and discomfiting stories. For instance, if you're in a meeting of people developing this year's strategic planning process, you might begin thinking about how frustrated you were during last year's because you felt embarrassed when it became clear that your department hadn't accomplished its goals. Unless you're aware of these associations, you can get cranky about this year's process. Practicing mindfulness enables us to notice the associations the brain is making so we can decide whether they're relevant to the current conversation or just an undermining distraction.

Finally, mindfulness practice improves the tone of the vagus nerve, which is a key part of the parasympathetic nervous system that can turn off fight-or-flight reactions and turn on what psychiatrist Stephen W. Porges calls the "social engagement system" (2011, p. 56). The tone of the nerve plays an important role in regulating the homeostasis of the body's internal organs, including the heart, lungs, and digestive tracts (p. 103). Higher vagal tone makes it less likely that we'll get angry and helps us recover more quickly when we do (Goleman, 2015, p. 27). It also means that we're able to better manage our attention and emotions (Goleman, 2013, p. 198).

Strengthening the Mind. Daniel Siegel defines the brain as "a collection of neurons distributed in the skull and throughout the body through which energy and information flow." He defines the human mind as "an embodied and relational emergent process that regulates the flow of energy and information" (Summer, 2011, p. 73). It's "embodied" because the process occurs in the body. It's "relational" because (a) energy and information flow within and among people on both a conscious and an unconscious level and (b) how we relate to ourselves and to others (and how they relate to us) affects this flow. We can experience and observe this flow as it happens. For example, when you see a good friend, you can feel excitement and happiness moving throughout your body and sense the same in your friend. It's an "emergent process" in that it's dynamic, always changing in relation to circumstances and attention.

Practicing mindfulness "promotes the growth of integrative fibers in the brain," thus increasing our ability to observe and manage the flow of energy and information in the brain, including the entire nervous system (Summer, 2011, p. 71). This practice opens up space between stimulus and response so we can make conscious choices. Through mindfulness meditation, we strengthen the uniquely human ability to decide how we want to respond to circumstances.

In other words, developing mindfulness enables us to use our minds to manage our brains. This occurs because mindfulness meditation increases and strengthens the connections between the prefrontal cortex and the amygdala. According to neuroscientist Richard Davidson, these connections promote equanimity and resilience, meaning we can avoid or recover more quickly from emotional hijackings (2012, p. 243).

You could think of mindfulness meditation as a kind of mental training in which you learn to use the mind (the embodied and relational process through which we manage the flow of energy and information) to help you consciously manage the brain (the collection of neurons through which energy and information flow) so you can make conscious choices about how to relate with others and the world at large. Over time, this mental training can help you move from states of mindfulness that come and go to a trait or characteristic of how you usually are in meetings and in your life.

I want to be clear. I'm not proposing we use the mind to control or override the brain or body. I am suggesting that we use the mind to engender more awareness of the brain and body so that we're better able to calm and manage the self-protective mechanisms in the older parts of the brain and have more access to the wisdom and compassion that are resident in the whole brain and body.

Here's what strengthening the mind might enable you to do in a work meeting: You notice that you're getting annoyed with a colleague who keeps talking about things that seem off topic. You also observe that your inner dialogue is intensifying the annoyance: "Why is she talking about this? It has nothing to do with what we're discussing. We have several more agenda items to cover, and her tangents are wasting our time." You pause, take a breath, pause the unhelpful thoughts, and ask yourself, "What is this?" You realize that you're annoyed because you're afraid the group might not get to your agenda item. You consider how you might get her back on track without offending her or disrupting the meeting—in other words, respond without causing harm. You decide to say, "Excuse me for a moment. We're getting short on time to finish all the agenda items we agreed we wanted to handle today. Could you help us understand how what you're saying relates to or might help us finish this topic?" Your tone and facial expression are crucial because they communicate how you're feeling, regardless of how much of a poker face you try to put on. This is why becoming less reactive to experience is helpful: You can really be calmer when you intervene, not just pretend that you are.

All said, the mind isn't as easily defined or delineated as the brain. Are they the same thing? Does the mind include the brain and body in addition to something else as yet to be defined? Where is the mind located in the nervous system? In the prefrontal cortex? The entire body? How does the brain affect the mind and vice versa? Perhaps one day we'll be able to answer these questions. For now, I approach the definition of *mind* with humility and respect, sharing what seems to be true both in terms of the neurological research—which is in its infancy—and my direct experience. Thus, I use Siegel's definitions of brain and mind as works in progress. The great gift and mystery of "mind" is that it does include the brain but refers to so much more, such as our ability to direct our attention and to observe our thoughts, emotions, and sensations as we experience them. We can be aware of mind itself: We can simultaneously experience something and know that we're experiencing it. As Delman wrote, "The knower, the known, and the capacity for knowing all arise together" (2007).

Despite our lack of complete understanding of the mind, Siegel posited the significance of using it in an interview in 2011:

> Mindfulness is a part of a much larger frame that society has to move to: embracing the importance of our relationships with one another and seeing that the mind, though it's not measurable like physical things are, is actually a real entity whose workings have monumental effects on the shape of our world—physical and otherwise. (Boyce, 2011, p. 50)

Increasing a Sense of Interconnectedness and Compassion. Mindfulness meditation strengthens our sense of interconnectedness with others, or the "resonance circuit" that helps us be aware of our inner state and attune to that of others (Siegel, 2011, p. 74). This means that mindfulness meditation alters how we experience and treat those around us. When we practice mindfulness, we tend to pay more attention to others, especially when they're in distress or pain. We're also inclined to help them, to try to relieve their suffering (Destano, 2015).

Being open to connecting with and caring for others is an essential part of interacting effectively. This is critical when we engage with people who differ and think differently from us. Our connectedness and compassion can help us maintain a sense of safety in a meeting instead of feeling threatened by the uncertainty that comes with differences. Although compassion doesn't mean we'll agree, it does increase the likelihood that we'll find some common ground.

Chapter 7 explores what compassion looks like in meetings and why it's essential to our solving complex issues together.

Despite all the good news about mindfulness meditation quieting the brain, strengthening the mind, and increasing compassion, we'll likely get triggered in meetings. Here's an in-the-moment meditation to help you calm yourself so you can make conscious choices.

When You Notice You're Getting Triggered . . .

With practice, these six steps can be done in less than a minute. Practice them in situations that aren't fraught with emotion so you can more readily follow them when a situation is.

1. **Ground yourself in your body.** Pay attention to the surface (floor, chair) under you that supports you. Notice the sensations in your body of weight or substance, your feet on the ground, and your buttocks on the chair. When you're about to be hijacked

by fear or anger, you'll feel it in your body first: increased heart rate, shallow or rapid breathing, tightening of muscles in legs or hands. Scan inside your body to see if you notice any other sensations. Body sensations are both the source of and part of the antidote to emotional hijacking.

2. **Pay attention to your breathing.** Pause and sense your breath. Notice whether you're holding your breath or breathing rapidly. Take three slow breaths in which you pay attention to all four parts of it: the exhale, the slight pause, the inhale, and the slight pause before the next exhale.

3. **Bring conscious attention to the external world.** While remaining connected to your body and breath, notice the colors and shapes in the room. Listen to the tones of people's voices. Bring awareness to the space around you, above and below, front and back.

4. **Notice and label what you're feeling.** Acknowledge and accept whatever emotions you're experiencing as best you can. Be careful not to judge yourself for them; doing so will only intensify the emotions. Remind yourself that whatever you're feeling isn't all of who you are ("I am angry"); it's only a part of who you are in this moment ("Part of me is feeling angry right now"). Another part of you is able to observe these emotions and make conscious choices about how to handle them.

5. **Inquire into the source of your emotions.** What has been threatened: your sense of status, certainty,

autonomy, relationship, or fairness? When you inquire into the source of your reaction, be careful not to exacerbate your emotions by judging or justifying them. Practice accepting and "being with" whatever you're feeling, even if it's unpleasant or uncomfortable.

6. **Make a conscious choice about how to proceed.** Here are some options:

   - Stop and take a break. (It's always possible and often wise to ask for a "time out" when you or a group needs it.)
   - Share how you're feeling.
   - Ask a question.
   - Talk about something unrelated to your emotion.
   - Make a process observation or suggestion.

If you decide to talk about your emotions, take responsibility for them by using "I" statements ("I feel frustrated" versus "You make me so frustrated"). Explain what evoked the emotion without interpreting or judging others' behavior. For example, say, "We seem to be jumping in quickly to talk right after one another. I feel frustrated because I'm finding it hard to track the group's thinking. I wonder if we could slow the pace down a bit and make sure we understand what someone has said before someone else jumps in."

Remember why you are doing this. You practice and follow these steps because you don't want to go on automatic, become mindless, and cause harm. Your intention is to work with others effectively so you can accomplish what all of what you set out to do.

Expand Awareness to Self, Others, and the Context

Being mindful in interactions enables us to expand our awareness to tend to the three components operating in every meeting: yourself, others, and the context.

1) Awareness of "Self." "Self" is in quotes here because, as we explore in Chapter 6, most of us have a fixed definition of "self" that blinds us to the dynamic nature of being alive. Paying attention to breath and body sensations in the present moment enables us to notice how they, along with our emotions and thoughts, reveal their transitory nature.

Being more aware of this dynamic inner world enables us to notice early warning signs of an emotional hijacking—tightening shoulders, elevated pulse, butterflies in the gut—so we can consciously manage our emotions, not deny or repress them. For example, suppose that at a meeting, you notice that your tummy is jumpy and that part of you is feeling anxious. You also notice that you're paying more attention to your opinions about what others are saying based on past experience than you are to understanding what they're saying right now. You can choose to become curious and listen more carefully to their words and tone in this moment. You might ask them questions to deepen your understanding of their perspectives: "How did you come to see the situation this way?" This self-awareness enables you to shift from past to present, from opinions to questions, and deepen your sense of relationship with others.

Two parts of the brain are instrumental in helping us develop the ability to be aware of our internal states and bodily processes: the vagus nerve and the insula. As noted earlier, Porges calls this ability to sense what's going on internally our sixth primary sense, or interoception. The vagus is a large nerve with many branches that enables bidirectional communication between the brain and the body, especially the internal organs. Deep in the cerebral cortex, the insula is also involved in communication between the brain and the viscera. Because it has links to all the visceral organs, including the heart and gut, the insula is a kind of map of our insides.

As already mentioned, mindfulness meditation increases the tone of the vagus nerve. It also increases the gray matter in the insula, enhancing its ability to sustain interoceptive connectivity and accuracy even in the face of external "stressors" (Farb, Segal, & Anderson, 2013). Paying attention to any of the organs in the torso—for example, the heart or gut—increases the insula's sensitivity to it. This in turn increases activity in the insula overall and supports greater levels of self-awareness (Davidson, 2012, p. 79).

According to Goleman, "Our 'gut feelings' are messages from the insula and other bottom up circuits" (2013, p. 66). Embodied moving and embodied listening are practices that enable us to listen to the integrated messages coming from our "wisdom body." In this way, mindfulness meditation helps us expand our awareness of ourselves so that we find and exercise options that are more life-giving than fighting, fleeing, or freezing in difficult conversations.

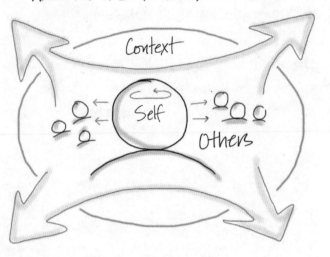

Awareness of Self, Others, and Context

2) Awareness of Others. It might seem counterintuitive, but the more self-aware you are, the more you're able to be aware of others. Our ability to sense the states of mind of others depends on how able we are to sense our own. The vagus nerve and the insula are part of a "resonance circuit" in the brain that enables us to sense what others might be feeling by noticing what is going on inside ourselves (Siegel, 2011, p. 62).

In addition to having an internal awareness of others, we can, of course, notice people's facial expressions, tone of voice, pace of speech, and posture as we interact with them. When we do, it increases our ability to understand their perspectives, feel what they feel, and build a sense of connection with them.

Although mindfulness meditation engenders individual aware-ness, more explicit action is usually required for a group to become aware of itself. One of the most powerful things to do is to hold up a neutral verbal "mirror" to a group by describing what you're seeing and hearing. For example, when you say, "I notice that we're starting to interrupt one another," a group automatically changes its behavior.

Increased awareness of others helps you see what's going on in the group as a whole. For example, you might notice the overall tone of conversation (friendly, combative, or engaged); its pace (slow and considered or fast and spontaneous); or how people are participating (debating and asserting or listening and asking questions). Such awareness helps you make observations and suggest course corrections to keep the conversation moving forward constructively. You'll find examples of how to do this in Chapter 9.

People tend to feel anxious in the unpredictable environment of group discussions, so it's easy to lose your ability to be aware of others and the group as a whole and become lost in your thoughts and feelings. As mentioned previously, when we're anxious, we tend not to care about or even notice others. If expanding your attention to others seems difficult, shift your attention up to the ceiling and pretend to be a bank camera surveying the group as a whole. Notice what stands out from that vantage point.

When I'm at my most calm, present, and expansive, I'm simultaneously aware of what's going on inside me and what's going on with a group. More often, my attention is like a toggle switch, shifting between self and others. The important thing is to be able to expand your awareness so you can either shift your attention back and forth between inner and outer or pay attention to both simultaneously. The ability to move our attention from inner to outer in an embodied way is essential to our ability to make conscious choices about how to help a group move forward in a constructive way.

Paying attention to others includes noticing how a meeting is affecting you along with everyone in it. Although mindfulness enables you to investigate what others are experiencing by observing your own body sensations, thoughts, and emotions, you need to remain differentiated. In other words, you need to be able to discern your perceptions and experience from those of others. For example, suppose you notice that you feel frustrated or annoyed in a meeting. Pause and ask what might be causing this. After a few moments of investigation, you conclude that you don't seem to be feeling annoyed about anything, so you wonder if you're sensing what others might be feeling. It's important to avoid making assumptions and to check your perceptions by making an observation or asking a question—for example, "I'm noticing a number of furrowed brows. How is everybody?" Asking this reminds everyone in the group to be aware of themselves and others. Without the ability to distinguish, you might have thought you were annoyed and unconsciously begun to say things that exacerbated people's distress, not realizing that you were mirroring the emotions of others.

Awareness of others' emotions is a critical component of being able to behave constructively in interactions. It enables us to make wiser choices about what to do or say.

3) Awareness of Context. Previously, I indicated that context includes two elements: the culture in which the conversation is occurring and people's stake in the content or outcomes of a meeting. I'd like to broaden this definition to include any of the conditions in which the interaction is occurring. For example, the context for meetings in organizations includes their mission, vision, strategy, business plan, customers or clients, suppliers, and financial health; the leadership style of their leaders; and the values and current circumstances of their employees. In communities, context includes the effectiveness and accessibility of governmental and social institutions; the financial health of businesses and families; the health of infrastructures; the leadership style of the leaders (both formal and informal); and the values and circumstances of the residents and the culture of the various communities that comprise larger communities.

Being aware of the context in which any interaction occurs is important because it influences what people say and do, how they feel, and what they might need in a meeting. For example, in planning and facilitating a series of community meetings about how to manage a county's primary water resource, I needed to understand that these gatherings were occurring in a state prone to drought and in a region still smarting from the extraction of its resources, especially timber and water, over decades. People along the political spectrum were bringing an already defensive and protective stance to these discussions. Thus, creating a safe and inclusive environment in the meetings was even more critical than usual.

When we mindfully pay attention to present experience—sensations, emotions, and thoughts—without liking or disliking it, things change in the brain, body, and mind. We're calmer and more compassionate; better able to prevent or manage destructive behavior; and capable of making more conscious and constructive choices about what to say, how to say it, and when to say it. In meetings, we need to develop our attention so we can pay attention to what's going on for us and for the group and how the context might be affecting everyone in the group. This is why mindfulness and the practice of making conscious choices is foundational to using the other seven practices that are the subject of ensuing chapters.

Key Points

- "Mindfulness is moment-to-moment, non-judgmental awareness, cultivated by paying attention in a specific way, that is,
  in the present moment, and as non-reactively, as non-judgmentally and as openheartedly as possible" (Kabat-Zinn, 2005,
  p. 108).
- Embodied movement and embodied listening are instrumental practices that complement mindfulness meditation.
- Practicing mindfulness calms the brain and body, makes us less
  reactive, weakens the chain of association of mostly negative
  thoughts, and makes us more resilient and compassionate.
- When we're aware, we can make conscious choices about what
  we want to say in interactions and how and when to say it. In
  other words, we can respond with care and consideration and
  not react from fear or anger.
- Practicing mindfulness enables us to strengthen our minds to
  more effectively manage the brain and its habitual self-protective mechanisms.
- In meetings, we need to have an expanded and mobile attention that allows us to be aware of ourselves, others, and the
  context in which we're interacting.

Questions for Reflection

Think about the last time you were alone and just listened
to *yourself*. What was that like for you? What did you learn?

How might you increase your ability to make conscious
choices in your meetings?

Chapter 5:
Defining Intentions

Do you create or destroy? That's for your ordeal-by-fire to answer.

— Daj Hammarskjöld

Daj Hammarskjöld, the second Secretary-General of the United Nations, thought the UN "should have one room dedicated to silence in the outward sense and stillness in the inner sense." Because of this, he personally planned and supervised the creation of the Meditation Room before he died in a plane crash in 1961 while on a peace mission in the Congo. There are only three things in this dimly lit, triangular room: the 9-by-6.5-foot abstract fresco you face as you enter; three rows of woven wicker stools; and a 6.5-ton, 4-foot-high rectangular block of raw iron ore in between the two. A single spotlight illuminates the polished top of this "altar."

The text that Hammarskjöld wrote for visitors to this room includes the following:

The material of the stone leads our thoughts to the necessity for choice between destruction and construction, between war and peace. Of iron man has forged his swords, of iron he has also made ploughshares. Of iron he has constructed tanks, but of iron he has likewise built homes for man. The block of iron ore is part of the wealth we have inherited on this earth of ours. How shall we use it?

Although the myriad decisions we make before, during, and after meetings at work and in our communities might not individually set the stage for us to create or destroy, cumulatively they do. Our choices either create or destroy a sense of connection and community, and they diminish or develop our ability to talk well together, solve difficult issues, and make wise decisions. Over time, the choices we make about how to interact affect our organizations, communities, and eventually who we are. What impact do we want such choices to ultimately have on our world? What are our deepest intentions for meetings with co-workers and neighbors?

Intentions Guide Us from the Inside Out

Our purpose—or intention—acts as an internal compass guiding our thoughts and actions when we interact with others. For example, regardless of whether I'm a meeting participant, a leader, or a facilitator, my intention is to help people (a) feel a sense of safety and belonging so that they can contribute their unique perspectives and experience and (b) work together collaboratively so they can solve tough issues and create a desirable future. Since we never know which meeting or interaction is going to make an important difference, I assume I might as well behave in all of them as if they were the lynchpin event in the life of an organization or a community.

Intentions reflect what is most important to us in working with others. Intentions help set the stage for what is possible because they shape how we think and behave. In turn, our intentions influence the same in others. Because of this, we need to carefully and consciously define our intentions. Ideally, our intentions live at the intersection between what we love and what the world needs—that is, they reflect "enlightened self-interest."

Building on the thoughts of Peter Block in "The Empowered Manager" (1987, pp. 80–87), our intentions are "enlightened" when they

- respond to a deep longing or value in us and include a desire to contribute something of real value, to be of service;
- incorporate a commitment to act with integrity: saying what we mean and meaning what we say;
- have a positive impact on people: treating people with compassion and caring about their well-being; and
- involve understanding as much as we can about the issues at hand: considering information that both confirms and challenges our current thinking.

In other words, our intentions of enlightened self-interest benefit us, those around us, *and* the situation at hand.

One hurdle to carrying out our intentions is to remember what they are so they guide how we interact. When we're under pressure or when we feel threatened, intentions can get lost as our self-protective instincts take over.

Realizing our intentions can sometimes put the brain's two survival instincts—to protect ourselves and to stay connected with others—into conflict. We might think that we have to choose between the two. What might happen if we were to perceive these instincts as complementary instead of conflicting? We can protect ourselves by maintaining a relationship with others, especially in a heated argument.

For instance, Mike is a member of a work team. Because the project's success is important to him, he decides he wants to help build good working relationships among all the members of the team. In a project update meeting, he's unpleasantly surprised when another team member, Tom, criticizes him in a harsh tone of voice. As Mike's heart starts to race, his face reddens. He doesn't feel safe, and defensive thoughts proliferate: "Where does this guy get off criticizing me? He knows nothing about it. What a jerk!" However, because Mike defined his intention beforehand, he pauses, takes a breath, and reminds himself that he wants to build good working relationships. So instead of acting defensively, he slows himself and the interaction down by checking his understanding of Tom's concerns. In a calm tone, Mike paraphrases what Tom said: "It appears you don't approve of the way I handled this." Then Mike asks for more information: "Can you be more specific about what I did that you think is a problem?" Once Mike better understands Tom's concerns, he evenly explains why he did what he did and why he thought it would contribute to the project and the team as a whole. Now that Tom understands Mike's logic, he describes how it created problems for him in more detail. Mike acknowledges that he didn't foresee how his work would interfere with Tom's. Team members join in to figure out how to prevent the problem from happening again.

Mike's intention is an example of enlightened self-interest. The intention had meaning for him, and it included a desire to have a positive impact on the team and to be of service to it. Remembering his intention—the hardest part—helped him to realize it by caring about Tom's well-being and to understand the issue at hand.

What would have happened had Mike forgotten or not defined his intention? He could have easily gotten defensive, disconnected from Tom and the group as a whole, and vehemently defended what he had done. If he'd really gotten hot and bothered, he might have even begun criticizing Tom. In doing this, he would have destroyed the teamwork necessary for the project to succeed.

Defining clear intentions before meetings primes us to behave in ways that are consistent with our intentions and helps us get back on track when we start to veer off course.

Three Ways to Clarify Intentions

There are many ways to clarify your intentions. Here are three: (a) ask good questions, (b) be a fair witness to yourself as you clarify them, and (c) develop metaphors that help you refine and remember them.

1) Ask Good Questions. The brain can't resist a question, so be sure to ask good ones. They don't need to be complex, just heartfelt. You could start with "What are my highest intentions for this meeting? " "How could I be of service to the group as a whole?" "What would help me act with integrity in this meeting?" or "How can I help everyone—including myself—feel safe and bring the best of who we are to the table?"

Our intentions for meetings often grow out of the ones for our lives. Here are some questions about your larger intentions for how you live your life:

- What is your purpose in life? What matters to you in life, ultimately?
- Circle back to the places and things of your youth. What were your original aspirations for yourself? What kind of person did you want to be?
- What has heart and meaning for you?
- What do you most deeply love and hope for? What intentions will help you take responsibility for that?
- What intentions could serve you, others, and your life as a whole?
- What kind of relationship do you want to engender with people at work or in your community?
- What impact do you want to have on those you interact with?
- What legacy do you want to leave behind?

Clarifying your most important intentions for a meeting, or for your life, takes effort. You'll likely need to reflect on them and test their veracity and importance to you with trusted mentors, friends, or colleagues. As you say your intentions aloud, pay attention to your internal response, including your body's sensations. When I ask myself about what's important, after the initial answer, I often follow it up with "Is that so? What is underneath this? Why is this important to me?" I ask this until I get to what I think is the essence of my intention. For example, what lies underneath my intention to help people have a sense of safety and belonging? It's my belief that in order to solve tough issues, we all need to bring the best of who we are to the table, including our compassion and wisdom. We can't do this when we're in the throes of fear or anger. I usually sense a "yes" inside my torso when I get to the essence of my deepest intentions.

It's not common for people to clarify their intentions before meetings in this way, but research indicates that when you ask people about their intentions, it influences what they do. People are more accustomed to clarifying their ambitions, what they want to accomplish, how they'll make the case for their point of view, or how to manage the interaction to get their way or win the day. I invite you to clarify the edifying, far-reaching intentions that might just underlie your ambitions. As philosopher Peter Koestenbaum said, "Unless the distant goals of meaning, greatness, and destiny are addressed, we can't make an intelligent decision about what to do tomorrow morning—much less set strategy for a company or for a human life" (Labarre, 2000, p. 224).

2) Be a Fair Witness As You Clarify Your Intentions. Ironically, as you unearth and define your deepest intentions, you might be surprised at the chorus of voices that arise to undermine them. They might sound something like "Who do you think you are, wanting to help others bring the best of who they are to the table?" "Given all you've seen and heard, what makes you think people can be wise or compassionate in this organization?" "Why do you think that you can help change the culture of conversation in this community just by how you behave as a participant?" or "When you listen, it only encourages those who already talk too much."

It's up to you whether you (a) listen to these critical voices and allow them to discourage you from your bold intentions, (b) argue with them, or (c) ignore them. None of these are helpful: getting discouraged is certainly not, and when you argue with critical voices or try to ignore them, they seem to get stronger. (That which we resist persists.) They tend to quiet down when we simply acknowledge that they exist and usually are trying to protect us from harm—for example, from being disappointed or hurt.

It's important to remember that these voices are part of who you are, not all of who you are. Acknowledge and accept both the critical, fearful, protective voices and the courageous and hopeful ones. You can acknowledge and accept them by saying something like "I notice that part of me wants to give up my enlightened intentions and stay hunkered down in business as usual. Another part wants to 'go for it' and help create the best possible conversation in this group."

Avoid labeling any apparently competing voices or attitudes as "good" or "bad." Simply acknowledging that they're there frees up space in which you can consciously choose where you want to turn your attention and what will motivate your actions.

3) Develop Inspiring Metaphors. Metaphors, or symbols of our intentions, help us stay aware of our intentions so we can act congruently. Metaphors can also help us define intentions. For example, as you ask yourself good questions about your intentions and wait for them to become clear, notice what images draw your attention. Listen to the lyrics of songs you sing in the shower or as you drive to work. They could be breadcrumbs leading you to your deepest intentions. For example, when I heard cross-cultural anthropologist Angeles Arrien speak many years ago of a "bamboo reed, firm and yet bending," this image helped me clarify my intention to communicate my ideas in a clear and inclusive way, meaning I share my point of view and am open to changing it based on what I learn from others. To this day, this image reminds me to not be attached to being "right" and to stay open to others' perspectives.

Another image that helps me is that of the bank security camera. After all my years of training and practice as a consultant and facilitator, I've become adept at seeing situations through the eyes of others. As a result, it's sometimes hard for me to know how *I* see it and contribute my own thoughts. My colleague and friend Dawna Markova encouraged me not to *give my eyes away*—to view circumstances primarily from the point of view of others or a bank camera—but to practice seeing the world through my own eyes.

Living our intentions is easier to write about than to do. Because of this, I encourage you to consider your intentions as "practices." Use them in low-stakes or low-conflict settings so they're more readily available in high-stakes, high-conflict interactions. "Constantly practice being who it is you want to be," said martial artist and action film actor Bruce Lee. "Under duress, we do not rise to our expectations; we fall to our level of practice."

Here are a few of the ways I practice my intention to create a sense of safety and belonging: I make an effort to learn and use people's names, I make eye contact with them, and I do my best to listen attentively and not interrupt them. I also ask questions of genuine curiosity and check my understanding of what they have said.

A poem by William Stafford helps me remember that even though I won't always be able to stay true to my intentions, my intentions will always stay true for me. "The Way It Is" (1998, p. 42) goes like this:

There's a thread you follow. It goes among
things that change. But it doesn't change.
People wonder about what you are pursuing.
You have to explain about the thread.
But it is hard for others to see.
While you hold it you can't get lost.
Tragedies happen; people get hurt
or die; and you suffer and get old.
Nothing you can do can stop time's unfolding.
You don't ever let go of the thread.

Make Intentions Public

Although it's not common for people to think about or make public their intentions for a meeting, doing so can help set a salubrious tone. One way to make intentions public is by asking the simple question "What are our highest hopes for this conversation (or meeting)?" Considering and communicating hopes is one way to help people define their intentions. Asking people what their hopes are primes them to behave congruently with them.

You can ask this question as a leader, facilitator, or participant. At the start of a day-long planning session with an executive team, here are some of the ways the leaders responded when asked what their highest hopes were for the day: "respect each other," "reaffirm who we are," and "collaborate well." These became the basis for how they wanted to conduct themselves at the meeting, or their "ground rules."

Intentions Prime Us for Good

Making conscious choices about enlightened intentions increases the likelihood that we'll carry them out. This is because they prime us to do so. *Priming* refers to preparing or influencing people to respond in a particular way. Priming occurs through such factors as words, images, or an entire environment that evokes, facilitates, or inhibits particular body sensations, emotions, thoughts, and behaviors. The cues in an environment that can affect us—consciously or unconsciously—are just about everything in it, including colors, pictures, and objects along with gestures, tones of voice, expressions, questions, and people's appearances.

The environment is part of the context for a meeting. And as noted in Chapter 3, the context influences the extent to which we react defensively to threats to our sense of status, certainty, autonomy, relatedness, or fairness (SCARF). We can consciously choose to hold intentions, create a meeting environment, and shape the context in which we meet to prime people to contribute the best of who they are to the conversation.

In a classic experiment, a group of college students (ages 18 to 22) was asked to create sentences from a set of words such as *Florida, forgetful, bald, gray,* or *wrinkle.* Other groups of students were asked to do the same thing but with words that aren't associated with being old. When the students who crafted sentences with words associated with the elderly were asked to walk down the hall to an office for another experiment, their pace was slacker than that of the other groups. Outside of their awareness, the words primed these students to move more slowly than peers who hadn't been primed in this way (Kahneman, 2011, p. 53).

Another striking example of just how powerfully priming can influence us was demonstrated in Ellen Langer's ambitious 1979 "counterclockwise study" (2009), in which she invited a group of elderly people to live as though it were 1959. The experimental group comprised men in their 80s who were all extremely dependent on relatives—that is, until the moment they were driven to a monastery in New Hampshire, where they lived and spoke as if it were 20 years earlier. They had access only to magazines and TV shows from the same week in 1959. *Life Magazine* and *The Saturday Evening Post* were strewn on side tables, and *Ted Mack's Original Amateur Hour*, Jack Benny, and Perry Como were on the TV. They discussed "recent" books like Ian Fleming's *Goldfinger* and Leon Uris's *Exodus* in the present tense. The control group lived at the same monastery at another time, but they reminisced about life in the past instead of living as if it were 1959.

Here's what the researchers found. The experimental group showed greater improvement in gait, joint flexibility, finger length (their arthritis had diminished), manual dexterity, vision, and hearing. On intelligence tests, 64 percent of the experimental group's scores improved, compared to only 44 percent of the control group's. And, finally, when reviewing before-and-after photos, independent observers noted that participants in the experimental group appeared "significantly younger" at the end of living as if it really were 1959 than those in the control group who only reminisced about 1959. Such is the power of priming.

Priming seems to occur most often outside of our awareness through the associative nature of the brain, with all its memories, ideas, and emotions. For instance, when I hear the word *grace*, I think of an old friend named Grace with whom I initially experienced Carl Rogers' groundbreaking work on listening and offering "unconditional positive regard" to another. This one word sparks a spider-web of associations and evokes a series of emotions, body sensations, and thoughts inside me, including poignant moments of when I was deeply listened to or when I listened deeply to others. I feel warmth growing inside and sense a slight smile blossoming on my face. All this in a few seconds from the word *grace*. Priming is a self-reinforcing dynamic of cognitive, emotional, and physical responses.

Clearly, priming can be done for a variety of reasons. Advertisers, pundits, and politicians prime us to adopt their perspectives: "If you buy this product, you'll be happy, successful, safe, popular, and of course, gorgeous, just like the models or actors in the advertisement." Politicians and pundits try to influence our thinking by how they frame issues in speeches, interviews, and political ads. For example, notice the different impact on you when you read or hear "getting fired" versus "getting outplaced," "gun control" versus "preventing gun violence," "freedom to choose" versus "right to life," or "performance management" versus "performance evaluation." Words in and of themselves prime us to think and feel in particular ways.

Because human beings both are influenced by and influence their environments, we can use the power of priming to help people feel safe and stay focused and to stimulate constructive conversation. To echo the choice Hammarskjöld posed, we can use priming to create or destroy. We can take advantage of the positive benefits of priming by making conscious choices about our intentions and by priming others in a meeting to follow suit. Our intentions will be mirrored in others through the mirror neurons that read our intentions.

Clarifying our intentions is challenge enough, but the bigger test is whether we can we stay true to them when we're standing in the fire of difficult conversations—when people disagree with us, question our character (especially with a few expletives thrown in), or simply ignore us. This is when mindfulness practice comes in handy: We notice when we are about to interact or are interacting in ways that aren't congruent with our intentions, and we choose to get ourselves back on track. Your choices about your intentions can have a positive impact on all your meetings—everywhere, every time.

Key Points

- Essentially, we have one choice to make: to be constructive or to be destructive in interactions.
- Intentions act like an internal compass during meetings. They shape how we behave.
- Our intentions are enlightened when they have deep meaning for us, include a sincere desire to be of service to people in a meeting, reflect a desire to behave with integrity, incorporate a commitment to treat people with compassion, and contain a desire to investigate issues and be open to information that confirms or disconfirms our point of view.
- There are three ways to clarify intentions: (a) Ask good questions, (b) be a fair witness as you clarify them, and (c) develop metaphors that help you refine and remember them.
- We can use our intentions, and the function of mirror neurons, to prime a meeting to be constructive and productive.

Questions for Reflection

What are your highest or deepest intentions when you interact with others? Do they reflect "enlightened self-interest"? What are your intentions for a specific meeting coming up at work or in your community?

How does it feel when you interact congruently with your intentions in a meeting? What happens in the meeting?

Chapter 6:
Opening to Change

Healthy change involves dynamic tension between
our habits and our pioneering spirit.

—Peggy Holman

Eighty people sat in groups of four around small tables spread across a gymnasium floor. The topic was water, always a touchy subject in California. This time, however, the problem wasn't having too little water; it was having too much. The state "owns" the water and grants rights to use it to various agencies throughout the state. There's a catch, however: If you don't use what you've been licensed to use, you can lose rights to the water. The challenge in this rural region, nestled in the northwest corner of a water-hungry, drought-prone state, was to protect rights to water no longer being gobbled up by the recently closed pulp mills. Some residents were keen to protect this natural resource—they had already lost much of the region's timber. Others focused on safeguarding it because water is key to the value of real estate and future development. All faced an unusual dilemma: how to use more water in order to protect the rights to it when most people are inclined to preserve it.

Many options generated in previous meetings were on the table, including selling water to nearby municipalities, creating a lake in a lakeless town with "lake" in its name, and transporting water to drought-stricken areas. Initially, one option seemed quite appealing: Take water out of the river in question and move it to restore another one that had been degraded by diverting too much water to yet another river further south, closer to densely populated areas. Among the concerns people raised, one stood out: "confuse-a-fish." Migrating fish, like salmon, imprint on the specific rivers in which they're born and to which they return to spawn. In addition to concerns about the cost and challenges of moving the water, people feared that transferring water from one river to another would discourage members of an already endangered species from returning to their birthplace.

As Karen, a dedicated environmentalist, reported the thinking of the groups who deliberated this option, she said, "I thought this was a good idea until I sat down and had a chance to talk about it with these folks." People burst into laughter, recognizing their own changes of heart about this and other options they had been strongly for or against at the start of the meeting.

When people listen and honestly consider new information or perspectives, they learn and often change their points of view and positions. Through the very process of meeting and relating with others, we change. All we have to do is get ourselves, or at least our fixed beliefs, out of the way. No movement forward can take place without change. Even an inchworm has to bend to move forward.

It's unfortunate and counterproductive that in some arenas, particularly political ones, the ability to change one's mind is perceived as a weakness instead of a sign of strength and wisdom. When we can separate ourselves from our beliefs, positions, or ideologies—or at least hold them more lightly—we reduce polarization and begin to build bridges across that which divides us. We might even begin to see the differences among us as assets, things from which we can learn and craft new solutions.

Change Is Unavoidable

To be alive means to be in a constant process of change. The only thing that is certain in life is that it's impermanent and that things change. The fact that the human brain changes in response to the lives we lead is emblematic of our dynamism as living systems.

Even our ideas about the human brain have changed: "For four hundred years . . . mainstream medicine and science believed the brain anatomy was fixed" (Doidge, 2007, p. xvii). We now know that the brain has the ability to change its structure and functioning in response to activity and mental experience; scientists call this *neuroplasticity*.

In addition, because people believed the brain couldn't change, they believed humans couldn't change. As research psychologist and psychiatrist Richard Davidson asserted,

> Much of psychology had accepted the idea of a fixed program unfolding in the brain, one that strongly shapes behavior, personality, and emotional states. That view is shattered by the discoveries of neuroplasticity. Neuroplasticity will be the counterweight to the deterministic view [that

genes have behavior on a short leash]. The message I take from my own work is that I have a choice in how I react, that who I am depends on the choices I make, and that who I am is therefore my responsibility. (Begley, 2008, p. 242)

In other words, the brain isn't fixed or immutable—and neither are we. We can intentionally shape the changes in our brain and our beliefs about who we are.

Change Is Paradoxical

On one hand, the brain loves certainty and predictability (i.e., no change). On the other, it's a living organ with a unique ability to change itself. Despite our dynamic nature, we try to hold the world and our beliefs about it still. Life feels safer this way. But avoiding change is a recipe for suffering and mindlessness, because the world isn't static, and neither are we. There's an ongoing tension between life's natural inclination to change and the brain's need for certainty and safety. In unrealistic and unsatisfactory attempts to satisfy this desire for surety, we resist changing our minds and work hard to defend beliefs, keeping them intact. "I think we sometimes buy into these concepts because it is so much easier to embrace absolutes than to suffer reality," writes Anne Lamott. "Reality is unforgivingly complex" (1994, p. 104).

Too often, our positions are based on unexamined "truths." We avoid examining them because it can be unnerving to discover that our positions are outmoded. Allowing in another's ideas can feel threatening. Although credos or "truths" can help us feel more secure in an uncontrollable, changing world, they also imprison us.

When we believe we "know," it's hard for us to hear each other and consider others' points of view.

Change Is Essential

When we embrace certainty or absolutes, we pay a price. We close ourselves off from possibility and shut the door on what might be. We forgo experiencing the energy and vibrancy that listening to and learning from others generates. Clinging to certainty—what any one of us thinks is "the truth"—pretty much guarantees that we won't be able to move forward together; we won't be able to satisfactorily solve complex issues; and we'll remain in a local or global stalemate, hobbled from progress.

Unless we work hard to prevent change, change is a natural and essential part of interacting with others. Just like Karen, the environmentalist, when we listen and learn, we can come to see the "good ideas" or "truths" we hold tightly as simply the tentative opinions that they really are.

Why even talk with others if we aren't going to listen to them, learn from their perspectives, and reconsider our own? If you don't learn and change and I don't learn and change as a result of our interchange, then why meet? It's stultifying to repeatedly think and say the same things or defend the same positions without pausing to check whether we still see the situation the same way or whether we're simply trying to protect a point of view that's become intertwined with our sense of identity and safety.

Fixed Beliefs Block Change

When we interact with others for the sole purpose of convincing them of our point of view, we widen divisions and slow or block the possibility of working with others to develop a more complete understanding of a situation and devise potential solutions. The past becomes the future through our current beliefs and behaviors. Do we really want more of the same?

When our beliefs remain fixed, the natural flow of change freezes. Five telltale signs that we are attached to our version of "the truth" include the following:

- holding onto and fiercely advocating for preconceived ideas;
- interrupting people in frustration;
- combatively and repeatedly disagreeing with others
- arguing ad hominem (i.e., questioning a person's character or competence instead of their point of view); and
- checking out or disengaging from the interaction.

Any of these actions can stop people in their tracks and spark an "emotional contagion" that infects others, leading them to either join in arguing or withdrawing. Either way, the interaction is now stuck with relationships battered and a sense of safety frayed. It can be very difficult for a group to recover and advance once this occurs.

Of course, people need to be able to disagree and share different points of view. The key is to do so in a way that doesn't imply that what we think is "the truth." In other words, we need to lay out our points of view as just that, in a way that doesn't threaten others' sense of safety with words, tone, facial expressions, or gestures. We need to learn to disagree without triggering people's survival mechanisms and evoking fear or anger. It's all in *how* we disagree that we can nurture understanding and constructive conversation. And when we listen and honestly consider different opinions, collective learning and thinking can progress. This is, of course, easier to describe than to do. Chapter 9 describes communication skills that help us interact effectively.

In an effort to prevent contrary beliefs from even getting on the table, people sometimes try to control conversations and make them more predictable. Unfortunately, this also takes the life out of the conversation. In work settings, managers sit at the head of the table and report decisions made higher up in the organization. In public hearings, elected or appointed officials sit on a dais and look down on individuals in rows of chairs affixed to the floor or standing in lines at a microphone. People are left in solitary islands of solidifying thoughts, with no encouragement or process for sharing their perspectives and learning from one another.

We can have fixed beliefs about lots of things, including what our bosses and co-workers should be doing differently and how our elected leaders and government workers should think and behave. Underneath these beliefs are deeper or more foundational ones. These are who we think we are, the way things are, and the way others are. The last, beliefs about the "way others are," is the focus of Chapter 8.

We Confuse Beliefs about Who We Think We Are with Who We Really Are

The brain connects current experiences and emotions with memories from the past, often creating a story that explains, rightly or wrongly, how our life experiences are connected. When we replay

memories or retell stories, we create a sense of a static or immutable self. For instance, one of my father's favorite aspects of his
self-identity was about being a "self-made man." He told tales of
delivering newspapers in Pawtucket, Rhode Island, and lighting
fires on cold Sabbath mornings for Jewish families in his neighborhood. I imagine that these anecdotes, along with many others, and
the identity they reinforced helped him feel more secure in the face
of an uncontrollable, ever-changing world.

Although it's comforting to have an identity that we equate
with a "self," that identity can imprison us in a fixed state, especially
when we confuse our stories or labels with who we are. We develop
labels—such as *tall, short, fat,* or *thin; strong-willed, weak-willed,* or
flexible; confident, timid, or *unsure; open-minded, hardheaded,* or *soft-
hearted*—that reinforce a fixed sense of self. These and other descrip-
tors might capture a part of our experience in any one moment, but
they aren't who we are, because we aren't unchanging.

Our ideas about who we are influence what we think, say, and do,
whether we're aware of them or not. If we aren't paying conscious
attention, we don't notice how these beliefs determine our behavior. And if we aren't aware of what our beliefs are—especially the
self-limiting ones—we can't change them. However, we are *Homo
sapiens sapiens:* We know, and we know that we know. We can be
conscious of what we believe and dig into it. We can decide whether
our beliefs are outmoded or unhelpful.

However, if we've begun to equate our *beliefs* about who we are
with our identity, changing them becomes difficult. This is not just a
psychological challenge; it's also a physiological one. Because beliefs
have strong neuronal pathways in the brain, it's easier to reinforce
them than to deconstruct fixed beliefs about ourselves. When we

hear someone say something about us that doesn't fit our self-image, we recoil and balk, sometimes even if it's complimentary. If their statement is similar or at least congruent with our self-image, we accept it as "true." Either way, we stay where we are, strengthening existing neural pathways.

The stronger the pathways, the more likely that beliefs about who we think we are get interwoven with a sense of identity and survival. Because of this, we'll do just about anything to preserve them. For example, at a pharmaceutical company, I worked with a scientist who needed to hold the belief that she knew more than anyone else in the room. Unfortunately, because of this belief, when her colleagues asked her questions about her research, she experienced them as threats to her concept of who she was, as an assault on her competence or status. Because of our work together, she knew this undermined, even stopped the collaborative learning that was important to her. She also understood that the tendency to defend her self-image was an internal reaction that she didn't have to act out. Over time, she learned to pause more frequently and listen to her colleagues' questions without needing to defend herself. With self-exploration, she realized that her professional and personal commitment to make sure that the drugs she helped produce were efficacious and safe was far stronger than any need to protect her self-image. She decided that her belief that she was the smartest person in the room was not only not necessarily true but also not helpful.

If we allow and even encourage it, our seemingly stable "self" is always changing. For instance, maybe yesterday, you felt uptight and defensive about your pet project, fearing it would be an embarrassing and abysmal failure. Today, after some sleep and exercise, you have more perspective. You stop taking the project and yourself so seriously. You remind yourself to hold more loosely your often tightly held sense of identity ("competent, rarely-makes-mistakes tough guy"). At a project status meeting, you ask your colleagues to help you assess the current status of the project and brainstorm ways to make it successful.

When we let go of our labels of who we think we are, not only do we learn some interesting things about ourselves, but we also open up new possibilities or ways to interact constructively. We don't have to hold onto a definition of ourselves so tightly. We aren't fixed, solid entities. What we think we are is not the same as what we can be.

When we allow ourselves to pause, notice, and observe how dynamic we actually are, we can join architect and inventor Buckminster Fuller in his observation that "I am not a thing—a noun. I seem to be a verb, an evolutionary process—an integral function of the universe." When we realize and behave as if we're verbs—in motion, changing—then the groups in which we interact can also be verbs: alive and changing, better able to learn and think collaboratively.

Investigating Your Beliefs about Who You Think You Are

Some of our deepest beliefs develop over many years, most often outside of our conscious awareness. If you want to be open to change in your interactions, it's likely that unexamined beliefs will get in your way.

You can start to explore your beliefs about who you think you are in three ways: (a) Unearth and test your beliefs about yourself;

(b) practice paying attention nonjudgmentally to the ever-changing parade of physical sensations, emotions, and thoughts inside; and (c) explore what you mean by "self."

Investigating your beliefs about yourself isn't an easy thing to do. However, it might allow you to hold your beliefs more lightly or modify them, especially if they aren't helpful or true. An interim step could be to hold them as working assumptions instead of as confident conclusions. As Leonard Cohen says in his song "Anthem,"

Ring the bells that still can ring.
Forget your perfect offering.
There is a crack in everything.
That's how the light gets in.

Forget strongly held beliefs. Listen to the perspectives of others. See the cracks in beliefs and positions. Allow light into thoughts and interactions. Ring the bells of change that still can ring.

When we learn to listen to ourselves mindfully, with open minds and hearts, and we pay attention to the impact of others' perspectives on our sensations, emotions, and thoughts, our perspectives change, and possibilities not yet considered emerge.

1) Unearth and Test Your Beliefs about Yourself. Unearthing and evaluating your beliefs about who you think you are is a powerful route to creating a more natural and changing self-identity. As you investigate your beliefs, discern which aspects of your self-image still ring true and which do not. However, as you do this self-examination, tread lightly, with a warm-hearted curiosity and acceptance of what seems true in this moment. Unless you feel "psychologically safe," it will be difficult if not impossible to find and honestly consider aspects of your self-identify. If you criticize yourself for a particular belief ("How could I have ever believed that about myself?"), you'll feel psychologically threatened, create resistance, and likely strengthen the aspect of your self-image you want to consider changing. Opening to change requires acceptance first.

One part of your self-image, for example, might be that you're logical and emotionless in meetings. We already know that every human experiences emotions and communicates them, whether they want to or not (see Chapter 3). So what do you say to say to yourself now? You could chortle at the illusion that you don't have emotions (humor helps!) and ask yourself how important it is to you to act as if you don't have emotions when interacting with others. You could also ask, "Is this belief beneficial? Does it help me grow and develop?"

Try a brief experiment. Think about a belief you have about who you are, particularly in interacting with others. Then ask yourself two questions: First, is it true? And second, can you absolutely know that it's true? (Katie, 2002, p. 26). One of my beliefs is that I get anxious in groups of ten or more when I don't have a role, such as leader, facilitator, or consultant. I believe this is true because I've experienced enough discomfort attending gatherings, parties included, where I don't have a specific role to play. When I check whether I know it's absolutely true, I remember times in groups when I didn't feel nervous. So sometimes I do, and sometimes I don't, depending on whether I know others, whether I've met with this group before, whether I know the purpose of the gathering, and whether I'm prepared. Upon investigation, I now think this self-perception is not absolutely true all the time.

Now, ask three more questions: How do you feel inside when you hold this belief as a fixed and unchangeable "truth"? (Consider both emotions and body sensations.) How would you feel without this belief? What might be possible if you held this belief more loosely? Continuing to investigate one of my beliefs, I realized that I feel physically constricted and awkward when I hold the belief that I'm anxious in large groups when I don't have a specific role. Sometimes I avoid gatherings simply because I don't want to feel this way. Without this belief, I might be able to be more relaxed and even have fun. I like this possibility. As a result of this exploration, I think I can hold this belief more lightly, perhaps even let it go.

2) Pay Attention Nonjudgmentally to Your Direct Experience. When we pay attention mindfully to the parade of ever-changing body sensations, emotions, or thoughts, we realize we're always changing. Mindfulness can lead us to a less static definition of "self." Practicing mindfulness enables us to have moment-to-moment awareness of the unfolding of sensations, feelings, and thoughts and to reduce the tendency to construct a narrative *about* what is happening.

According to psychologist Ronald D. Siegel, a part of the cortex called the *medial prefrontal cortex* is active when we're constructing stories about who we are. It's quieter when we pay attention to our direct experience through mindfulness (Siegel, 2011). The medial prefrontal cortex is involved in memory formation, memory retrieval, and decision-making. In this way, we construct a sense of self that can distance us from experiencing ourselves directly. In addition, once we construct a story about who we are, we stop paying attention. As psychologist Norman Farb wrote, "Mindfulness changes the very ground of the way we experience the self" (Baime, July 2011, p. 85). With mindfulness, we're better able to see the dynamic part of who we are and avoid getting caught in beliefs about who we are.

Practicing mindfulness meditation or being mindful—observant, careful, and alert—of whatever we're doing while we're doing it helps us become conscious of what's occurring inside and around us and of the self who is experiencing what's occurring. In other words, we develop the ability to discern between what we're experiencing and our thoughts and beliefs about what we're experiencing. There's an aspect of "self" that is separate from the thoughts and beliefs we normally identify with. We can even notice how our beliefs are shaping our experience and as a result are shaping how we behave. In a meeting, for example, I may notice butterflies in my stomach before I'm about to say something that I fear challenges the perspective of others in the room. I'm aware of the "me" that is experiencing the butterflies along with my beliefs about the importance of how one says things. Being aware of all this, I'm able to say what I want to say in as even a way as possible ("Here's my current understanding of the situation . . .").

3) Explore What You Mean by "Self." You know who you are, right? You have lots of ways to describe yourself. In my case, some of the ways I describe myself are as follows: born in New England of Irish and French-Canadian descent, an enthusiastic hiker with a pesky back, a lover of books and movies, a believer in the basic goodness of human beings, and too attuned to politics for my own good. But is this who I am? What if both you and I were to perceive ourselves as dynamic and complex collections of experiences, knowledge, desires, memories, beliefs, emotions, and body sensations that are in constant movement? That is, what if we were to recognize that we change from moment to moment as we interact with others?

This idea doesn't mean there isn't a "real" you or a "real" me; rather, it means that, just like a conversation, each of us is always in process, being affected by our relationships and experiences and inevitably changing. I experience this dynamism and complexity most clearly when I expand my awareness to include myself, those I'm interacting with, and the context in which we're talking. Let's take a brief look at the physiological "process" of "self." Settle into your chair. Follow three breaths mindfully, noticing where you feel the breath moving inside you. Now, bring your attention to your feet on the floor and your thighs and your seat on the chair. Notice the sensations in your feet, including the toes, heels, and ankles. Check to see whether you can detect any difference between your experience of the left and the right foot. How would you describe the variations? As you pay attention to your feet, do the sensations change? After experimenting with this for three or four minutes, what do you notice? I hope you were able to observe how even this small part of your body is dynamic, constantly changing in subtle and unsubtle ways. Your entire body is like this. It changes because it's alive; it also changes when you pay attention to it. If you're intrigued, continue this investigation with other parts of the body: thighs and buttocks, torso and back. Everything we experience is part of a process; it's not a single place in the brain or something static, unless we work hard to make it so. What is true about bodies is also true about brains: When we don't get in the way of this natural process by trying to freeze our brains with fixed beliefs, we change.

What might be possible if each of us were to bring a dynamic sense of self instead of a fixed one into our interactions? In other words, a "self" that pays attention to its body sensations, feelings, and thoughts as they alter when relating with others? A "self" that experiences and accepts a reciprocal causality, meaning that we both are influenced by and are shapers of our interactions with others? We co-create our experience in meetings. If we're able to live with this kind of uncertainty in our conversations, our meetings will be more vibrant, and new perspectives and solutions will emerge.

Beliefs about "The Way Things Are" Are Not Necessarily the Way Things Are

Just like our beliefs about ourselves, our convictions about the world can keep us stuck, getting in the way of our opening to change. Unless we learn to identify and investigate these convictions, we remain stuck in a fixed view of "the way things are."

Think of beliefs about "the way things are" as mental models that define our "deeply engrained assumptions, generalizations, or even pictures or images that influence how we understand the world and how we take action" (Senge, 1990, p. 8). At best, these assumptions about life are double-edged swords. They provide a framework that helps us order and interpret the world, that make it seem more coherent, understandable, and safe. Unfortunately, because they help us feel secure, we tend to hang onto our mental models like life preservers in tumultuous conversational seas.

Our assumptions work against us when they prime us to pay selective attention to information and experiences that support our beliefs and to ignore or discount those that don't. Unless we identify and investigate our mental models—and decide which ones are outmoded—we'll continue to have a distorted or partial view of reality.

What are your fixed or limiting beliefs about the world of interactions? Here are some examples:

- "People don't want to listen to one another, so it's impossible to find common ground."
- "I can't be honest in meetings at work because I'll get fired.".
- "Managers dominate conversations so they don't have to know what's really going on."
- "Meetings are a waste of time."
- "The world is going to hell in a handbasket. Talking isn't going to change this."

We take our certitudes about the world for granted so much that we think the world actually is as we define it. As psychologist Ellen Langer described it, "Most of us confuse the stability of our mind-sets with the stability of underlying phenomena and we come to think that things are, will always be, and even need to be a particular way without recognizing how they may also vary" (2005, p. 5). When we pause to investigate our "certitudes," we often discover unexamined beliefs that might be out of date. It would be closer to "the truth" if we were to communicate our beliefs about the world by saying, "This is the way I see it," rather than saying, "This is the way it is." Often, I add "right now." This alerts others and me to the fact that my understanding might change.

Just as it's possible to change our beliefs about ourselves, it's possible to change our beliefs about the world. This requires unearthing and testing foundational mental models to discern, if we can, whether they really are "true." This can be tricky to do for two reasons. First, many of our beliefs about the world are intermingled with our beliefs about who we think we are. Second, because we like to interact with people who think as we do, many of our beliefs are actually just shared assumptions. However, examining our beliefs is worth it because unless we do, we'll continue to be unconsciously influenced by them, regardless of whether they continue to make sense.

Investigate Your Beliefs about "The Way Things Are"

Following are some ways to investigate your beliefs about the world.

Asking Fundamental Questions about Your Beliefs. Because many of our beliefs about "the way things are" are fundamental and unconscious, they're rarely explored. Religious scholar Huston Smith identified three questions that can help us bring them to consciousness. He posits that how people answer these questions has divided us for centuries (1994, p. 81). The three questions are

- whether people are independent or interdependent;
- whether the universe is friendly or indifferent, if not hostile; and
- whether the best part of a human being is the head or the heart.

Usually, the beliefs we hold are unconscious answers to these questions. They're also the bedrock on which we build other beliefs. They drive our behavior—including how we interact with others—outside our awareness and therefore outside of our choosing.

For example, if I believe people are independent, then I probably think I have a duty to defend my individuality, protect my autonomy, and get my point across. However, if I believe we're interdependent, then I might think it's important to work collaboratively with others, including those who don't think like I do, and to consider the long-term impact of decisions on others. If I believe the universe is friendly, I might think that we need to take care of it, be friendly right back. If, however, I believe that the universe is indifferent or hostile, I'll likely think my job is to control it, use it, and protect myself from it. Finally, if I think the head is the best part of a human being, I'll put forth my ideas logically. But if I think the heart is the best part, then I'll likely focus on building relationships and appealing to people's sense of compassion.

Two additional questions can help us clarify our beliefs about the world:

- Is power a fixed commodity we use to control others, or is it an expanding resource that when shared with others expands our ability to get things done?
- Do human beings have dominion over the natural world, or are we an interdependent part of it?

How you define power significantly affects how you conduct and participate in meetings with co-workers or neighbors. If power means control over others, you'll likely try to dominate interactions. If power means getting things done with others, you'll tend to be collaborative in them.

If the world has no limits and human beings have dominion over it, then extraction of natural resources can continue forever. Those who contributed to the Dust Bowl in the 1930s in the United States might have implicitly believed both of these things. In an attempt to attract more settlers to the High Plains areas, the federal government distributed bulletins claiming that the land in the Texas Panhandle was the one "resource that cannot be exhausted." Hugh Bennett, who led the study into the causes of the Dust Bowl for Franklin Delano Roosevelt, said at the time, "I didn't know so much costly misinformation could be put into a single brief sentence" (Egan, 2006, p. 126).

Although such questions usually weren't on the table then, they are now. How we answer these questions in communities, organizations, governmental agencies, and nations affects the incremental decisions we make every day that in turn have a cumulative impact on our world.

I encourage you to consider answering these four questions about your beliefs:

- Where are your fundamental beliefs leading you?
- What would happen if everyone believed as you do?
- How do your beliefs affect how you interact with others?
- Do your beliefs help or hinder your ability to work with others to understand and solve complex issues?

Left unexamined, beliefs might have the effect of following a script that no longer reflects what we really think. However, it takes courage to honestly examine fundamental beliefs. Realizing long-held beliefs no longer make sense can be frightening. However, answering these questions helps you understand your worldview—either what it is or what you want it to be.

In considering these questions, I test my answers by asking, "Is this true?" or by simply saying, "Maybe," meaning, "Maybe this is true." My questions are inspired by an old story as told by philosopher Allan Watts: Once upon a time, there was a Chinese farmer who lost a horse when it ran away. All the neighbors came around that evening and said, "That's too bad," and he said, "Maybe." The next day, the horse came back and brought seven wild horses with it. All the neighbors came around and said, "That's great, isn't it!" The farmer said, "Maybe." The next day, his son rode one of the wild horses and attempted to tame it. The son broke his leg. All the neighbors came around in the evening and said, "That's too bad, isn't it?" The farmer said, "Maybe." The next day, the conscription officers came around looking for people for the army. They rejected his son because he had a broken leg. The neighbors came around that evening and said, "Isn't that wonderful!" The farmer said, "Maybe." This story reminds me that my beliefs might change over time in different circumstances, so it's advisable to always hold them lightly.

When we become polarized in our interactions with others, we often wage what I think of as "solution wars," not understanding that we're actually arguing about worldviews. This makes it very difficult to find promising ways forward. Because interactions seem to become polarized quickly, particularly when we're discussing public policies, delving into these deeper beliefs is a necessary step to finding common ground and a way forward. Consider posing the questions noted in this section to one of the groups you participate in.

Exploring Beliefs through Dialogue. Dialogue is another way to investigate your beliefs or mental models. Dialogue is usually characterized by explicitly identifying and testing underlying beliefs without judgment or criticism and by letting go of attachment to any particular outcome other than increasing everyone's understanding of their mental models (Isaacs, 1999; Ellinor & Girard, 1998). One of the keys to a successful dialogue is engaging with genuine curiosity and a desire to learn about different perspectives and how people came to them. This can occur only when people feel safe and are able to listen with an honest desire to understand.

Dialogue takes advantage of the paradoxical nature of change: When we understand and accept one another's point of view, we become free to change our own beliefs, and others become free to change theirs. Investigating our fundamental beliefs is especially helpful when we try to talk across social, economic, political, and hierarchical divides.

Dealing with Threats to Your Sense of Safety. Either way you approach investigating your worldview—by asking fundamental questions or through dialogue—doing so is both difficult and essential. It's difficult because most of us have so many unexamined assumptions about "the way things are"; it's essential because unexamined beliefs shape how we interact with one another. Leaving them unexamined denies us the opportunity to decide whether they're shaping us in ways of our choosing.

If you expect to confirm your beliefs about yourself, others, or the world and aren't able to do so for a variety of reasons—they no longer make sense, they don't fit with your recent experience, or you get disconfirming information—you might experience "error signals" in the orbital frontal cortex (Rock & Schwartz, 2006). This region of the cortex, located above the orbits in which eyes rest (hence the name), is closely associated with the amygdala, which is an important part of the survival mechanisms in the brain. Because of this, exploring your (or anyone else's) core beliefs needs to be done with kid gloves and soft slippers. No hobnail boots allowed. Chapter 9 describes behaviors that will help you do this skillfully.

How Neuroplasticity Can Help Us Open to Change

As I've noted previously, because the brain is designed to help us survive, it isn't fond of uncertainty and change. The good news is that although the brain might feel threatened by change, it's the only organ in the body that can change itself and enable us to be open and responsive to change. Changing our beliefs can help us change our brains: "Since the mental processes of attention and imagination change the firing in the brain, the brain can be changed by the mind," noted psychiatrist Daniel J. Siegel (de Llosa, p. 71).

When we investigate our beliefs, we activate neuronal activity in the brain and lay down new tracks or reinforce related ones. Our attention takes physical form in the activity of our brains. In other words, we embody our mental processes in neural networks that in turn influence our thinking and actions. We can strengthen the habitual routes of our thoughts, or we can create new routes with novel thoughts and experiences. How we take advantage of this neuroplasticity is up to us.

Think of your brain as if it were a web of country roads. Some roads have deep tracks with a grassy mound in the center that scrapes the bottom of your car. This makes it difficult for you to drive on different parts of the road. Even if you want to create new ruts, it's easier to just drive in the old ruts, thereby making them deeper. Beliefs are like ruts: We deepen the grooves when we follow predictable, familiar chains of thought and behavior. Over time, it can become difficult to drive anywhere but in the ruts. It takes conscious choice and effort to lay down new synaptic tracks.

"Neuroplasticity only occurs when the mind is in a particular mental state, one marked by attention and focus," according to science journalist Sharon Begley (2008, p. 130). Nascent research suggests that such attention and focus stimulates the *nucleus basalis*—a region near the brain stem—to secrete acetylcholine (ACh) into the brain. ACh is the primary neurotransmitter involved in thought, learning, and memory. According to Siegel, "It's a neuro-modulator whose presence enables any neurons that are activated at the same time to strengthen their connections to one another" (2011, p. 133).

Opening to change will become easier over time as the new neural pathways created by your investigations become the preferred ones. "Trained" neurons tend to fire faster and more strongly. Be patient with yourself. Our brains can understand information quickly, but changing deeply held beliefs takes time and attention.

Key Points

- To be alive means to be in a constant process of change. Our brains change in response to the lives we lead and our interactions with others.
- Despite our dynamic nature, we try to hold onto fixed and often unexamined beliefs about ourselves and the world. This interferes with our natural inclination to change.
- Being open to changing one's beliefs and opinions is essential to finding solutions to tough problems.
- We confuse our *beliefs* about who we are with who we really are: beings in motion.
- We can test our beliefs about ourselves by asking challenging questions, paying attention nonjudgmentally to our direct experiences, and exploring our definitions of "self."
- Beliefs about "the way things are" are not necessarily true.
- We can investigate our beliefs by asking fundamental questions and exploring them through dialogue.
- Investigating our beliefs can threaten our sense of safety.
- The brain's ability to change itself—neuroplasticity—can help us change.

Questions for Reflection

Do you believe it's necessary to be open to changing one's beliefs to effectively solve complex issues? Why or why not?

What are your beliefs about who you are? Do they still seem true? If not, how would you change them to better reflect how you see yourself now?

How would you like to describe yourself in five years? What beliefs would have to change in order to match that description?

What are your most deeply held, influential beliefs about the world? Do they still seem "true" to you? How do they influence your behavior in meetings? Are they helpful?

Section Three:
Interacting Constructively

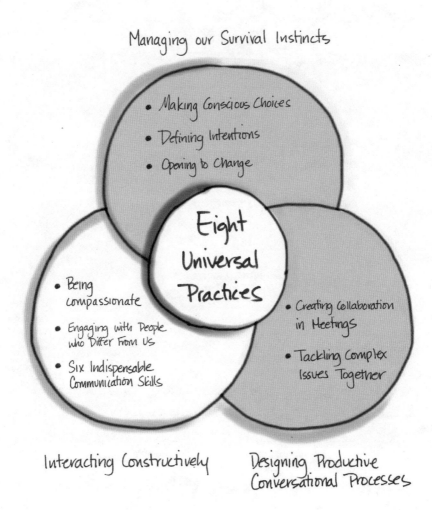

Managing our Survival Instincts

- Making Conscious Choices
- Defining Intentions
- Opening to Change

Eight Universal Practices

- Being compassionate
- Engaging with People who Differ From Us
- Six Indispensable Communication Skills

- Creating Collaboration in Meetings
- Tackling Complex Issues Together

Interacting Constructively

Designing Productive Conversational Processes

Chapter 7:
Being Compassionate

Can I be mindful and loving of whatever arises?
If I can't be loving in this moment, can I be kind?
If I can't be kind, can I be non-judgmental?
If I can't be non-judgmental, can I not cause harm?
And if I cannot not cause harm, can I cause
the least amount of harm possible?

—Larry Yang

While facilitating a series of meetings to assess community mental health needs, one of the questions we asked was "What would the local mental health system be like if it were working just as you want it to work?" This question elicited useful responses for the mental health agency sponsoring this data-gathering from the families, patients, and transition-age youths who participated in the meetings. However, in the meeting with "service providers" from outside the agency—doctors, nurses, police, and independent therapists—the 50 people crowded into the room did not want to answer this question or to talk in small groups as I suggested. Many had driven long distances to come to this event at the end of their workday and were loaded for bear. They wanted to vent their anger en masse to the agency staff representatives in the room, detailing all that wasn't working—and vent, they did. Doctors and nurses told horror stories about trying to treat emotionally difficult or disturbed patients with little or no help from the mental health agency. They knew, for example, that they couldn't effectively treat a cardiovascular condition without also getting the patient's depression or anxiety taken care of. Police officers were angry at having to arrest people and force them into already crowded cells because they didn't get their medications on time and were causing themselves and others harm.

Although I felt compassion for them, they felt none for the agency staff, whom they blamed for making their jobs more difficult and for what they saw as incompetence and carelessness. Having met with representatives of the staff previously, I knew that many of them felt the same frustration and anger as these service providers did. The needs far outmatched the help that was available. However, under attack, the staff hunkered down into folded arms, tight jaws, and silence. The director of the agency walked out of the meeting, fueling everyone's upset. No one could muster a word or sign of empathy for each other. It was a standoff among people experiencing "compassion fatigue" or "secondary traumatic stress disorder," a gradual decrease of compassion for others that's predictable among people who work in environments that frequently expose them to heart-wrenching, emotional challenges. Steeped in frustration and anger, they were cut off from a natural inclination to care about one another.

Tired and sobered, I left this meeting with rolls of chart paper—covered with words of rage, sadness, fear, and frustration—tucked under my arm. As I drove home, I thought about what possibilities might have opened had anyone in that room offered empathic words. Perhaps our ability to feel compassion for one another in society as a whole has diminished with the brunt of a 24/7 news cycle filled with stories and pictures of human suffering near and far. Has this inured us to the less obvious or hidden suffering that exists in more benign circumstances, such as meetings and conversations at work or in our neighborhoods?

What's Compassion Got to Do with Meetings?

Compassion—extending empathy to include offering kindness or help—might sound like a surprising, even unnecessary practice for meetings. However, to solve complex issues, we need to converse and build a sense of relationship with people who have different life experiences and points of view than we do. To find common ground and move forward together, at the very least we need to understand people's perspectives or have what Daniel Goleman calls "cognitive empathy." Two additional types of empathy are also needed: "empathic concern" or the ability to sense what another person needs, and "emotional empathy," or the ability to feel what someone else feels (Goleman, 2013, p. 55).

These three types of empathy are a prelude to compassionate action—listening, asking questions of genuine curiosity or concern, wishing for the well-being of others, doing something helpful—that in turn builds a sense of relationship and safety. This doesn't mean you need to agree with those for whom you feel compassion, but it does increase the likelihood that you'll be able to disagree in ways that don't evoke people's self-protective mechanisms and all the destructive behavior that accompanies them.

How might you avoid getting provoked by someone else's anger so that you can explore what might be causing it without aggravating it? The three kinds of empathy are a good start. Do you understand others' perspectives? Do you know what they need from you or the group as a whole? Can you feel how they're feeling right now? And, finally, a question of compassion: Do you want to be helpful? Although compassion for others in meetings at work or in your community might not be your first inclination, it's a key component of staying in relationship with others and creating a safe environment in which people can have a constructive conversation.

With these three kinds of empathy in place, you might even be able to experience a fourth kind: empathic joy, or feeling happy when someone else is doing well, being successful, or accomplishing something from which you don't benefit directly. This would be a boon to a sense of safety and relationship among meeting participants.

The brain is not just an organ that knows how to fight, flee, or freeze. It's also one that knows how to empathize and help others. As noted in Chapter 4, mindfulness meditation strengthens this ability by calming the brain, strengthening the mind, and increasing a sense of interconnectedness and compassion.

Here is compassion in action at a staff meeting in a unit of a research and development company: At a meeting of approximately 20 scientists and 6 lab technicians, one of the technicians, Sharon, unexpectedly burst into tears. She described how "pulled apart" she felt by all the competing needs and priorities of the scientists, and she wailed, "I am so frustrated that I can't do the quality of work I want to do because there is just too much of it, and there is no way to prioritize anything." Fortunately, the manager had been developing self-awareness and communication skills over the past several months, so he was able to pause, take a breath, and respond in a concerned and caring way. He reflected her words and feelings back to her and then asked, "Do I get what you are saying, Sharon?" His empathy for her shifted what had been an anxious, nearly combative tone in the room to one in which, as they charmingly described it, "we need to figure out better ways to get the work done without beating the crap out of one another."

The manager didn't leave it at that. He continued to ask questions of this technician and the five others present so he and the other scientists could better understand the conditions that led to the upset. This helped all of them figure out how to improve the situation and, they hoped, to decrease everyone's stress. This manager acted compassionately. He did something to understand and alleviate the conditions causing the distress of the lab technicians.

If this department manager had been gripped by fear ("She's challenging my authority!"), anger ("This makes me look like a bad manager."), or any of their cousins—anxiety, annoyance, and embarrassment—he would have gone on automatic and likely become hostile and inflexible. In this state, he would have lost access to his empathy and compassion. Fear and anger make us self-protective, unable to notice what others need.

A manager's role in extending compassion is important. The emotions of the most powerful person in the room are usually the most contagious. Because of this, a leader's responsibility to maintain a sense of equanimity and empathy, even compassion, is greater than anyone else's. Due to the resonance circuits among us, a leader's calm and compassionate state activates similar states in others.

True compassion is a relationship among equals. It is not top-down or feeling pity or sorry for another person. Pity is a "near enemy" to compassion because it distances us from one another. When we feel pity for people, it's as if we don't share a common humanity with them or as if those who are suffering are less human than we are. They're "beneath" us. Pity is a way of protecting oneself from other people's pain. However, all of us get afraid and angry. Life—and our meetings—are challenging for everyone. When you're truly compassionate, you recognize you're not separate from another's distress or exempt from distress in your own life. It takes courage to be compassionate because it opens us up to feel the pain of others.

We Are Wired for Empathy and Compassion

Although experiencing empathy, even compassion, for our co-workers and neighbors might feel like a stretch, remember that our brains are wired for both. They were a key part of how our ancestors survived in the distant past and how we will survive in the near future. It is only fear and self-protective habits that get in the way of our extending empathy to one another and ourselves today.

We are wired for empathy and compassion in four ways. First, when we empathize with someone else's pain, we're literally feeling their pain through the older parts of the brain, including the amygdala, the hypothalamus, the hippocampus, and the orbitofrontal cortex (Goleman, 2013). For example, when babies hear another baby cry, they start crying. In contrast, they rarely cry when they hear their own cries on a recording. After about 14 months of age, not only do babies cry when they hear the distress of other babies, they try to do something to alleviate it. The older they get, the less they cry and the more they just try to help (Goleman, 2006, p. 55).

Second, mirror neurons are special cells in the brain that "help us to be empathic and fundamentally attuned to other people" (Iacoboni, 2009, p. 279). In addition to enabling us to empathize with others, they allow us to "read" others' intentions and "see" things from their point of view (Ramachandran, 2011, pp. 22, 260). Daniel Siegel believes that "the mirror neuron system is the root of empathy" (Siegel, 2011, p. 59).

Mirror neurons create signals—physiological mimicry—inside us that clue us in on what might be going on for others. If someone else is scared and his heart is racing, yours might start to race too, even if you don't consciously know he's frightened or why your heart rate increased. When we're self-aware, meaning that we're conscious and noticing our own body sensations, thoughts, and emotions, we can pick up on the "messages" about what might be going on with others by paying attention to what's going on inside us. This doesn't mean we understand the cause of their upset; it just means that we can recognize when they're in a state of distress. Fortunately, another part of the brain, the temporoparietal junction, helps us distinguish between self and other, how they feel and how we do. This helps prevent compassion fatigue.

Third, visceral organs seem to communicate with us about what we're experiencing along with what others are, too. This is in large part due to the vagus nerve that serves as one of the primary pathways between the brain and the body's major organs. This nerve is the longest and most branched of the cranial nerves, with autonomic, sensory, and motor fibers. The vagus nerve is part of the "social engagement system." Learning to be aware of body sensations, particularly those in the central core where our organs are, is a critical element of self-awareness and of empathy and compassion for others.

Fourth, when we help others, activity in the anterior cingulate (ACC) increases (Keltner, 2010, p. 10). According to Siegel, the ACC "straddles the boundary between our thinking cortex and our feeling limbic regions. . . . The ACC plays a key role in the resonance circuitry that lets us feel connected to others and to ourselves" (2011, p. 125), thereby strengthening our ability to empathize and extend compassion.

Develop Your Capacity for Compassion

Although we're wired for compassion, it seems that the neural pathways for it aren't as strong as they could or need to be. There are several reasons for this. I've already mentioned one: compassion fatigue from all the tragedies we witness on the news and, for some, the tragedies they deal with every day on the job or in their day-to-day lives. Also, many of us live in cultures in which individualism and independence are more valued than collaboration and caring, as if it has to be one or the other. Furthermore, many people believe that asking for help or acknowledging that we need one another is a sign of weakness instead of one of strength.

Also, survival instincts take priority in the brain. They tend to trump the natural inclination to empathize with others. When your self-protective mechanisms are on alert, it's difficult to pay attention to or care about others. The competitive or combative tone of many meetings tends to make us self-absorbed individualists who pay attention only to our own agendas.

Finally, when people are in distress, they often behave in ways that trigger us, making it difficult to empathize with them, let alone be compassionate. It's difficult, for example, to empathize with people who vehemently disagree with you, adamantly espouse opinions that set your hair on fire, interrupt you, attack you personally, or simply check out and act as if they don't care. When people behave in difficult ways, you can usually safely assume that they're afraid and being driven by the older parts of the brain. However, when you're under fire, it's hard to remember that the soft underbelly of anger is self-protection.

Here are three ways to develop your ability to extend empathy and compassion to others.

1) Set an Intention to Treat Everyone, Including Yourself, with Compassion. When you're about to go into a meeting that you think might be difficult, take time to define a life-giving intention—for instance, to listen, stay mindful, and not become reactive. When you sense you're about to be hijacked by fear or anger, your intention can function as a life vest and enable you to respond to others with cognitive empathy, if not with emotional empathy or empathic concern. If you can't generate any kind of empathy, let alone compassion, you could make the intention in that moment to do the least harm possible. As psychotherapist and meditation teacher Larry Yang suggests at the start of this chapter, if you can't be loving, kind, nonjudgmental, or nonharming, can you do the least harm possible? This might be simply remaining quiet until your emotions have subsided and you can make a considered choice about how to proceed. Doing this takes intention and practice.

Empathizing with colleagues in a meeting at work might be easier than it is with people at community meetings. In organizations (business, nonprofits, government), to varying degrees, most employees understand the pressures everyone is under to do their jobs. There's also organizational context (mission, vision, goals and plans, customer or client needs, policies, and procedures, along with employment contracts and paychecks) that helps staff members understand and care about one another's circumstances. And in meetings at work, people usually know one another and sit in spaces where they can see one another.

However, public meetings make empathy for others less likely because people bring various agendas without that common context or glue. During meetings or public hearings, people often don't know one another and are asked to speak only to the elected officials or governmental staff members who convened the meeting during a period of public comment. In addition, people usually sit in rows facing decision-makers and have to walk to a microphone for their three minutes. All of these elements make it hard if not impossible for people to empathize with one another or with those not there who will ultimately be affected by the policy decisions made in that room. Such decisions could include, for example, everything from where to place street lights to budget priorities for the municipality as a whole. In this environment, it's nearly impossible to feel empathy across the multiple differences (age, gender, neighborhood, socioeconomic background, race, ethnicity, sexual orientation, and political leanings) or have compassion for people with such varying perspectives ("What do you mean you want to take my property for the public good?" "Are you suggesting we actually drink treated water?" "How dare you consider building low-income housing [or putting a food bank] in my neighborhood!" "You really think we need traffic calming on *that* thoroughfare?").

When I sense I'm about to be hijacked by what people are saying in meetings where people are allowed to interact, I do five things to help me do the least harm possible:

1. I pause and feel my feet on the floor and my seat on the chair. Then I notice the breath in my body, and in my best moments, I remember my intention.

2. I paraphrase (put in my own words) what I heard someone else say to check whether I understand what was said and to make sure the person or persons feel heard. This gives me a few moments in which I continue to sense my body and breath.

3. I ask a good question. The last two steps might sound something like, "You said you think I'm 'dead wrong' about the situation. Would you please explain how you think I'm off-base on this?"

4. I listen deeply to their answer and try to understand what they're saying, how they feel about what they're saying, what might be going on for them, and what they're concerned about. Depending on the circumstance, I might then repeat Steps 2 and 3.

5. When someone appears to be operating on automatic, I do the best I can to remember that they're likely suffering in some way. When people are hurt, afraid, or angry, they often lash out at others. To become or remain calm, I continue

sensing my body and breath in the hopes that I can infect others with it through positive emotional contagion.

2) Build Up Your Empathy and Compassion "Muscle." In a previous chapter, I described how mindfulness meditation increases our sense of attunement with and compassion for others. You can also deliberately cultivate empathy and compassion through a meditation practice designed to develop these qualities: compassion meditation.

Compassion meditation creates at least four changes in the brain that become a self-reinforcing pattern, enabling empathy and compassion to become a proclivity or even a trait:

- It quiets the amygdala, making the mind calmer and more able to read what is going on inside us (Davidson, 2013, p. 223).
- It amplifies activity in the insula region, enabling us to better track body signals, especially ones regarding emotions (Davidson, 2013, p. 214).
- The dorsolateral prefrontal cortex gets livelier during compassion meditation. This is important because this part of the brain is associated with goal-directed behavior—in this instance, to relieve the suffering of others (Davidson, 2013, p. 223). It also plays an instrumental role in being aware of one's internal state (interocepting) and therefore the mental states of others (Farb, Segal, & Anderson, 2013).
- Compassion meditation increases the links among the prefrontal cortex, the insula, and the nucleus accumbens (Farb, Segal, & Anderson, 2013, p. 223). The nucleus accumbens is the brain region where motivation and reward are processed. In other words, we're motivated and better able to be empathetic and compassionate toward others and feel good about being so.

One type of compassion meditation invites us to look at what we have in common instead of at what separates us. Because each of us has unique fingerprints and individual styles of dress and, for the most part, we look different from one another, it's easy to believe that we differ from one another in significant ways. The reality is that if we inventory how we're alike, we find more there than we might imagine. We aren't fundamentally different, only apparently different.

Here is a compassion meditation that can help you pay attention to how we're alike rather than how we differ. It's an adaptation of ones developed by psychotherapist and meditation teacher Rosamund Oliver (2013, pp. 189–190) and former Google engineer Chade-Meng Tan (2012, pp. 169–170).

Compassion Meditation

1. Sit in a comfortable, upright position that helps you relax while remaining alert. Take a few moments to bring yourself fully present into this moment by sensing the weight of your body on the chair and noticing how your feet, bottom, and arms are resting on whatever surface they're on. Take three mindful breaths, noticing where you feel it in your body along with the length of your exhale and inhale.

2. Think of an individual or a group with whom you'll be meeting. Imagine you're with this person or the group, as if they were here right now. Picture her, him, or the group in your mind's eye. If you haven't

met these people before and don't know what they look like, you can say their names to yourself.

3. As you hold the image of each person or the group as a whole, read the words below, pausing now and then to refresh your attention on the image and your words.

   - [Name] has a body and mind, emotions and thoughts, just like me.
   - [Name] has hopes, fears, and a deep desire for happiness and fulfillment, just like me.
   - [Name] has experienced physical or emotional pain, just like me.
   - [Name] has been sad, disappointed, afraid, angry, hurt, or confused, just like me.
   - [Name] wants to be healthy, loved, and included; to make a contribution; and to be heard and acknowledged, just like me.
   - [Name] wants to be free from pain and suffering and to be happy, just like me.
   - [Name] is a fellow human being, just like me.

4. Take a moment to put yourself in this person's or group's shoes and imagine you can see the world through her, his, or their eyes.

5. Bring forward wishes of goodwill for this person or group, such as the following:

   - May [name] be with their pain, heartache, or discomfort gently and kindly.
   - May [name] be free from fear, anger, and suffering in this meeting.

- May [name] have the strength, clarity, and calm to say what they need to say.
- May [name] enjoy talking, learning, and solving difficult issues together today.
- Notice whether you have more empathy and goodwill toward the person or people you're about to gather with.

Compassion meditation creates a supply inside us so that when compassion is needed in our interactions, it's available. Energy follows attention. So when we pay attention to developing and extending compassion to others, we activate and strengthen these pathways in the brain. And when we feel compassion for others, it quiets our discursive thoughts and proliferating emotions, helping us better understand what others need. Small acts of compassion in meetings help train the brain and get it ready for when larger acts are needed. These small acts include smiling, saying thank you, listening attentively when others speak, asking how you can be helpful, or silently holding a sense of warm-heartedness or goodwill for people in a meeting.

An essential part of developing compassion for others is developing it for ourselves. This is the ground from which all compassion grows. Being self-compassionate means we treat ourselves the way we would a good friend. We forgive ourselves when we think we have "screwed up" and speak kindly to ourselves instead of being harshly self-critical.

Notice how you talk to yourself. During or after a meeting, listen to the self-talk. What do you sound like: "You really screwed that one up. You're an idiot." Or "You handled those questions really well. I'm proud of you." A berating inner voice activates the amygdala, making us more reactive and less able to be compassionate with ourselves and others. A kind inner voice enables us to be kind to others. It's important to remember that the pain you feel in a frustrating meeting is the same pain that others feel. Our story lines might differ, but the experience is the same.

When I feel compassion for myself, I feel more spacious inside and more aware of what's going on inside me and around me. Our common humanity is more apparent to me. I'm more able to remember that everyone experiences pain, loss, and suffering—that life is hard for everyone. Unfortunately, when we're upset, forgetting this is all too easy. It can seem like we're alone on a stage, isolated and scared. We feel disconnected from others and overlook what we have in common: our shared human experience. This isolation exacerbates the fear and anger that might already be gripping us, making it impossible to be empathetic towards anyone else.

In your next meeting, look around the room. Do a mini version of the compassion meditation: Look at each person's face and silently remind yourself that life—and perhaps this meeting—is challenging for everyone. See whether you're able to develop a sense of warm-heartedness or goodwill toward each of them and yourself. Notice how this feels in the body, especially the torso.

3) Use Humanizing Thoughts and Questions. You can enlist the help of humanizing thoughts and questions to develop empathy and compassion.

When people are being "difficult," assume they're under the influence of the more primitive parts of the brain. When someone is being disruptive, how might you respond differently if, instead of getting fearful or combative, you consider the possibility that something has threatened their sense of safety (i.e., they're afraid) and that they're operating on automatic (behaving unconsciously)? You might wonder, "Why would a person behave this way? What might be going on for this person? What are they experiencing? What might they be needing?" Although you may have some good hunches about what they need, it's important not to make assumptions and act on them, lest you aggravate the situation.

Don't pull away into interpretations of or judgments about their behavior. This will unconsciously aggravate their sense of isolation and upset. Generate a sense of kindness inside yourself for them, or at the very least a neutral sense. Without a word being spoken, they'll sense the kindness through their resonance circuits and through your facial expressions and body language. This helps calm their survival mechanisms and enables them to feel safer. With a kind tone of voice, you might also ask a humanizing question aloud—for example, "How are you responding to what the group has said thus far?" or "What's the most important aspect of this issue for you?"

Questions that help you reappraise the situation can also help you manage your emotional reactions (Lieberman, 2013, p. 296) so you're better able to empathize with others. Reappraising includes asking questions about an upsetting circumstance so you can consider a different perspective and perhaps change how you perceive and experience it. Three fundamental questions can help you change your perspective:

- What's actually going on, separate from your thoughts and stories about it? In other words, question the accuracy of your thinking. ("Am I sure? Are my thoughts accurate?")

- What are the facts of the situation? ("What am I missing?")
- If you change vantage points and see the situation from this person's or group's perspective, what do you see? For example, in the mental health meeting at the start of the chapter, what if any of them had stopped blaming one another for the situation and looked at the facts of it—the number of people in need, the number of staff hours available to serve that number—and shared their perspectives on what was and wasn't working in the system? What solutions might have emerged if they had paused and attempted to see the situation from the point of view of others in the room?

It's tough to develop accurate and effective reappraisals when you're emotionally aroused and have little or no access to the prefrontal cortex. This is why setting the intention to treat everyone, including yourself, with compassion and doing mindfulness and compassion meditations are so important. They help keep you from becoming reactive and losing access to your natural ability to be empathetic and compassionate. Practicing reappraisals increases activity in the ventrolateral prefrontal cortex (VLPFC) and decreases reactivity in the amygdala. This is significant because the VLPFC is the hub of the brain's "braking system." In other words, it plays an important role in preventing us from behaving impulsively outside of our conscious control. Mindfulness meditation appears to be a great way to strengthen the braking system that is part of the VLPFC (Lieberman, 2013, pp. 208, 297).

Remember, compassion isn't about avoiding or denying disagreements or conflicts. Empathy and compassion are key to being able to work through disagreements effectively with minimal damage to relationships. When we're compassionate with one another, we're more likely to avoid unnecessary conflicts evoked by how we treat and feel about one another. This gives us more time and emotional wherewithal to work through the different perspectives on the real issues facing us.

Extend Your Sphere of Compassion

Thus far in this chapter, I've focused on developing compassion for those you're interacting with directly. However, our interactions affect more than just the people in the room. Usually, meetings at work and in our communities result in decisions that affect many who haven't been at the table or who haven't had a chance to influence the thinking that led to these decisions. How far can we or should we extend our sphere of compassion?

Chapter 8 describes why we need to extend compassion to those who will be affected by the results of any deliberation. As Mother Teresa explained it, "The problem with the world is that we draw the circle of our family too small." But compassion isn't just a matter of including these people in meetings or through other means, such as focus groups and the Internet; compassion asks us to honestly consider and care about how decisions made in meetings affect others near and far, now and into the future.

Key Points

- To solve complex issues in meetings, we need to have three kinds of empathy—*cognitive* (understanding people's perspectives), *concerned* (knowing what others need), and *emotional* (feeling what others feel)—along with *compassion*, a warmhearted desire to extend goodwill and be helpful to others.

- The human brain is wired for empathy and compassion. Fear and a culturally reinforced competitive individualism get in the way of our natural inclinations.

- Compassion meditation changes the brain in at least four ways, making it easier for compassion to become a proclivity or trait rather than a temporary state or something we have to work hard to do.

- Three ways to develop your capacity for compassion are to (a) set an intention to treat everyone—including yourself—with compassion, (b) strengthen your compassion "muscle" with mindfulness and compassion meditations, and (c) use humanizing thoughts and questions.

Questions for Reflection

How might exercising empathy and compassion in your meetings at work or in your community change the tenor of the conversation?

How might you extend empathy and compassion to those you disagree with, even adamantly?

Which approach might you want to try in order to develop your empathy and compassion: setting an intention, doing compassion meditation, or practicing using humanizing thoughts and questions?

Chapter 8:
Engaging with People Who Differ from Us

It is a fact: we are heading irreversibly into a multicultural and multipolar world. Those who do not understand that understand nothing.

—Václav Havel

The air was cool and moist in the gray light of dawn as I walked to my office in a redwood forest. As I slid the key into the door lock, I heard an unfamiliar and unmistakable cry of distress. It sounded close, but I couldn't see who or what was making the sound. I cautiously peered around trees and under bushes—there, just 3 feet away under a heather plant and leaning against the foundation of the building, was a newborn fawn teetering on its hind legs and front knees, trying to get up and run. To its dismay, and mine, it was too young to stand. Alert to the dangers of the mountain lions that frequent this area, I yearned to protect this wee creature. Yet I knew my presence increased its distress, so I backed away, promising myself to check in on it in a short while. I was relieved when, that afternoon, I saw the fawn following its mother and sibling on spindly, shaking legs.

There was tension in that brief encounter with the fawn. Although I yearned to calm and protect it, I knew my presence aggravated it. The fawn needed to be with someone like it, another deer—ideally, its mother. This tension is similar to what we feel when we meet people who differ from us in age, ethnicity, race, gender, sexual orientation, education, political persuasion, and economic or social class. Mentally, we might want to interact effectively with people who aren't like us, but doing so can feel uncomfortable, even threatening. We feel safer with people who are like us. Gathering in families and tribes is how we've survived as a species.

When the amygdala is activated by our interacting with people who differ from us (Fiske, 2008), our ability to engage effectively decreases. Although we might put up a polite front, the alarm center in the brain is sending out distress signals. Activation of the amygdala decreases the resources available to the prefrontal cortex, the area that's critical to paying attention and managing our emotions.

We differ from the fawn in that the newer part of the brain, specifically the prefrontal cortex, gives us options that the fawn doesn't have. We can make conscious choices about what to do based on our intentions. We don't have to be driven by habits of self-protection. We can be aware of anxiety brewing in the face of difference, we can notice and put on the back burner preconceived "truths" we might believe about "those people" and calm our fears. We can choose to be aware of our discomfort and still engage with those who differ from us. The very act of relating can alleviate our trepidation. Ironically, the source and solution to anxiety in an interaction is the same: Connect with others. Although survival in the past depended on being part of a family or tribe, it now depends on our ability to relate effectively with those whom we perceive as being *outside* our tribe or group.

As noted, to understand and solve complex issues, we need to work with people who have different backgrounds and points of view. Unless we engage effectively with people who differ from us, our solutions will be limited to our own perspectives. We create echo chambers when we primarily talk with like-minded people, and our beliefs and ideas are reinforced through repetition. This makes us surer of our own positions than we probably should be. In this way, we blindly continue on the same path and repeat or recreate the past at a time when we sorely need to forge a new future.

Engaging with those we perceive as different means including anyone who has a stake in the issue at hand. This usually means interacting with people of different backgrounds, areas of expertise, and points of view. To do this effectively, we need to make a conscious choice to mindfully manage the self-protective parts of the brain. The benefits are invaluable. Engaging with those who differ from us begins to dispel the myths we have about "those other people," thus increasing our understanding of the issues at hand and revealing common ground where we might have assumed there is none.

Identifying Stakeholders Who Need to Be at the Table

If we want to increase our chances of successfully tackling tough challenges, we need to put aside our inclination to gather primarily with people who think as we do. We need to carefully consider who needs to be at the conversational table, regardless of whether they think as we do or not. Doing something new like this takes more energy and an active prefrontal cortex. We need to be alert and not let our brains unconsciously slide into doing what's comfortable: talking with those who are like us.

In light of what you hope to accomplish at your meeting(s), identify the stakeholders you think need to be included. This means people who

- have decision-making authority over how the problem is defined and what solutions to pursue;
- care about or are being affected by the issue;
- have diverse points of view;
- have information and expertise;
- will likely be affected by solutions;
- will have the responsibility to implement solutions; and
- could block implementation of solutions or are considered "troublemakers."

These people are called "stakeholders" because they have a stake in the issue being considered. Each of these individuals or groups has important information or perspectives that are key to understanding what the issue is, seeing how it relates to other problems, and finding effective solutions that people support. It can be tempting to simply go into a room with a group of "experts" or like-minded folks and create what seem to be ideal solutions. However, solutions developed by an exclusive group rarely solve the problem or get implemented because they

- do not address systemic causes of the problem that are usually interconnected with other problems (e.g., protecting water rights in face of drought);
- do not solve the issue as perceived by those closest to it (e.g., making sales staff take customer relations training when, from their point of view, the issue is insufficient phone lines: By the time a customer gets to talk with the sales staff, he or she is angry from having to wait);
- are not understood or supported by those responsible for carrying them out (e.g., lab technicians drag their feet on using a new IT platform because they weren't consulted when the decision was made to change it and they don't know why the change was made);
- have unanticipated and negative impacts on other parts of the organization or community (e.g., to help patients feel more welcome when they check in at a hospital, attractive new tile flooring is installed in the main lobby to make it look more like a high-end hotel; however, patients experience significant discomfort when they bounce across tile ridges as they're wheeled in or out of the facility); and
- create other problems (e.g., in an effort to make a main thoroughfare safer, a municipality widens the road and removes trees that provided an aesthetic appearance along with a wind break for cars, bicyclists, and establishments along the road).

But getting people who differ from us to the conversational table is not enough. We need to be able to engage with them effectively so that all stakeholder voices are heard and understood. This means making conscious choices to be compassionate, define "enlightened" intentions, and be open to change.

When we dedicate ourselves to including diverse voices, we add life and creativity to interactions, especially when people are committed to finding common ground. However, the key is how we interact with "those other people" in our interactions. Diversity does not have to mean discomfort.

Building "Bridging Social Capital"

The term "social capital" was first used in 1916 by L. J. Hanifan, the state supervisor for rural schools in West Virginia, in regard to developing support for these schools. Quoted in David Putnam's *Bowling Alone*, Hanifan wrote:

> Social capital refers to those tangible substances [that] count for most in the daily lives of people: namely good will, fellowship, sympathy, and social intercourse among the individuals and families who make up a social unit. . . . If he comes into contact with his neighbor, and they with other neighbors, there will be an accumulation of social capital, which may immediately satisfy his social needs. . . . The community as a whole will benefit by the cooperation of all its parts. (2000, p. 19)

Just like when we accumulate financial capital we can draw on, we can build social capital in the form of trust and reliability among people, allowing us to do things in organizations and communities that we can't do in isolation.

Although the term languished in near obscurity for decades, the truth of it did not: We all understand but rarely discuss the fact that we are interdependent and need one another to survive and get things done. When the expression "social capital" was the focus of a World Bank research program in the 1990s and the subject of at least two mainstream books, including *Bowling Alone* by Robert Putnam and *Better Together* by Putnam and Lewis Feldstein, it resurfaced and moved into popular parlance. "As used by social scientists, 'social capital' refers to social networks, norms of reciprocity, mutual assistance, and trustworthiness," wrote Putnam and Feldstein (2003, p. 2). When we work in relationship with stakeholders, we can achieve things that no one of us could accomplish on our own. At the same time, we experience the satisfaction and comfort of being part of and contributing to a community of people.

Social capital has its upsides, such as lowering crime rates in neighborhoods where neighbors know one another well, and its downsides, such as political parties that punish members who don't toe the party line. To understand these two sides, let's consider two types of social capital: When we interact with people who are like us, we build *bonding* social capital, and when we interact with people who differ from us, we build *bridging* social capital.

Understanding Bonding Social Capital. Bonding social capital develops naturally among people who have something in common, such as similar goals, values, or points of view. The old adage "birds of a feather flock together" captures the essence of bonding social capital. Socially bonded groups tend to be homogeneous and focused on themselves and their goals, such as improving their children's school, advocating for a particular political cause, or simply providing camaraderie or protection for those deemed part of the group. Political parties, professional associations, civic organizations like the Rotary Club, labor unions, and youth gangs are examples of the various forms bonding social capital can take. Being with people who are similar to us in ways that are important to us increases our sense of safety and power: Together we get things done.

It's noteworthy that when people see themselves as power-less, their ties to their "tribes" can become very strong because the identity of the group becomes connected with the sense of identity and safety of its members. People communicate their ties to spe-cific groups in a number of ways, including wearing clothes with a group's logo or developing secret rituals that only those in the group know about.

Our long-ago ancestors survived by banding into groups and tribes that rewarded reciprocity, fairness, and loyalty. We continue to affiliate and bond with homogeneous groups because they provide the sense of belonging we all need along with the benefits of mutual support, trust, and cooperation.

People in bonded groups expect their interactions to be predict-able because they know, or imagine they know, that everyone shares the same values and beliefs. Anyone who challenges these can get pushed to the edges or entirely out of the group.

Seeking Bridging Social Capital. Bridging social capital results from interactions among people and groups who are *not* alike. At work, this might mean engineers talking with people in marketing or research scientists solving problems with their colleagues in man-ufacturing. In communities, building bridging social capital involves conservatives meeting with liberals; the middle class talking with the rich and poor; and the old, young, and middle-aged convers-ing together.

Building bridging social capital (i.e., trust and relationships among diverse groups) can be challenging because it usually doesn't happen without intention and effort. We have to make a conscious choice to interact with others who aren't like us. And when we do, we have to work harder to understand and be understood. We also have to manage the threat we might feel, albeit unconsciously, in the face of difference. Understanding this helps us to make sense out of our difficulty in interacting effectively in heterogeneous groups and to avoid being drawn into taking sides. Because our perspectives, beliefs, and values are interwoven with those of our bonded group, stepping outside of them in order to build bridging social capital with "strangers" is challenging. Not surprisingly, the etymological root of *stranger* means "beyond the usual boundaries" or "outside your group."

Let's try a thought experiment. Close your eyes and bring to mind images of two or three people with whom you feel safe and at ease. They could be colleagues at work, friends, neighbors, or members of your family. Identify a few of the ways they're like you. Notice your body sensations, thoughts, and emotions as you think about these people. For example, as I think about one of my favorite colleagues, a friend, and my husband, I feel calm, content, and safe;

I feel a sense of connection with them. There' a slight increase in warmth around my heart. We are similar in age, education, profession, and political views.

Now, do the opposite. Bring to mind two or three people with whom you're ill at ease when you interact with them. Note a few of the ways they are not like you and, once again, observe your body sensations, thoughts, and emotions as you think about them. As I think about the people with whom I feel a bit on edge, I feel a slight pressure in my chest and some constriction in my shoulders. We are dissimilar in political views and styles of interacting. For example, two of them tend to dominate conversations. Not only do I not sense a connection with them, but they also seem like "strangers."

Such kinesthetic clues are helpful. They alert us to the early stages of a sense of alarm so we can make a conscious choice not to let our fears distance us from others and so we can remember our intention (assuming this is an intention) to engage effectively with people who differ from us.

How Too Much "Bonding Social Capital" Creates Collateral Damage

Although building bridging social capital can be challenging, too much social bonding capital brings its own set of problems.

Talking across Differences Becomes Harder. When we become accustomed to talking with people who think as we do (or listen to media that reinforces our point of view), it becomes even harder to talk with those who don't think as we do. And when our version of "the truth" becomes connected to our self-image, then interacting in diverse groups can be quite difficult because we perceive different versions of "the truth" as a threat.

Conformity and Unanimity Silence Us. When groups bond, they tend to build cohesion around beliefs, goals, or values. Such groups reward conformity and punish the lack of it. Multiple studies confirm that conformity discourages different perspectives and crushes dissent, the very ingredients we need to understand and solve complex issues. You might think peer pressure ended in high school; it did not. We like to go along with the crowd so that we stay part of the crowd. Remember that a sense of relationship and belonging is an important part of feeling safe.

Solomon Asch conducted a series of landmark experiments to investigate this phenomenon. As a social psychologist, he wanted to understand how Nazism—an unnerving and extreme example of the results of bonding social capital—was possible. What he discovered was startling: Our need to belong and feel connected to others is so strong that it can change what we perceive, what we believe, and how we behave (Brafman & Brafman 2008, pp. 153–155).

In Asch's experiments, a participant was placed in a room with several others. They were all told that they would be tested for visual acuity. The group was shown three straight lines of varying lengths. Each person was asked to determine which of the three lines matched the length of a fourth line. It seems a simple enough task, doesn't it? What the participant did not know was that the other "subjects" were actors who had been told to give the same wrong answer. As the actors called out erroneous answers, the real participant became bewildered and began to doubt his own perception. In contradiction with his own senses, he gave the wrong answer in order to align with the group.

Seventy-five percent of the subjects in Asch's study gave wrong answers instead of being alone in their dissenting opinion in a group of strangers. It's important to note that such "conformity experiments" have been replicated more than 130 times in 17 countries with similar results. Brain-imaging work done in some of these experiments suggests that when people conform, they begin to actually see the situation as others do. However, when participants were asked to give anonymous answers, they conformed less frequently.

The power of conformity comes from unanimity. Unanimous agreements in a group provide a set of simple "truths" and an island of safety in a world of bewilderingly diverse beliefs and points of view. However, in a variation on his studies, Asch unearthed the promising power of one voice raised in opposition to commonly held views. When he added a single actor who gave the right answer, this single, solitary voice broke the trance of conformity and gave permission to the real participant to break ranks and also give the correct answer. Furthermore, even if the actor gave a wrong answer, if it differed from the majority, it gave the participant courage to speak up and give what he or she thought was the correct answer.

In interactions, if you suspect that people are silent because they want to belong, you can crack open the hold of conformity at any time. For each decision you're about to make, pause and ask yourself what you really think. Do you believe it's the right decision, or are you supporting it because you're afraid of damaging relationships with your colleagues or neighbors? You can help others resist the pressure to conform by expressing your opinion and encouraging others to express theirs. For example, you can say, "This is a complicated issue. We need to understand everyone's point of view, especially if you have reservations or flat out think this is the wrong thing to do. Please tell us what you think." Appreciating such differences can open the door to avoiding bad decisions or open new ways of thinking about the topic at hand.

Homogeneity Creates an "Us" and a "Them." Believing in an "us" and a "them" might be terrific for sporting events but wreaks havoc in organizations and communities. Homogeneity influences our thinking so that we see others as separate and different, defined by their roles, their positions on issues, or their place in a hierarchy or a community. The safety of bonded groups can lead to the stereotyping of other groups; we make up stories and develop beliefs about "them." These beliefs can become more real to us than our direct experience. We can become antagonistic and slide into labeling and even demonizing people.

What are your stories and labels for those who differ from you? What are your stories about "tree huggers," "the 1 percent" or the "99 percent," "the do-nothing Congress," or the people who live on "the wrong side of the tracks?" How about for "those people" who are employed by federal, state, or local governments? Or those who work in different functions in your organization: customer service, sales, manufacturing, or research?

A number of years ago, I had colleagues who were dedicated labor organizers and union officials. I also consulted with organizations whose employees belonged to unions. In most of these organizations, managers, supervisors, and union members worked together day by day to take care of patients, produce and distribute products and services, or convey passengers. However, when handling grievances or negotiating contracts, they unsheathed their swords of stereotype: Union representatives spoke of management with disdain and in clichéd terms, and managers spoke of unions likewise.

Needless to say, turning one another into "the other," or the enemy, undermines everyone's ability to find common ground. Although I appreciate the historical roots of this animosity, I bemoan the waste of effort and lost opportunities that these "us"and "them" negotiations exemplify.

In-group loyalty easily turns into out-group antagonism. Psychologist Daniel Goleman captured the dark side of bonding social capital when he wrote, "We confront challenges of living in a global civilization with a brain that primarily attaches us to our home tribe. . . . Once the others are set at a psychological distance, they can become a target for hostility" (2006, p. 299).

It seems that we unconsciously choose to dislike some people in order to feel bonded with others. The neurotransmitter oxytocin plays a role in facilitating this in-group bonding and out-group exclusion (Smith, 2014). In research conducted by social psychologist Jennifer K. Bosson and her colleagues (Bosson, Johnson, Niederhoffer, & Swann, 2006), it appears we bond more strongly— feel a sense of closeness and affinity—with our group when its members share negative attitudes about others than when we share positive attitudes about them. The allure of these negative stances seems to emanate from the certainties of in-group and out-group boundaries that boost self-esteem for members of the presumed "in-group." It's noteworthy that the participants in these studies were unaware of this predisposition. They believed that sharing positive attitudes about others promoted more closeness than negative ones.

The core question is who is "them"? Who are "those people"? Who is "the other"? Whom do we regard as unworthy of consideration, inclusion, and engagement in our meetings at work or in our communities? It's important to stay conscious of such predispositions if we want to engage meaningfully with people who differ from us. The price we pay for preferring to talk in homogeneous groups is high: polarization, divisiveness, sectarianism, ethnocentrism, and fundamentalism. Poet W. H. Auden entreats us to overcome this proclivity, stating, "We must love one another or die."

Difference Can Lead to Denying the Humanity of Others. When we meet people who obviously differ from us (in height, weight, race, gender, age, style of dress, etc.) or who do so more subtly (come from different functions or levels in the hierarchy of an organization or from different economic, social, or political persuasions), we can feel unsafe. In fact, such differences can prime us to be more sensitive to perceived threats to our sense of status, certainty, autonomy, relatedness, or fairness (SCARF). For instance, if you're the only black person in a meeting and people seem to interrupt you but not anyone else, this might exacerbate an already aroused amygdala. This makes it difficult to interact constructively.

When we add a sense of threat to any beliefs we might have about others ("All Hispanics/Latinos are . . ." or "All white people are..." or "Everyone from marketing is . . ."), we can start to turn these "others" (not of my tribe) into objects. Studies indicate that in extreme forms of prejudice, we can go so far as to deny those who differ from us their humanity. Social psychologists Lasana T. Harris and Susan T. Fiske (2006, pp. 847–853) found that the patterns of activation in the medial prefrontal cortex are the same when participants view pictures of inanimate objects as when they look at social groups that evoke their antipathy. We've seen how this kind of dehumanization can become violent and tragic: savagery in Germany in the 1930s and 1940s, in the United States before and after the Civil War as well as in the 1950s and 1960s, in Cambodia in the 1970s, and in Rwanda in 1994.

Given the significant downsides of talking only with people who think as we do and the need to interact effectively in diverse groups to solve complex issues at work and in our communities, it behooves us to become more adept at building bridging social capital.

If we look at this just in racial and ethnic terms, the need for us to develop bridging social capital in the United States is great. According to census figures released in 2012, by the year 2043, whites will no longer make up the majority of Americans. Already, eight of the ten largest metropolitan areas have child populations in which white children are a minority. Hispanic children are the largest demographic in six of these ten metropolitan areas, and blacks are the largest in the other two (Blow, 2012). According to a 2012 Associated Press poll, 51 percent of Americans express prejudice toward blacks (up from 48 percent in 2008), and 52 percent hold anti-Hispanic attitudes (Blow, 2012).

In addition to developing social capital across race and ethnicity, we need to develop bridging social capital across classes. It turns out that financial differences create behavioral and attitudinal differences. Two of these differences are critical to how we interact with one another at work and in our communities. First, research indicates that people of wealth blame poor individuals for their impoverished circumstances or "failures." They also credit themselves for their prosperity and triumphs (Miller, 2012). And there's a growing body of research that indicates that wealth makes people "selfish and antisocial" (Miller, 2012). According to psychologists Dacher Keltner and Michael W. Kraus, "Those with the most power in society seem to pay particularly little attention to those with the least power" (Goleman, October 5, 2013). Paying attention to the feelings and needs of others is essential to empathy and compassion and finding common ground. As previously noted, to solve complex issues, we need to interact with people who have different backgrounds and perspectives. Empathy and compassion are keys to doing this effectively.

Solving seemingly intractable issues and moving forward together requires all of us to learn how to engage effectively with people who differ from us. This is already a highly prized skill set that's important on the job but in short supply (Herk, September 22, 2015).

Four Requirements for Building Bridging Social Capital

To engage effectively with people who differ from us, we need to do at least four things:

- Because segregation between the rich and the poor and among racial and ethnic groups still exists in most of the cities and towns in the United States, we need to go out of our way to connect with people who differ from us. For many of us, it doesn't happen in the course of a normal day.
- We need to balance our attention between protecting ourselves and connecting with others. You've already learned how mindfulness and making conscious choices play a critical role in this.
- When we meet with others who are significantly different from us, we must try to see them as fellow human beings and stay curious about them.
- We need to be aware of our beliefs about individuals and groups and how these beliefs influence our behavior and

that of others. This is called a self-fulfilling prophecy or the Pygmalion Effect.

Go Out of Our Way. As the racial and ethnic composition of the United States becomes more diverse, we continue to live in separate enclaves. According to an analysis of the 2010 census, whites in 367 metropolitan areas across the U.S. live in neighborhoods that are at least 75 percent white. Blacks live in neighborhoods that average 45 percent black, 35 percent white, 15 percent Hispanic, and 4 percent Asian. The neighborhood percentages for Hispanics are similar. The figures shift some for Asians. Their neighborhoods average 22 percent Asian, 49 percent white, 9 percent black, and 19 percent Hispanic (Logan, 2011).

Segregation by income is increasing along with income inequality. Over the past four decades, the percentage of poor families and affluent families who live in isolated or segregated neighborhoods has more than doubled (from 15 percent to 31 percent). In addition, the affluent are more isolated from other Americans than the poor are. This is because fewer middle- and low-income families live in affluent neighborhoods and because fewer middle- and high-income people live in low-income neighborhoods (Reardon & Bischoff, 2011).

Living apart in segregated communities has sobering implications for our ability to include stakeholders and interact effectively with those who differ from us at work and in public processes. Increasingly, we're becoming strangers who are frightened of or annoyed by one another. If we want to solve complex issues that cut across multiple boundaries, including geographic ones, we need to go out of our way to include people from outside our neighborhoods and from different parts of our organizations. And when we're together, we need to go out of our way to work harder to understand one another. Overall, we need to create more time and safe spaces in which we get to know one another as human beings. If we don't feel connected as fellow humans, we don't have the opportunity to collectively pursue solving complex problems in ways that might succeed and transform our relationships in the process.

Manage the Tension between the Instincts to Protect and Connect. Despite the fact that we're ultimately and profoundly social beings interwoven with one another through the limbic system and mirror neurons, in the business of everyday life, our self-images and all the thoughts in our heads can lead us to feel separate, as if each of us were going it alone. When we carry this sense of separateness into interactions, we bring fear with us, especially when we relate with those who differ from us. And as we've already seen, fear evokes defensive behavior that separates or disconnects us from others even more. This happens in part because fear inhibits the release of oxytocin, the "trust hormone" that's instrumental in forging and strengthening relationships and reducing social fears.

Engaging with those who differ from us—often a perceived source of threat—is also the antidote to that threat. When we mindfully enlist the help of the prefrontal cortex, we can consciously choose to step into the space between instinct and action and extend ourselves to engage with "strangers." We can investigate how they *are* like us, increase our understanding of their personal story, and appreciate the differences. When we develop a sense of relationship with those who differ from us, we feel safer. Feeling safe engenders a sense of trust, a desire to contribute, and sometimes even a willingness to make sacrifices. All of these enable us to work together effectively and reach goals that can't be achieved by individuals working alone.

When you're with people who are not like you, ask yourself, "Am I thinking of these people as 'the other' and/or as a target for my arguments?" Instead, think of them as human beings for whom life—perhaps even this moment—is just as challenging as it is for you. Our ability to do this depends on whether we're able to notice and manage our self-protective reactions.

In the face of difference, instead of arguing or withdrawing, you can connect by saying what's going on for you ("I'm surprised you see the situation so differently."), asking questions of honest curiosity ("How did you come to this conclusion?"), listening attentively ("Here's my understanding of what you just said . . ."), or saying what's important to you and why ("Here's what really matters to me . . . and here's why.").

In addition, threads of connection with others can be woven in simple ways: through eye contact, a head nod, or statements like "Please tell me more" or "I'd like to understand how you see the situation. I'd also like you to understand how I see it." One word, phrase, or facial expression can make a big difference. It's surprising how easily emotional states can change. Simple gestures can help people feel safe, which in turn encourages them to stay engaged. These gestures also help trigger the release of oxytocin and create an upward spiral of trust, warmth, and engagement. This doesn't mean people will agree with one another. It does, however, increase the likelihood that people can disagree without disconnecting from one another and evoking the offensive, defensive, or checking-out behavior that blocks effective interaction. It's the old saying modified: It's not *what* we say that matters; it's *how* we say it.

Connect with and Stay Curious about "the Other." Two ways we protect ourselves from engaging with "the other" are by avoiding contact altogether or, if we have to talk with people who differ from us, by disconnecting from them even when we're with them. This usually triggers self-protection in them. They go on offense, go on defense, or also withdraw. But it is possible to make contact and maintain a sense of relationship with another, even in the face of differences that challenge everything you believe or hold dear. A South African woman has shown us the way.

Pumla Gobodo-Madikizela is a clinical psychologist who grew up in a black South African township and served on the Truth and Reconciliation Commission. In *A Human Being Died That Night*, she described how she witnessed traumatizing scenes of violence much of her life, the first when she was 5 years old. Describing the violence that had spread to her township from Sharpeville in March 1960, when 69 people were killed and 186 were wounded during a demonstration protesting laws that required blacks to carry internal passports, she wrote, "I was witnessing something I had until then never seen before: live shooting, blood, and human death" (2004, p. 9).

Despite this, or perhaps because of it, in 1997 she began a series of interviews with Eugene de Kock, the commanding officer of the state-sanctioned death squads under apartheid. She met him in Pretoria's maximum-security prison, where he was serving a 212-year sentence for crimes against humanity. At their meeting, de Kock wore bright orange overalls and was chained to a metal stool bolted to the floor in a "tiny" room with gray walls. Gobodo-Madikizela sat across a table from him on a chair with wheels "which I could scoot back with ease in the event of an attack by de Kock" (p. 18).

This was hardly a setting conducive for human connection, but in 46 hours over a period of six months, they did connect.

Listening to de Kock describe killing operations, torture, and murder, Gobodo-Madikizela wrestled with big questions. She worked hard to understand his context. She asked herself, "To what extent was de Kock a normal, ordinary citizen corrupted by the apartheid system, and to what extent was his mind already corrupted by his own upbringing? When someone as a part of his job must carry out orders that continually involve him in crimes against humanity, to what extent can he remain simply a person carrying out his instructions, and at what point does evil intrude into and compromise the integrity of his conscience?" She remained curious: "At what point did Eugene de Kock cross the moral line and take over—and upon himself, as a personal cause—the evil of the system for which he designated himself as crusader?" (pp. 54–55).

When de Kock expressed his internal torment, confusion, regret, and shame for his role and actions, Gobodo-Madikizela experienced empathy for him but then felt guilty and afraid to have done so. She forbore because "the absence of empathy, whether at the communal or personal level, signals a condition that, in subtle and destructive ways, separates people from one another" (p. 127). In a chapter titled "I Have No Hatred in My Heart," she added, "Philosophical questions can and should give way and be subsumed to *human* questions, for in the end we are a society of people and not of ideas, a fragile web of interdependent humans, not of stances" (p. 125).

Confronted with the tragic harm that resulted from the extremes of bonding social capital ("us versus them") in South Africa and the apartheid policies it created, Gobodo-Madikizela built bridging social capital in the hardest conditions imaginable to affirm human connection. Frankly, she stretches my imagination about what might be possible in human interaction.

To strengthen this fragile web Gobodo-Madikizela spoke of, we need to have a clear intention to understand and have compassion for others as human beings, even under the most difficult of circumstances. This doesn't mean we'll agree with or like them. To move forward, to save the world, we must intentionally stay in relationship with others, be curious about them, and at least try to understand their experience and perspective. Chapter 6 provides assistance in how to go about doing this.

Enlist the Help of the Pygmalion Effect. People's beliefs about us influence how we behave. This is known as the Pygmalion Effect, after George Bernard Shaw's play *Pygmalion* (1916). In it, Professor Higgins transforms a Cockney flower seller, Eliza Doolittle, into someone who passes for a duchess. As Shaw has Higgins express it, "The great secret, Eliza, is not having bad manners or good manners or any other particular sort of manners, but having the same manner for all human souls: in short, behaving as if you were in Heaven, where there are no third-class carriages, and one soul is as good as another."

The truth is we are all Eliza. We behave according to how we are treated. How might we all behave as Professor Higgins suggested when we interact with one another? The most important question is whether our beliefs about others bring out the best in them. As Nobel Laureate Nelson Mandela said, "It never hurts to think too highly of a person; often they become ennobled and act better because of it" (Kornfield, 2008, p. 20).

In a classic study of the Pygmalion Effect (Rosenthal & Jacobson, 1968, pp. 16–20), fourth grade teachers were told that certain students would "bloom" during the school year. Because the teachers were given what they perceived to be "credible" information, they had high expectations for those who were predicted to do well. What they didn't know was that "bloomers" had been selected at random—that is, without regard to actual potential. The teachers' positive expectations influenced them to behave differently toward bloomers than they behaved toward other students. Social psychologists Robert Rosenthal and Lenore Jacobson observed that teachers called on bloomers more often, gave them more time to respond, and provided them with more instructional feedback. Not surprisingly, bloomers demonstrated significant growth in academic achievement. The teachers' beliefs and behaviors created a self-fulfilling prophecy.

The results of an experiment with 51 women who signed up to be part of a study on communication are even more striking because the impact was created by the unconscious expectations of anonymous peers (Brafman & Brafman, 2008, pp. 101–103). No authority figure like a teacher was involved. The task put to the women seemed simple: Have a short phone conversation with a randomly selected man about ordinary topics like the weather, college majors, and so on. The men, however, were given biographical information and a snapshot prior to the conversation. What the men did not know was that the photos were fake and randomly assigned: Half of them were "pretty" women, and half were "ordinary." Prior to talking to the assigned "partner," the men completed an "Impression Formation Questionnaire." Regardless of what the bios said, the men who thought they were about to talk with a pretty woman indicated that they expected the woman to be "sociable, poised, humorous, and socially adept." The ones who thought they would be talking with a more ordinary-looking woman said that they expected their phone partners would be "unsociable, awkward, serious, and socially inept." The women had no idea that any of this biasing or opinion-forming was going on.

A third, independent group listened to the recorded conversations with the men's side edited out. They knew nothing about the study and hadn't met any of the participants. They were unaware of the biases the men may have held during the conversation. The independent group "attributed the very same traits to the women based on their *voices alone* that the men had attributed to them based on their (fake) photos."

How do you explain this? Once the men formed an opinion based on a random photo, it affected how they interacted with the women. The women in turn reacted to the cues from the men: "The researchers explained, 'What had initially been reality in the minds of the men had now become reality in the behavior of the women'" (Brafman & Brafman, 2008, p. 103).

The Pygmalion Effect works in two ways. We mirror people's expectations of us, and they mirror ours of them. Despite perceiving reality as something outside and separate from us, we all live in and co-create a "participatory truth"—our assumptions and expectations create our experience of one another. We live in a network of mutual influence. What we believe to be true helps to create what is true. In meetings, many of us underestimate the impact of our beliefs about others. These studies demonstrate that the beliefs we hold shape our behavior along with that of others in ways we likely don't realize.

In addition to behavior, our preconceptions about others influence our physiology along with that of those around us. When we have positive expectations, the levels of dopamine and norepinephrine in the brain increase (Rock, 2009, p. 66). Dopamine is a neurotransmitter related to interest, and norepinephrine is connected to alertness. When we have negative expectations, the levels of dopamine decrease. This neurochemical plays an important role in things that are consequential to how we interact: being open, curious, interested, focused, insightful, and able to learn (pp. 83, 144–147, 151). If your preconceptions about a meeting you're going to attend are negative—you assume nothing will get done and that you'll be bored and frustrated—you can be confident that your levels of dopamine will plummet and that you won't be a constructive participant. It'll be difficult for you to stay interested and curious, to focus your attention and be insightful about the situation at hand. You'll likely influence others to follow suit.

For example, suppose I'm in a department meeting at work, and I expect Michelle will not support my proposal. I believe Michelle isn't supportive of anyone other than herself and the people in her unit. As I present my idea, I wait for her to interrupt and challenge my rationale for the project. Because of this, I don't notice that she's smiling, nodding her head, and maintaining eye contact. When she briefly looks down to look at the project proposal, I assume she's no longer listening. In other words, I pick out "evidence" that confirms my preconceptions about her. Preconceptions blind us to what we don't expect. We forfeit the chance to notice what is different in the moment.

Annoyed by the story I'm running in my head about Michelle, I become defensive about the project. This frustrates Michelle and confuses my colleagues. Their enthusiasm for the project decreases. I incorrectly think that Michelle and the group are separate from me. What I don't realize is that there's an influential relationship among us: We are co-creating the interaction. A belief about Michelle alters my behavior, which alters hers, which in turn influences that of others. My defensiveness changes the dynamic of the group. What we believe about others influences our interactions for good or ill.

Here are some questions to help you investigate your beliefs about others:

- What beliefs or assumptions am I making about the people at this meeting? Are they true? Can I absolutely know they are true? (When we're hurt or scared, we tend to assume the worst.)

- What assumptions am I making about other people's intentions? What impact are these assumptions having on me? Are they true? Can I absolutely know they are true? (We can't know others' intentions unless they tell us.)

- What is my attitude toward these people and this meeting? Is this stance helpful to connecting with and building bridges among people? (Mindfulness can help you assess whether your attitude is based on past or current experience.)

Threats to a sense of safety can come from the very people we need to work with to solve a problem. To engage effectively with those who differ from us, we need to get used to doing so, manage our habits of self-protection, stay connected with them as fellow human beings, and make sure that our beliefs about them create desirable, self-fulfilling prophecies.

Key Points

- In the past, our survival depended on being part of a family or tribe—that is, those who were similar to us. Now, our survival depends on relating effectively with those who differ from us.

- To solve complex problems, we need to include and involve stakeholders: people who have important information or perspectives that are key to understanding the issue and finding effective solutions that people support. Stakeholders usually have different backgrounds and points of view than we have.

- Engaging with stakeholders can be difficult because the brain can perceive differences as a threat to our safety.

- *Bonding social capital* (affinity within and among homogeneous groups) is easier to create than *bridging social capital* (trust and relationships within and among diverse or heterogeneous groups).

- Too much bonding social capital creates collateral damage. When we primarily interact with people who are like us, it's harder to talk with people who differ from us; the need for belonging creates a unanimity and conformity that can silence group members. Homogeneity creates an "us" and "them," and when bonded groups feel threatened, they can slip into denying the humanity of others.

- Building bridging social capital by engaging effectively with various stakeholders requires four things: we need to (a) go out of our way to interact with people who differ from us, (b) manage the tension between the need to protect ourselves and the need to connect with others, (c) stay curious about those who differ from us, and (d) take advantage of the Pygmalion

Effect by holding positive beliefs about people who are not like us.

Questions for Reflection

What are the characteristics of the people it's easy for you to connect with (i.e., you feel safe with them)? What are the characteristics that make it difficult or evoke anxiety in you?

Remember a conversation that you had with someone who differed from you (e.g., in background, age, or point of view) and that caused you to learn and grow. What allowed this to happen? What made it work?

Think about someone else whose perspective differs from yours or with whom you strongly disagree. What questions might you ask to help her feel safe telling you how she came to her point of view or why it's important to her?

Chapter 9:
Using Six Indispensable Communication Skills

A popular joke at the time said that, faced with the country's daunting challenges, South Africans had two options: a practical option and a miraculous option. The practical option was that we would all get down on our knees and pray for a band of angels to come down from heaven and fix things for us. The miraculous option was that we would continue to talk with each other until we found a way forward together.

—Adam Kahane

When I teach listening skills, I sometimes ask people to *not* listen to one another for two minutes in pairs. That's right, not listen to one another. As if on cue, the designated non-listeners become riveted to their phones, nails, or the ceiling. They do not make eye contact, and they turn their backs to the speakers and whistle. They are surprised by how much they know about *not* listening—and they know that listening is the opposite of everything they were doing. The most important realization consistently comes from the designated speakers. They invariably report that when they're not listened to, they lose their train of thought along with their desire to speak. They feel isolated and disconnected. They get agitated and angry and want to go mute or strike out at the non-listener.

Listening is one of six communication skills that are critical to saving the world. These skills are indispensable because they

- help people connect with one another;
- engender a sense of relationship and safety;
- help people understand one another and become aware of the direction and dynamics of the group as a whole;
- enable individuals to manage overwhelming emotions and to prevent emotional contagion;
- equip people to consciously consider and carry out their intentions; and
- create an environment in which people can empathize and extend compassion to one another.

Because I believe so strongly in the power of effective communication to solve problems, this chapter describes each of the six in depth.

Six Indispensible Communication Skills

Listen Attentively

Ask Open-ended Questions

Speak in an inclusive & and embodied way

Summarize & synthesize interactions

Make Process Observations

Make Process Suggestions

Skill One: Listen Attentively

In meetings at work or in our communities, listening is more than just allowing each person to have his or her say. It means that each person has the experience of being heard. Listening attentively is the most efficacious and yet the most underappreciated and underutilized skill in meetings. It's understandable. Listening takes courage, time, and effort. Listening takes courage because it implies a willingness to change. Psychologist Carl Rogers observed, "Most people are afraid to listen because what they hear might change them" (Rogers & Roethlisberger, 1991, pp. 105–111).

A cross-functional team in a large organization disagreed about their core business strategy. They had been meeting weekly for several months and always sat in the same seats. One morning, when they started to cover ground they had covered many times before, I asked them to stand up and move to different seats in the room. I also asked them to pause and close their eyes for a moment and imagine they were meeting with one another for the first time. When they opened their eyes, I asked them to listen to one another with a sense of curiosity and wonder, suspending their opinions or judgments about people and their points of view. I promised they could pick all of these back up later if they wanted.

I then asked everyone to do two things: "First, notice what surprises you about what the person says and what you seem to have in common. Second, paraphrase each person after he speaks to make sure you understand him accurately. You cannot speak until the person who spoke before you indicates that you paraphrased him correctly." After everyone spoke, I asked people to share what surprised them and what they noticed about what they had in common. After weeks of to-ing and fro-ing, they amazed themselves by agreeing on the new strategy for their organization. All it took was listening more attentively in the present moment, setting aside their beliefs about one another, and noticing what they hadn't noticed before.

When you want to understand what others are saying, you need to first notice and then suspend—at least for a while—the chatter going on in your head, especially your beliefs about other people. This includes putting on hold the internal voice that "knows" what the other person is going to say and prepares your "Yes, but . . ." reaction to what they've said. It involves shifting into the here and now with a fresh stance toward yourself and others. Sticking with your breath and body sensations helps you make this shift.

Here's what listening might sound like. First, start with silence; all listening starts with it. Then check your understanding of what you think you heard: "What I think you just said is . . . Have I got that right?" Or "Sounds like . . . is important to you. Could you please help me understand why?"

You're listening for what others want to communicate: what they know, think, feel, and value. To understand these, listen to what people say and how they say it, including the metaphors, analogies, or images they use to convey their message. Listen to the pace, tone, and pitch at which they speak, and observe their gestures and expressions.

I learned an important lesson about listening and pace while participating in an international women's dialogue. One of the participants from South Africa noticed how quickly we "Westerners" were talking. "I don't know how you can understand one another. You all speak so quickly, sometimes interrupting one another," she remarked. "For me to understand what you've said, I need to let your message come into my ears and eyes, travel down through my throat and heart and into my belly before I can really understand. This takes time."

It can be difficult to listen because the breathtaking speed of most meetings or conversations does not encourage or allow for attentive listening. We're socialized to move through things quickly, and we're more practiced at speaking than we are at listening. The challenge, especially in interactions about important issues, is to keep the conversation moving at a human pace that allows us to listen attentively so we understand what people are saying, how they're feeling, and why what they're saying is important to them. As cross-cultural anthropologist Angeles Arrien noted, "There is no depth in the fast lane." If you have trouble with "slow," you might also have trouble with "deep."

Many of us have the habit of listening to what others say and quickly agreeing or disagreeing with it. Listening is not the same as agreeing or disagreeing. That is a different step. When we listen to others, we pay full attention to them and what they're saying. It's a state of mindful awareness. In order to understand what someone is saying or feeling, we need to pause before responding. This does *not* mean simply saying, "I know what you mean" (What exactly do you understand?) and then continuing with "but/and I disagree (or agree) with you because . . ." Listening is about trying to make sure we actually do understand what the person intends to communicate. Sharing our opinion or stating whether we agree or disagree, although important parts of conversing, are not the same thing as listening.

I know when someone isn't listening when I'm speaking. I assume you do, too. We know whether people are really listening or whether they're just waiting to jump in to talk, getting judgmental or reactive, or tuning out because they believe they know what we're going to say. We also know when people are simply listening to gather data to rebut what we're saying. There are costs to this non-listening.

The Costs of Not Listening Attentively. Given all the obstacles, why would we want to listen attentively? The primary costs of *not* listening are undermining people's sense of safety, not understanding the issues at hand, shutting the door on possibilities, and damaging relationships.

When we do *not* experience ourselves as being listened to and heard, our desire to connect and contribute is thwarted. We can feel isolated and unsafe. This can quickly evoke frustration, anger, or hurt and the unproductive behaviors that often accompany these emotions.

If we don't understand one another's thoughts and feelings, we can't get to the essence of the issue at hand. Because issues at work or in our community are usually multifaceted and linked with other issues, it's important to understand everyone's perspective on them.

When we don't listen, we also miss the new ways of thinking or novel approaches to solving problems that usually emerge when we're focused on listening to one another and on the task at hand.

When we don't listen to others, they're disinclined to listen to us. Relationships are weakened, and we might want to avoid working together again.

Finally, the invisible costs of not listening attentively occur when people's relationship with themselves is damaged: They can lose their train of thought or try to convey their thinking in a superficial or modified way, something they imagine is more palatable and less controversial—in other words, in a way that will allow them to be heard.

The Benefits of Listening Attentively. Think about the last time you experienced yourself as being listened to and heard. What was the impact on you? People usually say that when they feel heard, they become clearer and calmer, their desire to listen attentively increases, they feel more a part of the group, their energy increases, and they're receptive to changing points of view—theirs and those of others—as a result of the conversation.

When we listen, we create a safe environment in which new possibilities can emerge and be earnestly contemplated. For instance, when you tell another person your understanding of what they said, not only do they feel heard and connected to you, but their connection to themselves also deepens. Their understanding of their own thoughts increases. They might fine-tune, change, or expand that understanding. Our attentive listening evokes similar behavior in others and slows the pace, allowing more space for people's curiosity and thinking to blossom. This kind of listening helps people see the relationships and connections among their individual perspectives. Listening is the ultimate antidote for what ails most meetings.

When we listen, really listen to understand others, we create a resonance among us that increases the comprehension of what is being said. One part of this resonance includes the listener's brain activity mirroring that of the speaker's. A "neural coupling" develops between speakers and listeners during successful communication (Stephens, Silbert, & Hasson, 2010). As psychologist Uri Hasson described it, "Coupling . . . is the neural basis on which we understand one another. We are suggesting that communication is a single act performed by two brains" (Hasson, 2010).

When we listen with attention and genuine curiosity, with a desire to understand a situation through the eyes of others, the impact on speakers can be profound. They feel safer and sense that we are listening and are connected to them. Because they aren't diverting attention to protect themselves, they have better access to their whole brains. People disclose only what they really mean and want to say when they feel safe. Our listening encourages people to listen to themselves, to dig for the deeper wisdom they carry inside.

Listening attentively is especially important when we talk with people we know: Familiarity creates the illusion that we understand and blinds us to what is being communicated in the present moment.

Listening attentively has a more powerful and positive impact on our meetings than you might imagine. In an environment of attentive listening, a way forward usually emerges: a new solution, a next step, a desire to continue working together.

Here are the six essential aspects of listening attentively:

Prepare yourself to listen. Quiet your mind by mindfully tuning in to your body sensations and breathing. To truly listen to and understand others, you'll need to silence (or at least suspend for a time) the internal chattering, including and most especially your judgments, expectations, and stories about the speaker.

Be patient. This does not mean forcing yourself to endure someone else's talking or suppressing your thoughts or feelings. Patience means opening space in which a person can express herself without feeling rushed or pressured to finish. It might also mean noticing and simply sitting with any restiveness and remaining silent until someone finishes speaking.

Encourage people nonverbally and verbally. If you're on the phone, you can say, "I'm listening." In person, if the person seems comfortable with eye contact, use it. If not, nod your head. You can also make sounds like "hmmm" or say, "Please tell me more."

Restate what you hear in your own words. Paraphrase what you hear others say. Check to make sure you understand what they said accurately: "What I understand is that you . . . Do I have that right?" or "So, from your point of view, you would . . . Do I understand your point accurately?"

Describe your perceptions of people's emotions. This can be tricky because reflecting back what you perceive about others' feelings could seem invasive or inappropriate. The speaker might not even know how she feels, so your description could seem presumptuous. So you need to do this carefully and kindly. For example, you might say, "It seems this project is really important to you. Is it?" Or "You sound like you might be upset about this. Are you?" Or "You sound like you might be really excited about this option. Are you?"

Listen to yourself. Track your inner experience. Notice what you're thinking and feeling so you can sidestep anything that might be interfering with your listening, such as preconceptions about the speaker or reactions to what she is saying.

You probably know these listening skills and use them with some regularity. However, my decades of experience indicate that few of us use them as frequently and as optimally as we could. One way we can increase our own and others' attentive listening is to ask others to use them too.

For example, when you suspect someone has misunderstood your words, ask the person to repeat what she heard you say: "I don't think I'm making my point of view clear. Would you be willing to say back what you just heard me say?" You can then affirm or correct the paraphrase: "No, that's not what I said or meant to say. What I mean to say is . . ." Or if others interrupt you, ask them to stop: "I'd like to finish my thought, and then I'd like to hear your response to it."

Skill Two: Ask Open-Ended Questions

After listening, asking open-ended questions of genuine curiosity is the second most underutilized and useful skill in meetings. This skill has immense potential for opening doors to new ideas and new relationships among people, especially ones who differ from us. However, one has to appreciate and be patient with the process of attempting to respond to these questions. They can evoke fear because they ask that we go into uncertain and unknown territory, both inside ourselves and with others. It's often in the journey of trying to answer them that new possibilities for solving seemingly intractable problems emerge. The poet Rainer Maria Rilke communicates his understanding of this when he writes,

> Be patient toward all that is unsolved in your heart and try to love the questions themselves like locked rooms and like books that are written in a very foreign tongue. Do not now seek the answers, which cannot be given you because you would not be able to live them. And the point is, to live everything. Live the questions now. Perhaps you will then gradually, without noticing it, live along some distant day into the answer. (1934, p. 35)

Attentive listening and open-ended questions are the keys to collaboratively solving complex problems. Asking open-ended questions indicates that you're interested and want to learn and understand. They build relationships and a sense of safety. Open-ended questions are ones that cannot be answered with a "yes" or a "no." They usually begin with "what," "how," or "why." Psychologist Marilee Adams (2004, pp. 31–54) identifies two types of questions: "learner questions" and "judger questions."

Judger Questions. You might be familiar with judger questions. They shut down productive conversations and trigger people's self-protective mechanisms. They're often the source of people's checking out or becoming defensive, truculent, or passive. Judger questions tend to be "I" or "you" oriented, and they focus on winning or losing. How often have you heard the following questions asked directly or implicitly?

- Who's responsible for getting us into this mess?
- Why can't you just let it go and move on?
- What possible evidence do you have that supports your position?
- How could we (you) have been so stupid?
- What makes you think it's our job to fix this?
- How could this group possibly think this is the way to go?

Judger questions are more available to us when we're scared or angry because their purpose is to attack or defend. They're often asked in a hard, clipped, or sarcastic tone of voice and can reflect a desire to maintain a fixed sense of self ("What gives you the right to criticize my ideas?"), a fixed sense of others ("You just don't understand the situation."), or fixed beliefs about the world ("In what world is this idea feasible?").

Learner Questions. Questions of genuine curiosity are learner questions. They deepen our understanding of others and the topic at hand. They also unearth what's important to people, help them find common ground, and often connect people to a larger collective purpose.

Learner questions tend to be "we" oriented, focus on the situation as a whole, and seek win/win outcomes. Genuine curiosity is a bridge between authenticity and collaboration. Here are examples of learner questions:

- How did you come to see the situation this way?
- What other factors or points of view should we consider?
- What's at stake for you? Your colleagues? Your neighbors?
- How does this issue affect you? Your colleagues? Your neighbors?
- What leads you to believe this is the right way forward?
- What's the potential impact of this change? On whom?
- What questions should we be asking ourselves?

Journalist and author Joan Ryan described the power of questions in her article "The Path of Honest Ignorance" (1998). As one of the first female sports columnists in the country, Ryan believed that asking seemingly naïve questions was key to her learning and success. She asked people in professional sports simplistic questions. For example, she asked a famous baseball player, "How do you hit a baseball? What are the mechanics?" She asked a quarterback what "he sees and hears when the ball is snapped"; a baseball manager, how he "knew when to take a pitcher out." She even asked him "what it was he loved about baseball and how that was different from his love for, say, fishing or his wife." Although she sometimes got blank stares or nervous laughs, "Mostly I got great answers." She opined, "What you really need to know is what you don't know."

Learner questions can help us connect with one another and with the executive functions in the prefrontal cortex. It's ironic that they're the hardest to ask when we need them the most: when we've been emotionally hijacked and our energy and attention are focused on protecting ourselves. Thus, you might have a hard time remembering what to ask, let alone how to do so effectively. Here are three types of learner questions.

1) Questions to understand what people want to communicate. Start by using the skills noted earlier: paraphrasing and reflecting feelings. After you've confirmed that your initial understanding is correct, you can increase your understanding by asking them to say more or asking a question about what they've said. For example, "What about this situation is important to you?" or "How is it affecting you and your team members?"

One town convened a series of public meetings to consider how to handle the transient and homeless populations that were credited with increasing crime, vandalism, and fear. There were multiple perspectives on how to approach the situation. When the town had tried to tackle this issue in the past, the various sides had ended up yelling at one another. The primary divide seemed to be between those who wanted to provide assistance and those who wanted to send the transients and homeless away or put them in jail, fearing that treating them humanely would only draw more of them to town. In an effort to set a different tone, I and my co-facilitator, Roger James, asked meeting participants to begin the meeting by agreeing on ground rules for the evening and then asked the approximately 50 participants these questions: "How does this issue affect you? Why is it important to you to try and figure it out with other community members?" Talking at small tables, they shared their responses to these two questions and created an atmosphere in which they could continue talking with one another. They proceeded to identify what they saw as the major issues and the existing forces that were helping to improve the situation and those that were impeding progress. As the meeting closed, they expressed appreciation for everyone's behaving civilly. They agreed to meet again to develop ways to strengthen the supporting forces and remove the impediments.

2) Questions to humanize meeting participants. Comedian George Carlin once asked, "Have you ever noticed? Anybody going slower than you is an idiot, and anyone going faster is a maniac?" A common cause of conflict in meetings is sticking strongly to our beliefs about others. When we do this, either we don't listen to others or we listen only to things that confirm our preconceptions about them.

There are three ways to get out of this trap. First, we can notice our judgments and start to listen to the other person instead of to our evaluations of the person. Second, we can ask ourselves, "Why would a reasonable person think this way?" Third, we can imagine stepping behind their eyes for a moment to see the situation from their vantage point. We might directly ask, "How did you come to see the situation this way? Please help me understand your perspectives or concerns." A corollary question to ask yourself is "What might this person need?" Unfortunately, because people often cloak their needs in positions they take, it can be hard to get to what they really need. Sometimes the most direct route is the most effective one: Ask them what they need.

3) Questions to expand and deepen the conversation. For many of our interactions, we need to go beyond questions that help us understand one another to evocative questions that deepen and expand the conversation along with our sense of interrelatedness. Evocative questions inspire hope, evoke creativity, and tap into a greater wisdom. They can also energize people and help them focus on what's most important to them individually and collectively. In other words, they invite us to interact from a place of "enlightened self-interest," tending to ourselves, those around us, and the larger situation at hand.

Questions such as these have an impact even before they're answered. They can build bridges among people and connect them to the larger and longer view of the situation in which they find themselves. However, they also ask the unaskable and invite people into the unknown—not the brain's favorite place to be. Novelist Milan Kundera (1999) captures the spirit of evocative questions when he writes, "Only the most naïve of questions are truly serious. They are the questions with no answers." Because of this, such questions can also threaten us.

Questions that Deepen and Expand Interactions

- What question(s), if explored deeply, could give us a real breakthrough with this issue?
- What is it that unifies us or could unify us? What possibilities might we create with this common ground?
- What do we want to create? How do we want tomorrow to be different from yesterday?
- What are the "undiscussables"? What do we avoid talking about?

- How could we interact so that that we increase the likelihood that we'll find common ground and not become polarized?
- What are our stories about how we got to or created this situation?
- What's most alive in this organization? In this group? In this community?
- What's emerging in this conversation? How can we build on it?
- What are the deeper questions underneath our concerns?
- What assumptions are we making?
- If we do this, what do we think will happen? What do we want to happen?
- How else might we think about this situation? What if we thought about this from the point of view of the stakeholders (e.g., the river, the forest, our grandchildren, our ancestors, the founders, the lab technicians, the customers, the suppliers)?
- If we assumed we would be successful, what would we do?
- What would be a home run in this endeavor? What is our vision of full victory?
- How might we strengthen the health and prosperity of this organization or community?

Skill Three: Speak in an Inclusive and Embodied Way

Speaking in an *inclusive* way means talking from your point of view as just that: your point of view, not as "the truth." It also means being aware of what we're saying and noticing its impact on others. Speaking inclusively solicits participation because you also express your interest in hearing the perspectives of others. Speaking exclusively suggests you know it all and discourages participation.

Speaking in an *embodied* way means that we experience what we're saying within and from the body. As we're speaking, we're aware of our thoughts, body sensations, and emotions, noticing whether what we're saying is as close to our honest perceptions, points of view, and experiences as possible. When we speak in an embodied way we intentionally pay attention to our experience as it is unfolding in a nonjudgmental way.

When you prepare for an interaction, you most likely prepare the content: what you want to propose, the positions you want to take, the counterarguments you want to be ready to wield. All of this can be very helpful to clarify your thinking beforehand so you can articulate your point of view when the time comes. The downside is that as you think through the content, you solidify your opinions and beliefs so that when you interact with others, you risk sounding more adamant about your "truth" than you might really be. You might become oblivious to the impact a super-confident delivery has on others and the conversation as a whole. Speaking in this way can engender a combative tone in a meeting and make it less likely that people will be open to being influenced by one another's ideas and less willing to explore new ways of thinking about the topic at hand. This is especially true if the interaction is occurring in an organization and you're the highest-ranking person in the room.

If you pay attention, you might notice that the more you try to convince people you're right, the more they resist, push back, or give up. When this happens, everyone's prefrontal cortex gets overloaded and exhausted, and people's brains revert to instinctive, self-protective behaviors. As mentioned previously, the prefrontal cortex uses up lots of oxygen and glucose that is, metabolically speaking, expensive for the body to produce.

It can be tricky to find the right balance: to be clear on one's perspective and present it in a cogent way while still remaining open to the perspectives, emotions, and needs of others. This balance is to be found somewhere between pushing and not holding back. Here are six aspects of communicating in an inclusive and embodied way.

1) Prepare Your Inner State. Practice mindfulness before important conversations, remembering that what you think and feel affects how you communicate and that these in turn impact those around you. If the stakes in this meeting appear high to you, and if as you prepare yourself for it, you sense your heart and breath quickening and your muscles tightening, pause and bring your full attention to your breathing. If you've added mindful moving and/ or embodied listening to your meditation repertoire, practice these. Inquire into why you perceive the stakes to be high. What's going on underneath the anxiety you might be experiencing? Surface and test the beliefs that are shaping your perceptions. If you're inclined to speak adamantly, it often means you're afraid of something: for example, not getting your way, not being liked, or having something taken away. In other words, you perceive a possible threat.

If I'm really scared, I ask myself three questions that seem to engage the prefrontal cortex and help me ground myself in my body. First, "What's the worst thing that could happen?" This gives me a chance to check the "catastrophizing" I can do unconsciously. Second, "What's the best possible thing that could happen?" My answer allows me to understand what my hopes are. Third, "What most probably will happen?" This question allows me to find some equilibrium in the middle ground between my highest hopes and my most frightening fantasies.

It's possible to say what you think and what you believe without getting so vehement that you upset the equilibrium of others such that they feel threatened. However, when you solidify what you think prior to a meeting, you create a tension between what you think is right and what others think is right. When you're able say what you want to say in an inclusive and embodied manner, there's more space for others to be curious about what you've said and for you to be curious about others' responses to what you've said.

2) Clarify What You Want to Say and How You Might Express That in an Inclusive Way. Take a new, fresh look at what you believe about the situation. Ask yourself some tough questions: "What do I really think? Am I absolutely sure that what I think or believe makes sense?" Think through how you came to see things as you do—facts, assumptions, and experiences—and why whatever you want to say is important to you. Knowing this will help you personalize your message and make it easier for others to feel included. The key question to ask is "How can I say what I want to say in a way that creates a sense of connection and belonging among people?"

A president of a community college ended her opening state-ment in a planning session with a jocular "That's my story, and I'm sticking to it." This let people know that despite her authoritative manner of speaking, she was open to different points of view. A CEO of a manufacturing company often shared his opinion by starting with "This is how I think about it at this moment." When possible, he also connected what he was saying with what others had said. And the president of the board of a large nonprofit frequently said what he wanted to say and then added, "This is how I see the situation. How do the rest of you see it?" He then waited for people to respond and listened to what they said.

3) Define your Desired Relationships with Others. What's the implicit message you want to communicate to others about your relationship with them? Is it "I know what's what, so you should listen to me"? Or is it "We face a complex issue, and the only way to solve it is for us to work together"? Getting clear about this will influence not only what you say but also *how* you say it. This includes tone, timing, posture, gestures, and intensity.

This third aspect of speaking in an inclusive and embodied way is more important than you might realize. When you say things that might be difficult for people to hear with "positive" emotional signals or "warmth" (e.g., friendly eye contact, soft tone of voice, open body posture), others can hear what you're saying without becoming reactive (Cuddy, Kohut, & Neffinger, 2013). In fact, they can hear those difficult messages more easily than they can hear agreeable ones communicated with negative emotional signs (e.g., stern facial expression, a loud or harsh tone of voice, and a finger pointing at them). This is because we feel threatened by stimuli we're not conscious of—for example, sighs or gestures that communicate superiority (eyes rolling), pushiness (harsh, rapid-fire speech), or speaking exclusively, like you have the corner on the only possible right answer (higher pitch and tone). The bottom line is, if you want to people hear you and contribute to constructive conversations, give no one cause to fear you.

4) Practice "Embodied Speaking" in Meetings. It's possible to listen to and observe inner sensations, feelings, and thoughts so that when you speak, not only are you speaking about what you already know, but you're also sharing what you're beginning to understand as you're saying it. When you're able to speak in this way, listening to yourself and speaking become one integrated action. When you practice embodied speaking, you'll likely hear yourself say things like "I never thought about this issue in this way before this moment" or "I need to pause for a moment so I can communicate this nascent thought clearly." Or, after you've spoken, you might say, "Let me pause for a second. I'm not sure what I just said is what I think."

When we express thoughts and feelings that seem to be alive kinesthetically (e.g., producing an increased heart rate, energy in the throat, butterflies in the gut) or that seem to emerge in us moment to moment—things that we've likely never expressed before—we're speaking in an embodied way. Sharing ideas that are on the edge of what we "know" or that are becoming known as we speak helps everyone open to new possibilities in their own thinking and in the situation at hand.

As pointed out in Chapter 4, mindfulness, embodied movement, and embodied listening prepare us to "hear" and communicate what is becoming apparent in the here and now. Because "here and now" is where we've never been before, it's the perfect time to move into uncharted territory and away from repeating preconceived points of view.

To say what's emerging in one's mind in this moment, even if it's only a fragment or a few breadcrumbs of what we're beginning to think, can be scary. You might feel exposed as you grope for words and sound less articulate than you expect yourself to be. You might want to hurry past these moments in the hope that you'll get to something clear, explicable, and known—in other words, certain and safe. It takes faith and courage to stay with something when it's fuzzy. My experience is that when I'm in what I call "fuzzy-land," the seeds of some new way of thinking, a fresh possibility for myself and the group, are sprouting. I just need to be patient and mindfully wait for the insights to become clear enough for me to find words to communicate what's surfacing.

To the extent that we can remain open and mindful to what's unfolding inside us is the extent to which we might be functioning as a microcosm of the whole. In other words, we'll likely be bringing forward a piece of a puzzle the group is trying to put together. My experience teaches me over and over again that what is emerging in me will resonate with others. In Carl Rogers' words, "What is most personal is most universal."

When I hear myself or others slow down and speak more hesitantly, sometimes in phrases and made-up words, I know that what's being communicated is hot off the presses and needs space and time to develop. Such sharing is usually coming from a deeper, wiser place inside people. To let people know this is the place I'm speaking from, I usually introduce my comment with something like "This is a thought that is just surfacing . . ." or "There's some-thing about what was just said that sparks something in me. It's not clear yet, but I think this is what's becoming apparent to me . . ."

It's important for those listening to respond with warm-hearted attention and patience, lest the speaker's thoughts wither in the face of implicit or explicit criticism. Listening is key to drawing forth whatever is emerging inside others. Things that come from deep inside can't be expressed in a few simple words. Remember that our internal states of being extend beyond our physical boundaries and affect those around us. Listening and asking genuine and appreciative questions can help. For example, you might say, "Sounds like this idea is just coming into view. Here's what I understand of what you've said . . . What else is arising or alive in you at this moment?"

5) Express Objections as Concerns. When you disagree with or want to express your objections to someone else's point of view, frame it as a concern instead. Others are better able to hear a concern than a criticism or objection. If you want to avoid triggering defensiveness in others, don't begin with "I disagree with you because . . ." Respond by first checking your understanding of what the person said, identifying the elements you like or support, and then expressing your concerns. It might sound something like "Here's what I think you said . . . Do I have that right? What makes sense to me about what you said is . . . My concerns are . . ." These actions, done with a neutral tone, will help you understand others' perspectives and help maintain a sense of inclusion and connection among people.

6) Communicate Appreciations. We are social creatures who need love and appreciation. Express yours early and often. Thank people for their perspectives, for their willingness to say difficult things, for caring about the topic at hand, for showing up in the room, for listening to others, and for being willing to participate. It's easy to take one another for granted in meetings at work and in our communities. If we're to bridge differences and tackle complex issues effectively, we need to appreciate every moment and everyone when we connect and make progress on tough tasks and strengthen our relationships.

Ultimately, saying what you think and feel in an inclusive and embodied way involves moving easily among speaking, asking questions, and listening deeply to yourself and others. For example, you might share your point of view and then ask, "How do you respond to what I just said?" or "What might I be missing?" Or you could ask others what they think: "How do you see the situation?" Then follow up by paraphrasing the key points of the other person's response to make sure you understand them correctly. Orchestrating these three skills—speaking inclusively and in an embodied way, asking questions, and listening—in combination sends signals that you don't think you have a lock on "the truth." This is a good thing. I don't know that I've ever been in an interaction where any one person had a complete definition of the problem, the causes underlying it, and what potential solutions might work. It's always a case of putting together pieces of a jigsaw puzzle, with the various players in the room adding a bit of the picture here and others adding pieces there. Saying what you want to say in an inclusive and embodied way helps a group collaborate to put the pieces together in a way that engenders forward movement.

Skill Four: Summarize and Synthesize Group Interactions

Most meetings involve freewheeling discussions. Because of this, it's easy to lose track of all the perspectives or options on the table. The optimal number of different ideas to hold in mind at one time is in fact no more than three or four. When there are too many, people start to get anxious because they can't remember them all. In self-defense, they either withdraw or keep adding ideas. The latter approach makes the conversation more difficult to follow and escalates people's anxiety. Tones of voice rise along with everyone's shoulders. When there are more than three different ideas or options on the table, it's time to summarize.

Summarizing. When you summarize, you paraphrase the key points of a group conversation. Summarizing is like paraphrasing what one person says but can be more challenging because you're paraphrasing what several people have said. A *summary* is a concise restatement of the key points, ideas, or options that have been raised in a conversation. Regardless of whether you're leading or participating in a group interaction, it's invariably useful to summarize: "Let's try to summarize the options we're considering. The first option we are considering is . . . ; the second one is . . . ; and the third one is . . . Have I captured them accurately?" Ideally, you have a place to write these (e.g., on a flip chart) so the summary is both verbal and visual.

Summarizing helps calm any agitation resulting from too many open topics on the table and enables a group to focus their discussion. Summarizing a conversation periodically also helps a group to become aware of the patterns or direction of their collective thinking and to make a conscious choice about whether they want to continue the current conversation or move in a new direction.

Synthesizing. *Synthesizing* is combining diverse or contradictory concepts or ideas into a larger whole. This often helps people see where they have "common ground." As with summarizing, synthesizing is usefully done periodically during a meeting. A synthesis might sound something like this: "Even though we have diverse, even contradictory ideas about how we want to proceed, they all seem to reflect an implicit belief that solutions to the lack of low-income housing need to come from people in the community in collaboration with the city's planning department. Is that what you're hearing?"

Skill Five: Make Process Observations

Making process observations means saying what you're seeing without blame or judgment. For example, "I'm noticing that we're starting to interrupt one another." When you make a process observation, you help others notice process, or *how* a group is interacting. This enables people to make conscious choices about their process.

As we've seen, we need effective process to help us work together effectively. Thus, we need to develop the ability to observe and describe process and to make it explicit so we can modify it when it's no longer working. A good process observation is as clarifying as watching a DVD of a group interaction. Its purpose is to raise awareness so conscious choices can be made about how people want to conduct themselves.

One of the most powerful ways to change a group's behavior is to describe what's happening without blame or criticism. For those observations to be effective, they need to describe people's behavior, not your interpretation or judgment of their behavior. Stick with what you see and hear, not with what you imagine is going on.

This is easier said than done. Because of the negativity bias in the brain, we quickly judge what we see based on what we assume are other people's intentions. Our interpretations and assumptions about what is going on becomes "the truth" instead of what we actually see and hear. We do this so quickly we don't realize we've done it. Perception and evaluation are nearly simultaneous. The truth is we can't know others' intentions unless they tell us.

Suppose three people from sales and marketing look at the clock while Joan is talking. Joan assumes that they aren't listening and that not only are they not listening, they disagree with what Joan is saying. Suddenly, she blurts out, "You sales and marketing people just don't understand the challenges that those of us in manufacturing face every single day." Stunned by her comment, the people in sales start defending themselves. They have no idea that their looking at the clock provoked her comment. Anyone making a process observation such as "I notice a few of you looking at the clock. I'm wondering if the meeting is running late" could have avoided the misunderstanding and hurt feelings.

All you know is what you see and hear. Not only will your interpretation of what's happening probably be wrong; it may also provoke conflict. Stay with what you can observe and describe: It increases the likelihood that people will listen to your observation instead of feeling threatened and falling into an argument or wanting to leave the meeting. When you describe only what you see or hear, it allows people to consider whether they want to modify how they're interacting.

It is so very difficult to refrain from judging or interpreting people's behavior. Here's another example of the difference between observing and describing what you see and hear and judging or interpreting what is going on:

Observation: "I notice that whenever we get close to making a decision, one of us raises another objection. What do you think might be going on?"

Judgment/interpretation: "This group is unable to or doesn't want to make a decision."

The observation focuses on behavior, and the judgment focuses on an interpretation of behavior.

It's helpful to add a question at the end of a process observation so the group can explore what's driving the process they're engaged in.

There are at least four areas of process that are useful to pay attention to and comment on, especially when things are starting to go awry: (a) what is being talked about and how, (b) communication patterns, (c) decision-making patterns, and (d) group norms.

Observations on What Is Being Talked About and How. You can make a process observation about which topics appear regularly on meeting agendas and which ones are rarely or never included. For example, are the causes of quality defects in the organization's sacred-cow product discussed? Do elected officials talk about how they plan to balance the interests of their constituents with the interests of a whole municipality? Two such observations might be "At the past three meetings, we've postponed talking about the issues with one of our best-selling products. I'm wondering what's going on" and "As we discuss transportation challenges, I notice that we aren't talking about the tension between meeting the urgent needs of one area of the city and the needs of the city as a whole."

Bringing people's attention to how a topic is being considered is also instructive. For example, you may say, "When we start to talk about balancing the needs of one area of the city with the needs of the city as a whole, we move onto other issues without figuring out a way to do this" or "We seem to be blaming the other department for this problem."

Observations about Communication Patterns. Who talks to whom, who listens, who talks more frequently or less, who people look at when they talk, who interrupts, who gets interrupted, and who is never interrupted are all part of a group's communication pattern.

Here are examples of observations about patterns of communication: "I notice that everyone seems to be looking at Joe when they speak," "Several of us have spoken two or three times while some of us haven't spoken yet," and "It seems that whenever Michael speaks, he gets interrupted." Patterns also include the balance among how frequently the group members as a whole speak, listen, and ask questions. For example, you may say, "We seem to be making a lot of statements and asking very few questions of one another. I wonder how well we understand one another's points of view."

Observations about Decision-Making Patterns. Groups can slide into making decisions unconsciously, especially about meeting processes. Decision-making patterns can develop without anyone noticing. Because decision-making is such a key issue in organizations and communities, it's critical to clarify how decisions will be made about both process and content. (Decision-making is discussed in detail in Chapter 10.)

For example, in the weekly staff meetings of a philanthropic foundation, a staff member noticed a pattern at the start of their weekly meetings. As each week's meeting facilitator reviewed and confirmed the agenda that had been distributed a day prior to the meeting, a senior manager added another item. The group then launched into discussing that item right away, ignoring and often not getting to the other agenda items that people had contributed to the agenda and prepared for beforehand. After several weeks of this, the staff member said, "I notice that when a manager adds an agenda item at the start of these meetings, we jump right into that discussion without deciding whether there's time on this agenda to add it. I suggest we first decide whether this has to be discussed at this meeting and, if so, where it fits into the prepared agenda. Would that work for everyone?" Most people hadn't noticed that this was occurring. They agreed to follow her suggestion.

Observations about Group Norms. *Norms* are the written and unwritten guidelines for acceptable behavior in a group. Sometimes the rules for appropriate behavior in a meeting are explicit, as in agreed-upon ground rules. Most often, norms develop unconsciously, based on people's experiences in other meetings, or they reflect the culture of the organization or community in which the interaction occurs. For example, at the automobile manufacturer mentioned in Chapter 3, one of their norms was that expressing anger was acceptable, even expected, while communicating appreciation was not. Concurrently, I consulted with a medical center where appreciation was expressed frequently and anger never was. These norms interfered with each group's effectiveness because only a portion of what people were thinking or feeling got communicated.

When norms get in the way of effective interactions, it's time to bring them to light so the group can consciously choose what they want to do. Examples of destructive norms are not raising difficult questions, not speaking the truth, and not bringing destructive group norms to awareness. Here are some example observations that can bring potentially destructive group norms to everyone's attention:

- "Every meeting seems to focus on who did what wrong with this project."
- "I like how we always express our appreciation for one another. I notice, however, that we seem to shy away from describing what frustrates us."
- "We seem to quickly jump to *how* to go about implementing a project before we've agreed on whether we want to do it or not."
- "All of the opinions expressed about the new staffing procedure have been positive."
- "I notice that we start our weekly meetings 15 minutes late and then are rushed at the end to complete the agenda."

Skill Six: Make Process Suggestions

Sometimes a process observation is enough to bring an ineffective process to people's attention, and they change it without any discussion. For example, saying, "We're starting to interrupt one another" usually stops it from happening, at least for a while. If it happens again, you could make the same observation and add a process suggestion—in other words, suggest what you think would keep people from interrupting one another. For example, "I suggest we let people finish their thoughts before we jump in. Are you all willing to do that?" It's important to include the process observation first—"I notice we're interrupting one another"—so that people understand why you're making a process suggestion.

The question at the end of a process suggestion, "Would you be willing to do that?" is also consequential. People need to decide for themselves how they want to operate. Even an agreement this small can help restore a sense of status, certainty, autonomy, relatedness, and fairness in an interaction. This is especially true if there have been a number of interruptions that are tending to make the interaction feel unsafe for participants.

Here's another example of a process observation combined with a process suggestion: "I notice that some of us have spoken several times already in this fast-paced conversation and that others haven't spoken at all. I suggest that we slow the pace a bit and allow those who haven't had a chance to speak the opportunity to do so. Is that acceptable?"

In a meeting of an executive team of a large nonprofit organization, a brave and astute manager said, "I notice that as we tackle each agenda item, one or more of us says, 'We've got too much to do and too few resources or time to do it.'" She then suggested that the team review the organization's current mission and vision at the next meeting and develop criteria to screen new potential projects.

Chapters 10 and 11 include a number of processes you can suggest to make meetings more productive.

Words of Caution

When learning new skills, we often use recipes that, to others, can feel a bit formulaic or stiff. Recipes are terrific to help us learn, but we need to replace them with our own terms as soon as we're more comfortable with the skills. You can help yourself do this by replaying conversations later and identifying when you used a recipe and how you might say it differently next time. For example, instead of starting a paraphrase with "what I hear you saying is . . ." you can begin with "I want to make sure I understand what you just said.

What I think you said is that . . ." I encourage everyone to practice using these six indispensable skills in conversations with friends so we can use them more naturally and have more ready access to them in meetings. Meetings can threaten our sense of safety, whereas conversations with friends tend to feel safe.

Key Points

Six indispensable skills based on brain science, mindfulness, and effective process can help us save the world because they integrate and apply what we know from all three bodies of knowledge:

- listening attentively to understand what others are saying and feeling and to learn why what they're saying is important to them;
- asking "learner" questions rather than "judger" questions to deepen your understanding;
- saying what you think and feel in an inclusive and embodied way (i.e., not as "the truth");
- summarizing and synthesizing group interactions;
- making process observations in nonjudgmental ways; and
- making process suggestions to help move a group forward.

Questions for Reflection

When was the last time you felt heard and understood? What were others doing that led you to feel this way? How and when could you adopt these behaviors to listen attentively to others?

What genuine questions could you ask to deepen your understanding of what someone else has said, humanize those you might be judging, or expand and deepen an interaction?

Are you someone who tends to speak as if you have the corner on "the truth"? If so, how might you present your perspectives in a more inclusive and embodied manner so that people feel included and believe that you're open to change?

When might a summary or synthesis be helpful in an upcoming meeting? What would help you summarize or synthesize group interactions?

When would you want to make a process observation or process suggestion during an upcoming meeting? What would help you separate your observations from your judgments or interpretations about what you're seeing and hearing?

Section Four: Designing Productive Conversational Processes

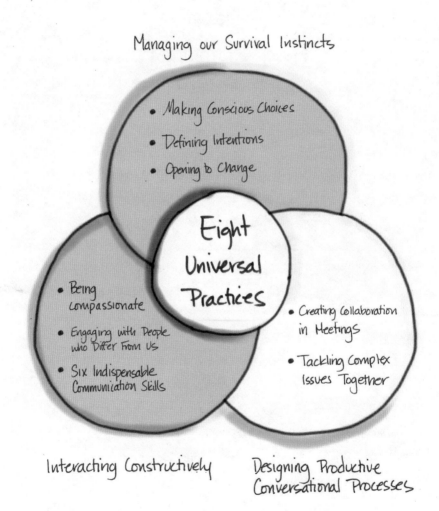

Chapter 10:
Creating Collaboration
in Meetings

*This is a world . . . that constantly surprises us with the
wisdom that exists not in any one of us but in all of us.
And a world where we learn that the wisdom we need to
solve our problems is available when we talk together.*

—Meg Wheatley

Imagine two artists—Camille Pissaro and Paul Cézanne—paint-
ing look-alike bridges straddling streams in two different forests.
Pissarro's fine, small strokes and soft colors capture light in slow-
moving water and slender, lacy trees. His *Le Petit Pont, Pontoise*
(1875) is delicate, calm, and harmonious. Cézanne's broad, angular
strokes and dark colors capture analogous water and woods, but his
Le Pont de Maincy, prés de Melun (1879) is hard-edged, dramatic,
and foreboding.

Over two decades of friendship (1865–1885), Pissaro and Cézanne carried on a mutually respectful and influential relationship in which they admired and learned from one another's markedly different styles while remaining true to their unique perspectives. Pissaro, the older and more established of the two, even advocated for the importance of Cézanne's originality and acceptance in an art world that initially shunned him. Because of their collaboration, the art world has been blessed by their innovative visions.

We can create equally influential and productive collaborations in our organizations and communities by consciously designing and conducting meetings that help people feel safe enough to bring the best of who they are to the table. This includes designing meetings to avoid unnecessary threats to people's sense of safety and considering how the process of a meeting could support people using the practices I've already described: making conscious choices, being compassionate, identifying intentions, opening to change, engaging with people who differ from us, and using six indispensable communication skills.

Meetings Have Ripple Effects

Creating collaboration in meetings is important because what happens in them affects us far beyond the moment. Depending on how we're treated or what we accomplish, we return to work or to our neighborhoods feeling isolated, angry, and weary or connected, content, and energized. If you're interrupted or ignored or your ideas are dismissed or discounted, you'll probably feel disheartened. If you're able to say what you want to say, you receive acknowledgement and understanding, and you're able to contribute to the meeting's outcome; you'll mostly likely feel uplifted. Either way, meetings affect your emotions, thoughts, and behavior for hours or even days afterward. What we experience in one meeting shapes our expectations, and therefore our behavior, in the next.

In meetings designed to engender collaboration, good things can happen: People have a better understanding of the situation from a variety of perspectives; the list of innovative ideas is long and robust; people have strong relationships and trust one another; and people want to work together again. And after a collaborative meeting, people are more likely to implement solutions they helped develop. The investment of time and effort to create meetings that engage people in the process instead of treating them like spectators always pays off.

Collaboration

Although the dynamic nature of participatory meetings can threaten people's sense of certainty and safety, it can also bolster people's sense of status, autonomy, relationship, and fairness. We can prevent a number of threats from occurring before or just as the meeting begins by making sure that the purpose and process of the meeting are clear. We do so by defining desired outcomes, developing a detailed agenda, clarifying the decision-making process, agreeing on ground rules, making sure people understand their roles, and arranging the room so people can see one another.

Collaboration = Cooperation

In meetings, especially when people feel threatened and become reactive, it might seem as if competition for airtime and for who has the best ideas is the norm. However, as we learn more about the brain, a different view emerges, one in which "natural cooperation" or collaboration becomes "a third fundamental principle of evolution beside mutation and natural selection" (Benkler, 2011).

Political economist Elinor Ostrom's research into the cooperative management of common property demonstrated that enlightened self-interest can trump individual, self-protective survival instincts. Examples of people cooperating to serve themselves, a group, and a larger situation or goal include the five-centuries-old self-regulated irrigation districts in Spain and the meteoric rise of open-source software. According to Ostrom, one of the principles that characterizes such cooperation is "collective-choice arrangements" (2005, p. 259). People who create the rules can change the rules. Such an arrangement is important to people's sense of autonomy and fairness. In looking to apply the principle in practice, this Nobel Laureate asked an important question: "How can we enhance the participation of those involved in making key decisions about this system?" (p. 271).

This is a paramount question for our meetings. How can we enhance people's participation in making decisions about important issues facing their communities and organizations? Creating collaborative meetings is critical.

Evidence is mounting that, in addition to naturally feeling compassion for one another (see Chapter 7), we're also predisposed to cooperate. If we think about it from an evolutionary perspective, it makes sense. We gathered in groups to survive. Cooperation was essential to gathering food, finding shelter, raising the next generation, and fending off predators. Today, we can activate this natural inclination by framing issues in neutral or inclusive ways. This can activate people's predisposition to cooperate and prime their brains to follow suit. For example, in an experiment labeled "Community Game," 70 percent of the group cooperated throughout the entire test. When the experiment was labeled "Wall Street Game," only 30 percent cooperated with one another (Benkler, 2011). We can achieve similar effects on cooperation through inclusive wording of a meeting's purpose and desired outcomes.

Collaboration is its own reward because we feel good when we do it. When we cooperate with others, the reward circuit is activated. And when we trust people enough to cooperate, oxytocin—a neurotransmitter that's instrumental in developing caring relationships—is released.

You can create collaboration in meetings by designing the process to build it, conducting the process to strengthen it, and following up to make it real. In all of the elements of The Meeting Cycle, the intention is to develop clarity and certainty about process so that people feel safe enough to wade into the difficult and uncertain waters of dealing with complex content. This doesn't mean that the process won't need to change during a meeting. But when you start by developing a sense of safety and clarity, changing the process as needed becomes easier. In addition, cooperating in the beginning of a meeting builds confidence that people can continue cooperating as the meeting proceeds.

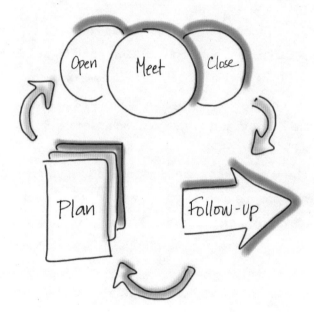

The Meeting Cycle

Open Meet Close

Plan

Follow-up

Plan: Design the Process

For people to bring the best of who they are to the table, they need to feel safe, know what's expected of them, and understand why the meeting is being convened. They need to know how people will work together, how decisions will be made, and how they should prepare themselves to participate. To achieve these things, you'll need to take the following steps *prior* to the meeting (i.e., during meeting planning):

- Define the purpose and desired outcomes.
- Clarify the decision-making process.
- Develop a detailed agenda.
- Identify participants and their roles.
- Arrange the meeting space so people feel safe and connected to one another.

If you're convening the meeting, you can take these steps on your own or, ideally, in collaboration with some or all of the people who will be attending the meeting. If you're facilitating the meeting, you would work with whoever is convening the meeting.

Define Purpose and Outcomes. Spontaneous interactions or scheduled meetings often occur without a clear purpose or desired outcomes. *Purpose* is the overarching reason for a meeting. *Desired outcomes* are the more specific and measurable end results. They're written as nouns, in terms of the end results you hope to achieve *from the point of view of participants.*

Specifying purpose and desired outcomes for a meeting does the following:

- allows for the development of a detailed agenda;
- helps people feel safe (they know what they're trying to get done and when they've done it);
- prevents unnecessary uncertainty that generates fear, frustration, or conflict;
- primes everyone to stay focused on achieving the purpose and outcomes; and

- enables everyone, not just the leader or facilitator, to keep the conversation on track and productive.

For example, a purpose might be "to create a common understanding of the mid-year budget status." The outcomes might be "understanding of the status of projected versus actual expenditures" and "agreement on a process and schedule for submitting final department budget projections."

Admittedly, not all interactions lend themselves to framing the destination in concrete terms. You don't need to force fit your reasons for meeting into a purpose and outcomes, especially if they're yet to emerge from a group's deliberation. There are times when a vague purpose is the closest you can get. Even a vague purpose can, however, be helpful. For example, the purpose could be as broad as "understanding people's points of view and hopes for the future so that we can determine if there's enough common ground to move forward together."

Clarify the Decision-Making Process. How decisions are made is an important aspect of any meeting because decision-making is central to what's expected of participants. As indicated in Chapter 3, *how* a decision is made is just as important as what the decision is.

In organizations, the leader's choice of process determines the kind of relationship that he or she has with employees. In governmental bodies, how decisions are made determines the relationship leaders have with residents. In both settings, there's a spectrum of possibilities for the decision-making process, all the way from simply informing people of decisions to involving them in decision-making.

In hierarchical organizations, the manager decides how decisions will be made. Here are some potential options:

1. A leader makes the decision and announces it.

2. A leader proposes a decision, asks for feedback, and modifies the decision based on the feedback.

3. A leader asks for input before arriving at a decision and then makes the decision.

4. The group decides by consensus.

5. A leader identifies the criteria or constraints for a decision and delegates it to an individual or group.

Although participation increases as you move from Option 1 to Option 3, the leader still makes the decision. The difference between asking for feedback and asking for input is significant. When a leader asks you for feedback, she already has a possible decision in mind: for example, "I think our organization should develop this new product. What do you think?" When a leader asks for input, she doesn't have a decision in mind. For example, she may ask, "Do you think our organization should develop new products? And, if so, what do you think those new products should be?"

Option 4 (deciding by consensus) and Option 5 (delegating a decision) involve more participation than Options 1 through 3. However, consensus does not mean unanimity. *Consensus* means that everyone in the group, including the manager, is able to say, "I understand the decision. I've had my say. I can and will actively support this decision." Consensus works best when there's still a way to make a decision if the whole group can't reach a consensus. This is known as a *fallback*. In hierarchical organizations, where there are varying levels of decision-making authority, the highest-ranking leader is usually the fallback decision-maker.

In "horizontal" organizations where everyone has equal decision-making authority (e.g., a board of directors), the fallback is usually a vote. This is also true in public processes convened by governmental bodies (e.g., a city council or a planning commission) where elected or appointed officials who have equal decision-making authority make the decisions.

Here are some options for elected officials and governmental leaders that roughly parallel the ones outlined for organizational leaders:

1. Leaders inform/educate the public by providing the public with balanced and unbiased information about the problem, the alternatives, and potential or already-determined solutions. (Although this isn't a decision-making process, it's an essential step in any public decision-making process.)

2. Leaders make a decision (a solution, policy, plan, or regulation), gather feedback, and finalize the decision based on the feedback.

3. Leaders gather input *prior* to framing the issue or making a decision.

4. Leaders collaborate with citizens in each phase of the decision-making process: defining the issue, understanding the causes, developing and evaluating potential solutions, and determining preferred solutions. (These then usually need to be affirmed in whatever formal decision-making process is required by law [e.g., a vote by elected officials]).

5. Leaders delegate decision-making to the public via referendum or ballot.

Option 2 (gathering feedback on proposed decisions) usually involves traditional methods such as public hearings, citizen advisory councils, or public comment periods. None of these encourage or enable citizens to consider issues with other citizens of diverse opinions and experiences. They don't allow areas of agreement to surface, nor do they allow people to develop collective recommendations. If the impact will be great and buy-in from the public, essential, then Option 3 (gather input) or 4 (collaborate with citizens) is the way to go. (*Note:* I use "citizens" to mean inhabitants or residents, not to refer to legally recognized subjects of a state.)

To determine which decision-making option makes the most sense, consider the following criteria:

- **How much time do you have to make the decision?** If the problem is urgent, then you have less time for people to participate. If you have time to involve people, then use the other criteria to decide how much you want to involve them.

- **What is the potential impact of the decision?** If there will be little impact on people or how they do their work, then it might not be worth anyone's time to make the decision in a collaborative way. If, however, you anticipate substantial impact, consider involving stakeholders because they'll have invaluable information about whether the decision makes sense and how best to implement it.

- **Will you need buy-in to get the decision implemented?** If commitment is essential to getting a decision put into effect, then involve large numbers of stakeholders. Without their participation, you might get only compliant stakeholders, meaning either the decision will not be implemented or it will be enacted in a lackluster manner.

- **Do stakeholders have the information and expertise they need to help make a sound decision?** If not, and the decision will have a significant impact and require buy-in, you'll need to develop a process to educate the stakeholders whom you want to participate.

- **Is making this decision a developmental opportunity?** If so, then by all means delegate it and set the individual or group up to succeed by providing adequate information about the constraints and/or criteria for the decision.

- **As a leader, are you flexible, or have you already made the decision?** If you've already made the decision, don't engage people in a puppet process.

In public processes, elected officials and governmental administrators also need to consider the level of polarization among citizens that already exists or could be evoked by a decision. Option 4 (leaders collaborating with citizens) is the most auspicious option if there is or could be significant conflict among citizens.

No matter how decisions are going to be made, the key is to make the process known to everyone involved and then follow the process as advertised. If people think they're providing feedback, offering input, or building a consensus (or collaborating with elected officials and governmental leaders) but the decision has already been made, they'll likely feel betrayed. Their sense of status and fairness will be undermined, and they'll be leery of engaging in a participatory process in future. They might also try to block implementation.

Develop a Detailed Agenda. Too often, agendas are simply lists of topics to be covered with no clarification of what the leader wants to accomplish. For example, a topic might be "budget." This could mean updating the current one, planning the next one, cutting staff, reallocating resources, or a number of other things. Such ambiguity makes it hard to know how to prepare or participate effectively.

When working alone, it's easy to jump around in one's mind from a problem to potential solutions to potential challenges to implementing solutions and back to the problem. When you're working with others, this more mercurial process can be less effective and undermine people's sense of safety in unhelpful ways. The challenge is how to design an agenda so that people can stay on the same topic using the same process at the same time.

A detailed agenda includes the purpose and desired outcomes for the meeting, the content and process steps to achieve those outcomes, who is responsible for the content of each step, the approximate time frames that will be needed for each of the steps, and if decisions are going to be made, how and by whom decisions will be made. A detailed agenda also includes a time to build agreement on ground rules and to clarify people's roles in the meeting.

Whenever possible, the agenda should include the preparation that people will need to do. When participants prepare for a meeting, the quality of thinking and interaction increases dramatically. After you've defined the purpose and desired outcomes for a meeting, identify what people need to know, do, or think about in order to be able to participate in an informed and thoughtful way. Preparation lays the groundwork for collaboration.

Distribute the agenda before the meeting and post a large version of it on a flip chart in front of the room so it's visible throughout the meeting. This helps people stay focused and keeps them from shuffling through the paper that seems to pile up in front of them in meetings.

Here's an example of a detailed agenda:

Purpose   Update project plan

Desired Outcomes   Agreement on priority goals for the next month
                               Revised project plan to meet new timelines
                               Agreed-upon plan and next steps

Preparation   Review the attached draft project goal list and project plan.
                               Come with suggestions.

Proposed Agenda

What	How	Who	When
Opening	• Review and confirm purpose and outcomes. • Clarify decision-making process. • Agree on roles and ground rules.	Leader	10:00–10:10 (10)
Priority goals	• Review draft list. • Propose changes. • Agree on goals for next month.	Leader/All	10:10–10:40 (30)
Current project plan	• Review plan. • Brainstorm and prioritize likes and concerns. • List potential changes to plan. • Agree on revised plan.	Project Manager/All	10:40–11:10 (30)
Next steps	• List, clarify, & sequence. • Identify who will do what by when.	All	11:10–11:20 (10)
Close	• Summarize agreements. • Evaluate the meeting (what worked, suggested changes).	Leader/All	11:20–11:30 (10)

Identify Participants and Their Roles. Meeting participants are usually stakeholders. In organizations, stakeholders are usually easier to identify because meetings occur within units or across functions around particular tasks, products, or projects. In public or community meetings, participants are usually whoever shows up. In either setting, people can cooperate better if they know what their roles are. Usual roles are the leader or whoever convened the meeting, a facilitator, participants, and a recorder.

Leader. In organizations, leaders are the ones who usually convene meetings. Their role is to determine whether a meeting is needed, what needs to be accomplished, who should be there, and how decisions will be made; they also hold people accountable for assignments after the meeting. If you as a leader want to create a more collaborative environment in your organization and in your meetings, then you'll also need to pay attention to including others in deciding what needs to be accomplished and *how* the meeting is conducted.

Facilitator. A facilitator pays attention to the process. As graphic facilitator David Sibbet described it, "Facilitation is the art of leading people through processes toward agreed-upon objectives in a manner that encourages participation, membership, and productivity from all involved" (1994, p. 2). A facilitator works with the meeting convener beforehand to clarify the purpose, outcomes, and decision-making process and to develop a detailed agenda. During the meeting, the facilitator keeps the group on topic and on time and helps them change the agenda when needed.

A facilitator should describe and get agreement on his role at the start of the meeting: "My role today is to help you achieve the outcomes of this meeting. I will not contribute to the content, but

I will make process suggestions as needed to keep things moving forward and to make sure each of you has a chance to participate. If I step out of my role, please let me know. Will you do that?"

If you want to be a "facilitative leader," you can do two things to help you tend both process and content. First, acknowledge at the start of the meeting that you'll be wearing two hats, and second, ask for help: "My role today will be to keep us on track and make sure everyone has a chance to participate. I'll also be contributing my ideas. If I spend too much time on the content and not enough time facilitating, please let me know, will you?" Pause and wait for people to agree.

At times as a leader, you might need to enlist the help of a neutral facilitator to lead the meeting. A facilitator is essential under the following conditions:

- You're so invested in the outcome that it would be hard for you to pay attention to the process.
- The meeting involves more than 12 people.
- The stakes are high for everyone and conflict is likely.

The facilitator could be from inside or outside your organization. If you decide to enlist the help of a facilitator, you'll need to work with him prior to the meeting to build a detailed agenda and plan how you'll work together during the meeting.

Participants. The decision-making process defines the role of participants to a great extent. Are they listening to understand already-made decisions, providing feedback on proposed decisions, providing input to a leader who will make the decision, or helping to make a decision in collaboration with others by consensus? If you're leading or facilitating the meeting, clarify the role of participants. For example, a leader could say, "Your role today is to contribute your ideas and listen to those of others. Although I'll be making the final decision, I hope we can come as close as possible to consensus on your input to me. Please help us stay on track by letting everyone know when we're off topic and suggesting ways we might move forward more expeditiously. Are you willing to do that?" Pause and wait for people to agree.

Recorder. The recorder creates a visual record of people's thoughts and group agreements on large paper in view of the group. Recording involves writing what people say, as they're saying it, on large pieces of paper in front of them on a wall or an easel with a flip chart. The recorder creates what is called the "group memory." He works with the facilitator before the meeting to prepare any needed charts and to organize the room for recording.

Either the facilitator or the recorder should describe the role of the recorder at the start of the meeting: "I'll be capturing your ideas up on paper in front of the room. Please let me know if I don't capture yours accurately." If the recorder is a part of the group that is meeting, someone else could step up to capture the recorder's thoughts when he wants to speak. If the recorder is neutral, he remains silent unless he needs to clarify an idea.

The *group memory* is a visual, written record of the meeting as it's happening in real time. It creates focus and clarity, reduces misunderstandings, minimizes repetition, and helps people come to agreement. It also helps participants summarize and synthesize a group's deliberations during the meeting.

The recorder and group memory help protect the prefrontal cortex (PFC), which would get overloaded if it tried to perform all its functions at once: understanding, deciding, recalling, memorizing, and inhibiting. As mentioned in Chapter 2, each of these processes involves billions of neurological circuits. When we try to do all of this at once, the PFC is taxed and our ability to function decreases as our anxiety increases. This can trigger some unhelpful, self-protective behaviors.

Capturing people's thoughts visually while an interaction is occurring is a powerful way to help people feel heard, safe, and connected with others.

Listening to and acknowledging people through visual recording also does the following:

- helps people feel heard and included as they contribute their thoughts ("I see my ideas on the wall.");
- increases listening and participation ("I become more engaged when what I say is written down.");
- creates focus, especially during freewheeling discussions ("After three ideas are on the table, it's hard to keep track of all of them. Seeing them helps me concentrate.");
- increases understanding and reduces misunderstanding ("I thought we had agreed on X, and you're saying we agreed on Y. Let's look at what the recorder wrote down.");
- engenders a more humane pace and draws out more introverted thinkers ("It's a relief to slow down to make sure the ideas are being captured on the flip charts. This provides an opening for me to add my thoughts and see what might be missing.");
- minimizes repetition and rehashing ("This idea and our thoughts about it have already been captured on the charts. What do we want to add that hasn't already been said?");
- helps people see the patterns of ideas ("Many of the ideas on the chart relate to the quality of customer interactions. Let's add ideas about product quality.");

- enables people to see connections among ideas to create new ones and to find common ground ("The idea on page 3 is similar to the one on page 4. This inspires another idea that integrates these two.");
- tracks agreements or decisions ("Being able to review our decisions at the end of the meeting helps me understand my role moving forward and brings closure to the conversation.");
- assists latecomers in catching up quickly ("Sometimes I just can't make a meeting on time, so it's helpful to see what the group has already achieved. That way I don't have to interrupt to get caught up."); and
- shortens the time to achieve desired outcomes. ("With all the information right in front of us, we were able to get through the agenda quickly and more easily than anticipated.").

If you're leading the meeting, ask someone else to record, especially if there are four or more people. For more information about visual recording, I recommend any of the books by David Sibbet. Here are a few tips to get you started:

- Arrange the room in a semicircle or open "U" so everyone can see the surface (wall or row of easels) you'll be writing on.
- Hang banks of pages taped across a wall or a large (4-x-8-foot) sheet of paper across a wall instead of using a single easel. This enables the group to keep working and to see progress as the recorder writes and moves from left to right.
- When recording, use people's key words and phrases and remain neutral.
- Put headings and page numbers on the top of each page.

All these roles—leader, facilitator, participants, and recorder (along with the group memory)—are instrumental to creating collaboration in meetings. For further reading about these roles and about facilitation in general, in addition to the works of David Sibbet, I recommend those of Michael Doyle, David Straus, and Sam Kaner.

Arrange the Room for Safety and Connection. Arrange the room to fit the purpose of the meeting and the number of participants. If the meeting is to solve a problem, make a decision, develop policy, or create a plan, place chairs and tables in a semicircle or open "U" facing away from the doors and toward the wall where recording is being done.

In meetings of 18 or more, vary the meeting process so people talk in groups of two, four, or six. Conduct meetings of 18 or more sparingly, and keep them to a maximum of 60 to 90 minutes. Interacting in large groups can threaten people's sense of safety and spark conflict. There are fewer opportunities for individuals to contribute their ideas in a group of 18 or more. This tends to diminish people's energy and desire to engage. When you use small groups, you can assign a question to a group or to a table and have people rotate among tables so they can address a number of questions throughout the meeting. For more information about this World Café style of meeting, I recommend the work of Juanita Brown and David Isaacs (2005).

Conduct the Meeting to Build Collaboration

Meetings have three equally important parts: the opening, the middle, and the closing. Think of a meeting as a sandwich. The top slice of bread is the opening, the interaction itself is the filling, and the bottom slice is the closing. Many interactions jump into the middle without a clear opening or closing. Just like a sandwich filling with no bread, meetings can get messy.

Open Meetings to Create Safety, Clarity, and Commitment. It's tempting to get right into the content, the issues at hand. But we need to talk about process first. Our ability to work together on today's issue and the next hundreds of issues we'll face is vital to our future. The first 5 to 10 minutes of any meeting lays the groundwork for what follows. This time should focus on making agreements about process.

When people show up to an interaction, they bring the worlds they carry in their heads with them. Their bodies often arrive before their minds and hearts. They're often in a rush, having just run out of another meeting or torn themselves away from their to-do lists. The challenge is to help people connect, feel safe, and align around a common purpose or set of outcomes. You create safety, clarity, and commitment by doing four things at the start of any meeting:

1. connecting people to one another;
2. building agreement on the purpose, desired outcomes, and agenda for the meeting;
3. clarifying roles and the decision-making process; and
4. developing agreement on how people want to relate with one another (i.e., ground rules).

First, help people feel included and connected by asking them to introduce themselves to one another. In addition to names and perhaps their role in the organization or community, ask them to respond to a question that helps them get to know one another and gets them thinking about the purpose of the meeting. Even if participants already know each other, use a question to help them connect in that moment and engage their minds in the content of the meeting. For example, "Why is the topic of this meeting important to you?" "What is your highest hope for this meeting?" or "What question is on your mind about the topic of this meeting?"

Second, build understanding of and agreement on the purpose and desired outcomes of the meeting along with the detailed agenda. Doing this right at the start satisfies the brain's quest for certainty. You may say, "What I hope we accomplish in this meeting is . . . Are you willing to work with one another to achieve these outcomes?" And "Here's the agenda. Please notice the time frames allocated for each topic. Do these time frames seem reasonable?"

Ask these as real questions, not rhetorical ones. It's better to know earlier rather than later whether someone isn't willing to work toward achieving the outcomes and why they aren't. It's easier to change the agenda in the beginning than to handle disruptive behavior that will likely emerge later if people don't agree on the agenda.

Agreements about the purpose and desired outcomes change the interaction from being "your" meeting to "our" meeting. However, these agreements shouldn't be restrictive. You, and the group, might need to modify them during the meeting.

Ask people to think of the purpose, outcomes, and agenda as a road map from which the group can consciously deviate when needed. Purposes, outcomes, and agendas need to change as people's understanding of one another and the content at hand changes during the course of the interaction—to tend to the brain's need for safety, make changes to any of these three elements explicitly. Groups can't make the same leaps or changes in direction that we can make individually in our heads. If one or a few people switch gears without making sure everyone is on board, that causes unnecessary anxiety and people heading off in different directions. Making a change might sound something like "We initially agreed to generate solutions today, but it's beginning to sound like we have yet to agree on the critical issues we want to solve. I suggest we agree on the issues before starting to generate solutions. Is this okay?"

Third, clarify people's roles and the decision-making process. As we saw earlier, the decision-making process should be explicit and understood by all participants so they don't have incorrect expectations about their roles in the meeting. People aren't usually accustomed to having this amount of clarity about their roles and the decision-making process, so making these two items clear can feel awkward. However, doing so avoids confusion and uncertainty that can create unnecessary conflict.

Fourth, as part of the opening, it's critical to agree on ground rules for the meeting. Each of us comes to interactions with often unconscious expectations about how other people should behave. Here are a few of mine: Listen and make eye contact, don't interrupt, and talk about what is important to you. However, not everyone has the same expectations. Some of us grew up in families or cultures, work in organizations, or live in communities where interrupting, minimal listening and eye contact, and speaking impersonally are the norm.

People don't like having their expectations violated. They get anxious, get angry, or check out. The key to preventing unnecessary upset is to make the expectations we have of one another explicit in a set of agreed-upon ground rules. Sometimes these are called *conversation guidelines* or *rules of engagement*. For example, do people really want to start and end meetings on time? If so, then make a specific agreement to do so.

When we agree on how we want people to conduct themselves in a meeting, it helps us feel safe and encourages us to bring our ideas and perspectives to the table and participate with confidence.

You can translate the intentions you identified in Chapter 6 into proposed ground rules for a group. For example, your intention to have equitable participation in a meeting can be turned into agreements to "Let people finish their thoughts. No interrupting." The following image lists some tried and true ground rules.

Ground Rules

- Listen to understand first
- Let people finish their thoughts
- Be pithy, succinct. Share the airtime
- Encourage everyone to participate
- Stay on topic & on time
- Turn off or mute devices
- Start & end on time

Building agreement on ground rules at the start of any meeting that you anticipate might be contentious can be a groundbreaking first step. It primes people to believe they'll be able to find common ground and avoid the dysfunctional behaviors that derail interactions.

You can propose ground rules and ask a group to add to them or to generate the list themselves by asking questions such as these:

- "What would help you achieve the purpose and outcomes of this meeting?"
- "What guidelines or ground rules would help you live out your highest hopes for the meeting?"
- "What agreements would help you work together during this meeting?"

Record people's ideas on a flip chart in front of the room, check for clarifying questions, and then build agreement on them: "Are you willing to follow these guidelines?" Do not let silence mean consent. Ask for an outward sign of agreement: a head nod or verbal "yes."

One of the ground rules that people frequently suggest is "Respect one another." Don't let this stand as is. Ask, "What would I be doing if I were respecting you?" People usually have some specific behavior in mind when they mention respect. Add that behavior to the list so people know what "respect" means and what they're agreeing to do.

Agreeing on the ground rules increases the likelihood that participants will follow them, in part because of the effects of priming and because people tend to do what they've agreed to do. It's tough to hold people accountable for following rules they haven't agreed to. You can ask for this agreement as a leader, a facilitator, or a participant.

To keep ground rules alive, post them in the meeting room. Go over them at the start of every meeting, even if you're just pointing to them and asking, "Do we commit to continue to follow these ground rules?" During the meeting, remind people of them: "We seem to be violating our ground rules by not staying on topic and on time. Should we modify the ground rules?" At the end of the meeting, ask, "How well did we follow our ground rules?"

Increase Collaboration during the Meeting. All the agreements you make at the start of the meeting help you grow collaboration during it. You can increase collaboration during a meeting in five ways:

1) Remind people of the agreements they made about the purpose, outcomes, agenda, roles, and ground rules. You can use two of the six indispensable communication skills to do this: process observations and process suggestions. For example, you could say, "We seem to be off topic right now. Do we want to continue talking about *X*, or do we want get back to talking about *Y*?" Or "We have only five minutes left on the agenda for this item. Do you want to expand the time, or should we identify a next step for this item and move on to the next topic on the agenda?" Or "We're starting to interrupt one another. I'd like to stick to our ground rules. How about the rest of you?" Usually, just calling attention to an agreement is sufficient to get people back on track.

2) Use all six of the indispensable communication skills identified in Chapter 9. Listen attentively, ask "learner" questions, say what you think and feel in an inclusive and embodied way, summarize and synthesize the conversation, make process observations, and make process suggestions.

3) Employ as many of the other seven practices as you can.

- During the meeting, stay mindful (Chapter 4) so you can make conscious choices about what to do and say.
- Define your intentions (Chapter 5) before the meeting and keep them in mind during it. When possible, suggest ground rules that might help you live them.

- Remain open to change (Chapter 6) by examining your own beliefs and holding them lightly.
- Experience three kinds of empathy (Chapter 7): cognitive empathy (you understand the perspectives of others), concerned empathy (you listen to find out what others need), and emotional empathy (you feel what others feel). Extend warmhearted compassion to others and yourself.
- Engage effectively with people who differ from you (Chapter 8) by going out of your way to understand them, by managing your self-protective mechanisms, by not disconnecting from others when you disagree or feel frightened, and by holding positive beliefs about others.

4) Build agreements on content as you go. The initial agreements are about the process of the meeting: what you want to get done, how to do it, when to do it, and how you want people to conduct themselves. This builds a foundation for making agreements throughout the meeting. For example, a group might start by agreeing on what the issues are and what's causing them. Then they agree on ways to solve the issues. And finally, the group agrees on how and when they want to implement the solutions and who is responsible for doing what.

A recorder is critical to capturing these agreements and creating the group memory. Just seeing them posted on the wall builds a sense of accomplishment and confidence that people can work together.

5) Maintain a human pace. Ask people to allow one another to complete their thoughts without interruption. Build in time for quiet reflection. ("We're going at a fast clip. Let's pause for a moment so each of us can reflect on whether we think the most important aspects of this issue are on the table.") The pace in many organizations can be nearly inhumane. The anxiety this generates undermines our ability to think clearly together. We can slow the pace in our meetings to help us collaborate effectively.

Close a Meeting to Build Safety, Clarity, and Commitment. This bottom bread slice in the meeting sandwich is usually forgotten or ignored as people dash out the room to get to their next meeting or task. The final five to ten minutes of any meeting is as critical to its success as the initial five to ten minutes. Close a meeting by summarizing agreements, confirming action items and responsibilities, and evaluating the meeting:

1) Summarize what you accomplished or the agreements made in the meeting. You can do this by reviewing the desired outcomes and noting which ones were accomplished and what decisions were made: "How did we do? It looks like we accomplished three outcomes and identified the next steps to accomplish the fourth outcome between now and the next meeting. Is that how you see it? And here are the decisions we made." If decisions are listed on a separate sheet from the rest of the group memory, you can point to them and/or say them aloud.

2) Review and confirm action items generated at the end of each topic on the agenda. If you haven't already, identify and record specific commitments about who agreed to do what by when. Also make note of any open issues or agenda items that need to go on an ensuing agenda. Assign responsibility to someone to make sure these items don't get lost. For example, "Here are the action items. Joe agreed to do *X* by *Y.* Roxanne, you said you would do *X* by *Y* . . . Is everyone committed to following up on these items? What issues are still open, or what items need to be taken up the next time we gather? Who will make sure these get on the agenda?"

3) *Evaluate how you accomplished what you did.* Ask questions such as "What worked well today?" "What do we want to do again?" "What didn't work well?" and "What happened today that we want to avoid in future?"

Action Items

What	Who	By When
Transcribe action items & decisions; distribute to project team	Lee	June 5
Finalize list of goals for next month; distribute to all staff	Nancy	June 10
Make agreed upon changes to project plan; distribute to project team	Peter	June 10
Include update re: status of goals on next week's agenda	Denise	June 11

Follow Up on Meetings

Following up on meetings—and doing what we said we would do—builds confidence in our ability to collaborate and get things done together. It helps us avoid the "broken windows" syndrome, the idea that if I break an agreement and then you break an agreement, others will follow suit, and we'll destroy our trust in one another and become wary of collaborating in the future. (The term *broken windows* comes from a criminological theory about norm setting. The theory is that if a few windows in a building are left unrepaired, vandals will break more, eventually break into the building, and become squatters or light fires inside. Over time, broken windows affect entire neighborhoods. [Wilson and Kelling, 1982].)

Following up on meetings involves three important steps that can be taken by an organizational leader, the leaders of a stakeholder group, or those who took responsibility for action items at the end of a meeting:

1) Send out meeting notes within 24 hours. Usually one page will suffice to capture key ideas along with decisions and action items. More detailed notes can be attached as an appendix.

Notes remind people of what they agreed to do, inform those who weren't there about what happened, and help keep everyone on the same page. And if you're trying to limit the number of people in your meetings, notes help people feel informed and included, even if indirectly.

2) Track and coordinate the accomplishment of action items. Tracking commitments sends a message that you and the group take agreements seriously. Let those with action items know that if something unexpected comes up and they can't keep their agreement, they need to communicate that and either renegotiate the due date or request that the task be assigned to someone else.

Often, one person's steps are dependent on another's. Make sure people are keeping their agreements and coordinating their actions to avoid duplication of effort and to ensure that everyone is heading in the same direction.

3) Thank people for their work. This is such an easy thing to do and makes such a big difference. We all appreciate being appreciated. Be specific with your gratitude verbally or in writing. For example, say, "Thank you for synthesizing everyone's contribution to the criteria that the group wants to use to generate and eventually evaluate solutions. You captured everyone's perspective in a succinct way. This will help the group move more quickly to generating solutions." Gratitude is especially important in community groups where people are volunteering their time.

Key Points

- Meetings have ripple effects. Plan, conduct, and follow up on meetings to build collaboration.
- Planning meetings includes
  - defining the purpose and outcomes;
  - clarifying the decision-making process;
  - developing a detailed agenda that includes the preparation required;
  - identifying participants and their roles; and
  - arranging the room so participants feel safe and connected to one another and so they can see the visual recording or group memory.
- Conducting meetings includes
  - opening meetings to build safety as well as clarity about and commitment to the purpose, outcomes, agenda, roles, decision-making process, and ground rules;

- increasing collaboration during the meeting by using the six indispensable communication skills (see Chapter 9);

- employing as many of the practices learned in previous chapters as possible: making conscious choices, defining intentions, being open to change, being compassionate, and engaging with those who differ from us;

- using visual recording to create focus and build agreements as you go; and

- closing the meeting to build safety, clarity, and commitment by summarizing decisions, confirming action items, and evaluating the meeting.

· Following up on meetings includes

- sending out meeting notes within 24 hours;

- tracking and coordinating the accomplishment of action items; and

- thanking people for their work.

Questions for Reflection

How do you plan your meetings now? What is one action you might want to take beforehand to set them up to be even more successful than they already are?

What do you do in your meetings now as a leader, facilitator, or participant to build collaboration? What might you want to do differently or add to what you already do?

How do you open and close your meetings? What changes might you want to make to make them more collaborative and productive?

How are decisions made? What is your preferred decision-making process? Is it helping you create the relationship you want with your employees or the residents in your municipality?

Chapter 11:
Tackling Complex
Issues Together

Understanding complexity: the capability to see patterns of
interdependency underlying problems, and to distinguish
short- from long-term consequences of actions . . .

—Peter Senge

The elected board of directors of a regional water district on the coast of northern California (described in Chapter 1) wanted to consider a proposal it had received from an Alaskan-based consortium that hoped to buy the district's water and ship it to southern California in water bags. From the district's point of view, it was a proposal worth contemplating. They were about to lose their major commercial customers, pulp mills, who paid for the majority of the costs of operating and maintaining their water system—just as the 50-year-old infrastructure needed significant upgrading. In addition, since the pulp mills used four to five times more water than the rest of their domestic customers, the board was concerned about being forced to raise prices and losing their rights to the water. Water rights are granted by the state on a use-it-or-lose-it basis.

However, many in the region didn't want the district to even consider the proposal. Angry citizens crowded the boardroom. Some made threatening phone calls and sent hostile letters to the district office. After years of losing their local resources, especially timber, residents had had enough. They wanted to protect their water.

The situation was fraught with complexity. As noted in Chapter 1, issues are complex when they have a number of diverse, interdependent elements that can't be understood or solved by tackling any one of them. Tackling complex issues is a challenge for any organization or community because they have few precedents and there are rarely clear-cut or permanent solutions. In addition, it's hard to predict the consequences of actions in both the short term and the long term. Complex issues also require working with diverse stakeholders who have different points of view. Any of these can evoke the survival mechanisms in the brain. In combination, they can feel overwhelming.

In Section One, we explored the conceptual and scientific foundation for the eight practices that are the focus of this book. Section Two described three practices to help us manage the survival instincts in the brain. In Section Three, you learned how insights from neuroscience and social psychology can be applied toward improving our ability to interact with others constructively. Section Four examined meeting processes that encourage cooperation and collaboration. In this chapter, we explore what's called *process architecture*. This means carefully designing a series of meetings to tackle complex issues that require sustaining effective interaction among multiple stakeholders over time. You also learn how to develop sponsorship and leadership of the process and which steps to take during it to prevent "cognitive hijacking" (Russell Delman, December 10, 2015, personal communication). Aspects of cognitive hijacking include confirmation bias (ignoring evidence that contradicts one's beliefs or cherry-picking information that supports them), intolerance of cognitive dissonance (reducing the dissonance or discomfort of holding conflicting ideas through *either/or* thinking), and loss aversion (going to great lengths to avoid loss or maintain the status quo).

The intention of designing clear and understandable process architecture is threefold:

- It should help people feel safe so they can engage with one another and with complex content with their whole selves.
- The process itself should help participants understand the complexity of the issues and the multiple perspectives on them. The result should be decisions that serve the needs of multiple stakeholders.
- The design should help people delve into the content in constructive and productive ways and should prevent cognitive hijacking.

To be successful, the architecture of a collaborative problem-solving process needs to have clear sponsorship and leadership and enlist the invaluable help of visual recording. Sponsorship provides resources and legitimizes the process. This is critical particularly in processes convened by a nonprofit, for-profit, or governmental organization. Leadership provides the day-to-day focus and glue of a process. Visual recording is essential because it helps people visualize and understand the relationship among the diverse and interdependent aspects of issues.

To illustrate the steps in designing and conducting process architecture to tackle a complex issue, I'll use the water district example throughout this chapter. I worked with the water district board as a process design consultant and facilitator to help them tackle the complex issue facing them. For the water district, protecting their water involved multiple, interconnected environmental, economic, and political concerns. Further complicating matters for the water district board was the presence of volatile, activist residents.

Please note that I'm not suggesting that the water district's process is the right one for all situations. It was custom-designed to fit their situation, as all process architecture should be.

Designing Process Architecture

Six steps are essential in designing process architecture.

Step One: Define the Purpose and Desired Outcomes in Neutral and Inclusive Ways. Just as in planning collaborative meetings, designing an effective architecture starts by defining a purpose and a set of desired outcomes for the entire process. How you frame the purpose and outcomes primes how people participate. Because the process will involve multiple stakeholders, it's critical to frame what you hope to get done in ways that are as neutral and inclusive as possible. This helps prevent people from polarizing around their positions before meetings even begin.

Formulate the purpose and desired outcomes in ways that help people feel included and connected to the topic. For example, if the water district had described the purpose as "figuring out ways to use more water to protect water rights and generate more revenues for infrastructure projects," this would have provoked the environmentalists and anti-government activists and pitted the water district against its customers, the municipalities to whom it sells water. Although water rights and revenues are key to the situation, defining the purpose of the process in these terms would have interfered with the district's larger purposes of strengthening relationships with the people they serve and generating creative ideas about how to deal with a difficult situation that included protecting water rights and fixing an aging water system.

Here's how the water district framed the purpose and desired outcomes of their process:

Purpose: To engage citizens in policy planning regarding water use in the region

Desired outcomes: By the end of the process, the water district board hopes residents will have

- an understanding of the key aspects of the situation facing the water district;
- an understanding and buy-in of the overall planning process;
- an understanding of the critical role they play in the process along with how decisions will be made and by whom;
- agreement on criteria to evaluate potential solutions to resolve the situation;
- a prioritized list of "hot ideas" for water use and the conditions under which they would be acceptable; and
- an understanding of next steps.

By framing the purpose and outcomes as they did, the elected Board of Directors helped residents work collaboratively with one another and with them to find a way out of a tough situation. The board knew they were on the right track when, at one of the large public meetings, business developers, realtors, and environmentalists began speaking in terms of "What are *we* going to do about this?" not "What are *you* going to do about this?" This is a significant change from how most public policy planning efforts go. It's hard to imagine anyone saying this if the board hadn't started with a commitment to creating a collaborative process in which they were genuinely asking for help to solve a problem.

Step Two: Develop Principles to Guide the Process. The principles you want to guide the process describe its desired characteristics. Here are three of the principles the water district used to design and guide their process:

Participatory: The process engages a broad spectrum of people, especially those who could be impacted by the board's decisions in meaningful ways through a variety of methods, including face-to-face meetings in various locations and online.

Educative: People understand the issues and challenges and are able to engage as informed participants.

Respectful: Participants listen to one another and consider each other's point of view, even when they disagree.

It's crucial for conveners of a process to define the principles they want to guide its design and implementation.

Step Three: Make the Process Transparent by Defining Phases and Outcomes. Process models can help you determine what the phases and outcomes of the overall process architecture should be. *Process models* are generic and symbolic representations of the elements and relationships of a method or approach. Models can help you think through how you want to define your specific process.

The Visioning and Problem Solving Model is the model that I use most often. It includes the following elements:

- Plan the process.
- Understand the situation, including the context in which it's occurring.
- Define the problem, its causes, and its relationship with other problems.
- Develop a vision and/or evaluation criteria.
- Develop and evaluate solutions to solve the problem and/or achieve the vision.
- Develop a plan to implement the solutions.
- Implement the solutions and evaluate the impact.

The first two components always come first, and the last two always come last. In between, the path can go in several directions and turn back on itself, as you can see in the Visioning and Problem Solving Model here:

Visioning & Problem Solving Model

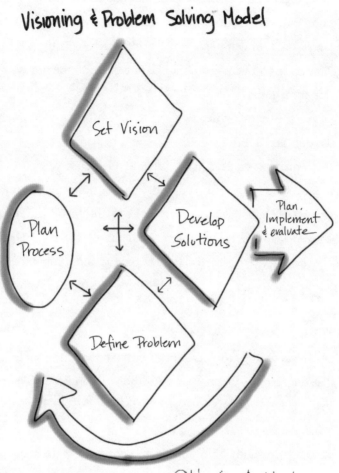

© Interactions Associates, Inc.

Within each phase of the process, identify outcomes that are more specific than the ones for the process as a whole. For example, within "Understanding the situation," your desired outcomes could include the following:

- understanding of the most pertinent aspects of the context of the issue;

- understanding of all the parts of the issue and how they're interconnected with other issues;
- agreement on whether we want to tackle this issue;
- agreement on who else should be involved in the process going forward; and
- agreement on whether to move to a next phase and which one (vision or solutions).

Other process models have different elements you can use to design a process to fit your situation. For additional process models, I recommend *The Change Handbook* by Peggy Holman, Tom Devane, and Steven Cady (2007). Various elements of the models can be used in any of the phases of the Visioning and Problem Solving Model described above. Here are three examples. Appreciative Inquiry questions and interviews can help develop the vision or evaluation criteria. A World Café can be an effective approach for multiple stakeholders to develop and evaluate potential solutions. In the Planning Phase, Open Space Technology can help stakeholders understand the complex variables that the Process Architecture will need to consider.

Although it might be tempting to adopt one particular model, I encourage you to use process models as springboards to help you develop a process that suits your particular situation. No single process model fits all circumstances.

The water district board decided that helping people understand the situation and involving key stakeholders was critical to the success of their process. Thus, the first phase was Education and Outreach. They conducted more than 50 educational sessions for stakeholder groups and encouraged people to participate in the process.

Understanding a situation is a critical part of any process. Do not underestimate the power of developing people's understanding of the issue at hand and the context within which it exists. Stakeholders need to understand as much about the issue that they're about to tackle as they can.

When designing process architecture and developing a process map, make sure there's a phase or step in which everyone involved receives unbiased information so people can participate in an informed and responsible manner. For example, in addition to the 50 educational sessions, the water district continued to educate people about the issue and its context at the start of each public meeting. In the feedback gathered during the nine-month process, participants cited education as one of its most effective aspects.

The water district also decided to ask residents to develop criteria to evaluate solutions *before* generating potential solutions. Although this seemed counterintuitive to some on the board, I encouraged them to follow this unusual sequence in order to build people's confidence that they could agree on what one staff member helpfully called "community values" and to avoid the solution wars that frequently compromise public policy decisions. The phases of their public process were as follows:

Education and Outreach	Start-Up	Develop Evaluation Criteria	Generate Options	Consider and Evaluate Options	Agree on Recommendations

In addition to defining phases and outcomes, you can make the process even more transparent to participants by documenting it visually in a process map. Process maps provide an overview of the entire process and act as a path for participants. Give each phase a memorable name across the top, as we did with the water district's project. Include a timeline running from left to right on a large chart. Make sure the project is set up to succeed with a reasonable timeline.

Whatever model you use to develop the process map, post a large version of it on a wall or have it available on a slide so you can remind people at the start of each meeting where you are in the process. This helps people feel safe, engaged, and focused. Working with complex issues evokes anxiety in and of itself; uncertainty or confusion about the process only exacerbates it. As with agendas, when the overall process design needs to change, make course corrections explicitly on the process map so people can focus on the same phase, the same outcomes, and the same time frame at the same time.

Process maps are invaluable when people join the process after it starts. This is a normal occurrence in public processes where people come and go. Maps help people jump in more quickly and help them to be more effective because they can see what has been achieved and what people are working on now. These maps also appeal to both hemispheres in the brain. The left brain likes the detailed steps. The right brain likes that the map shows the whole process and the relationship of its parts.

Here's what a process map could look like:

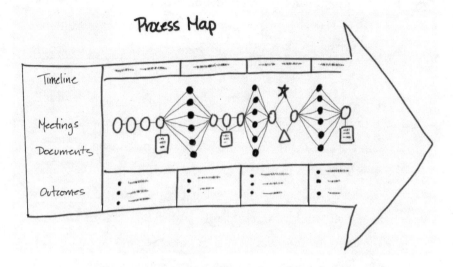

Process Map

Step Four: Make Sure People Understand and Own the Process. Building understanding and ownership needs to occur at multiple levels and is therefore usually an iterative process. It starts by building understanding and ownership of those who are convening the process. For example, I worked with the board of the water district over several months to help them frame the purpose and outcomes, develop guiding principles, and define the phases and outcomes. Building agreements on the process strengthened their relationships and ability to work together. This became an important foundation for their ability to collaborate effectively throughout the process.

In the water district's effort, we then developed the understanding and ownership of the process with the stakeholder advisory group that the board had selected from a group of applicants to help them conduct the planning process. Building understanding and ownership continued throughout the process at each public meeting.

It's important *not* to leave the understanding and ownership of the process solely in the hands of "expert" process consultants. Regardless of whether I'm consulting to a change process in an organization or a policy planning initiative with a governmental agency, after helping people clarify what it is they want to get done, I draft a process plan and then review it with people to modify it to make sure it works for them and to build their ownership of it.

Because I'm called in to be a "process expert," I often have to play devil's advocate and argue against what I've proposed so they don't defer to me and simply agree to follow it. Regardless of whether you're the convener (a leader in your organization or community) or a participant in a process, make sure that people at least understand the process and at most agree that it makes sense, and make sure they commit to be part of it.

The benefits of building ownership of a process are as follows:

- It increases the likelihood that the process works for everyone and increases people's commitment to stick with it.
- When people support the process, they're more inclined to support what comes out of it—an essential component of the successful implementation of decisions.
- It builds process savvy. When people learn about effective processes, they're more able to create them.

After you've published the process, follow it as faithfully as possible while still achieving the purpose and outcomes. It's easier to change direction in a meeting than it is to change the purpose and outcomes of a process involving multiple phases, outcomes, and meetings that have been publicized in an organization or municipality. It's a tricky balancing act to make sure the process remains explicit and understandable while also making it flexible enough that people can change it as their understanding of the issues evolve and as the stakeholders who want or need to be involved changes.

When you change a process, make sure you have a compelling rationale. Skeptics will cry foul if they think that changes to the process are being made to reach predetermined outcomes that advantage some and disadvantage others. In other words, they might see the process as unfair and contest what comes out of it even if they agree with the results. Remember that challenges to people's sense of fairness trigger defensive, self-protective reactions.

Step Five: Clarify Who Will Make Which Types of Decisions, How, and When. Defining the decision-making process can be a chicken-and-egg question. In a hierarchical organization where an executive is leading a process, she or he would determine the decision-making process. However, if the process is being led by a cross-functional team of peers, then they would need to determine their own decision-making process. The same is true in a community-based process. What decision-making process would they use to decide on their decision-making process? To keep people's heads from spinning, I usually recommend that they use consensus to agree on how they want to make decisions.

People are more ready to support or own a participatory process when they understand up front who is making the decisions, when they're being made, and how. In participatory processes, it's easy to equate collaboration with consensus decision-making. They aren't the same thing. There are varying degrees of collaboration, including providing feedback on proposed decisions and providing input before decisions are proposed. (See Chapter 10 for information on decision-making options.) What's important is that people know who is making which decisions, when, and how—and that they know the decision-making is done as advertised.

Step Six: Involve as Many Stakeholders as Possible in Meaningful Ways. Involve as many stakeholders as possible when the impact of decisions on them is likely to be significant and you need their buy-in to implement the results. (*Stakeholders* is defined in detail in Chapter 8.) The challenge is to do this without jeopardizing the process's and participants' ability to progress due to the numbers involved. Certainly, the use of technology for online or face-to-face participation has radically increased the number of people who can be involved in any process. For more information on the use of technology and other approaches to increase participation, I recommend Carol J. Lukensmeyer's *Bringing Citizen Voices to the Table: A Guide for Public Managers* (2013), Tina Nabatchi's and Matt Leighninger's *Public Participation for 21st Century Democracy* (2015), and the resources from the International Association of Public Participation (http://iap2usa.org) and the National Coalition for Dialogue and Deliberation (www.ncdd.org).

You can use decision-making options to help you define the level of involvement you need or want from various stakeholders. See the examples below to help you define levels of involvement for a public process convened by a governmental body or for an internal process in a for-profit or nonprofit organization. Potential stakeholders are listed on the vertical axis, and levels of involvement are on the horizontal axis. (See Chapter 10 for more information on these levels of involvement in decision-making.)

Determining Stakeholder Involvement in a Public Process (Example)

Stakeholders	Level of Involvement				
	Be Kept Informed	**Provide Feedback**	**Provide Input**	**Develop Recommendations**	**Participate in Making Decision**
Residents	At public meetings, online, and in the media	At public meetings and online	At public meetings and online		In public comment periods of board meetings
Environmental groups	At public meetings, online, and in the media	At public meetings and online	At public meetings and online		
Executive director of Sierra Club	At advisory group meetings, online, and in the media			Participate in stakeholder advisory group	
Business Community	At public meetings, online, and in the media	At public meetings and online	At public meetings and online		
President of Chamber of Commerce	At advisory group meetings, online, and in the media			Participate in stakeholder advisory group	
Builders and Realtors	At public meetings, online, and in the media	At public meetings and online	At public meetings and online	Participate in stakeholder advisory group	
Advisory Group		Listen to feedback	Listen to input	Develop recommendations for board	
Board of Directors		Listen to feedback	Listen to input	Two participate in advisory group	In public meetings

Determining Stakeholder Involvement in an Organizational Process (Example)

Stakeholders	Level of Involvement				
	Be Kept Informed	**Provide Feedback**	**Provide Input**	**Develop Recommendations**	**Participate in Making Decision**
Employees	Online and in meetings	Online surveys and participation in meetings	Online surveys and in multi-level and multi-departmental meetings	Two employees (one from shipping and one from customer service)	
Research Department	Online and in meetings	In multi-level and multi-departmental meetings	In multi-level and multi-departmental meetings	Senior manager participates in advisory group	
Marketing & Sales	Online and in meetings	In multi-level and multi-departmental meetings	In multi-level and multi-departmental meetings	Supervisor of marketing and supervisor of sales participate in advisory group	
Manufacturing	Online and in meetings	In multi-level and multi-departmental meetings	In multi-level and multi-departmental meetings	Night and day supervisors participate in advisory group	
Customers	Emails	Focus groups			
Advisory Group		Listen to feedback	Listen to input	Develop recommendations for Executive Team	
Executive Team		Listen to feedback	Listen to input	Two members participate in advisory group	In team meetings

Sponsoring and Leading the Process

Processes are most successful when they have clear sponsorship and leadership. In organizations, the management team is usually the sponsoring body. They could be the managers of a whole organization or a portion of it (e.g., the management team of a manufacturing division). In a governmental or public process, elected officials such as a board of supervisors or a city council are the sponsors. *Sponsors* provide the money and support to conduct the process and are usually the final decision-makers on the results.

In ad hoc community processes, the sponsoring bodies are usually less clear because it's more of a bottom-up than a top-down process: Identifying sponsors tends to occur spontaneously based on who shows up and who's willing to take the lead at any one time. Sponsors (who usually are also the leaders) can be anything from an ad hoc group of neighbors who want sidewalks installed in their neighborhood to the leaders of various food banks who want to coordinate their collection and distribution efforts.

The ongoing involvement and support of sponsors is critical to the success of any project. When they don't involve themselves in the process or provide the resources necessary to implement the process, it fails; people in the organization or community notice that the leaders aren't taking it seriously, so they don't either.

Sponsors are more likely to succeed in tackling complex issues if they enlist the help of a stakeholder advisory group to help them plan and lead the process. Leading the process entails planning and conducting meetings, summarizing and synthesizing input and feedback gathered during meetings and online, and drafting recommendations based on all the information gathered during the process. The challenge in organizing such a group in an organization or a public process is to make sure the group is sufficiently representative of diverse perspectives and stakeholders so that it's perceived as legitimate. One significant challenge for stakeholder advisory groups is to be perceived as honest brokers of people's input and feedback and to accurately reflect what people have said in summarizing and synthesizing the information gathered from stakeholders.

Members of stakeholder advisory groups in organizations or governmental processes can be identified in one of three ways: They're recruited by the sponsors, selected from a pool of applicants, or formed by a group of volunteers. It is usually a top-down process.

Here are important criteria for sponsors to use in selecting members of stakeholder advisory groups. Members should

- come from various functions, levels, locations, and stakeholders of the organization or community;
- bring a variety of points of view;
- be respected "thought leaders";
- have content expertise relevant to the focus of the process (or be willing to learn);
- want to work with people from different functions and levels in the organization or from diverse perspectives and backgrounds in the community; and
- have process savvy (i.e., they know how to ask good questions, listen, and plan, lead, and participate in productive meetings).

Providing an explicit and thorough charter for a sponsoring body or a representative stakeholder group helps the participants understand their role. Such a charter helps make the process understandable and transparent. Charters summarize the essential elements of the process architecture, including the following:

- the purpose and outcomes of the process;
- the process map and timeline;
- process principles;
- decision-making processes for the advisory group and the process as a whole;
- roles of the leaders and members of the group;
- roles of consultants, facilitators, and recorders; and
- operating procedures, including how, by whom, and when agendas will be developed and how, by whom, and when notes will be taken, transcribed, and distributed.

When a project involves several organizations of various types—governmental organizations, nonprofits, and businesses—that want to work together to have a collective impact on a complex issue in their community, having an explicit charter for the project's sponsoring body is critical. For the project to be successful, the charter needs to include an explicit process through which the various organizations develop a common agenda and approach along with an effective decision-making process (Kania & Kramer, 2011). A steering committee that represents the various organizations could sponsor the process while selected members of the community could lead it, supported by staff from the organizations.

The process through which a sponsoring group and a stakeholder advisory group comes together to lead a collaborative effort to tackle a complex issue is crucial to its success. Such efforts require dedication, engagement, reflection, vulnerability, and constancy. By *constancy*, I mean the intention and ability to stay mindful of oneself, the group, and the situation at hand so all three move forward in positive ways. This means using all the practices described in this book when working with one another and in leading the process.

I admired how the members of the board of the water district and the stakeholder advisory group worked together and led the 11 public meetings. They asked participants good questions, listened to them in small groups, and recorded their thoughts on large sheets of paper. At the start of each new phase, the advisory group tested whether their summary of the input or feedback from the previous phase was on target. The advisory group's recommendations to the board of directors reflected what they heard in the public meetings, and the district is implementing those recommendations.

How people are treated during any collaborative process determines their evaluation of the process itself and their perceptions of the convening body. Residents of this region continue to support the water district and its efforts to protect the water.

Preventing Cognitive Hijacking in the Design of Process Architecture

Chapter 4 described how we can get emotionally hijacked when we feel threatened and the survival mechanisms in the brain take charge. We can also be hijacked cognitively when we perceive, think, and make decisions with unconscious biases and impaired access to the prefrontal cortex. Emotional hijacking is usually the precursor.

Cognitive hijacking occurs in at least three ways. First, we all tend to look for and interpret new "facts" in ways that confirm what we already think; this is called *confirmation bias* (Haidt, 2012, p. 79). Second, holding conflicting ideas simultaneously is uncomfortable. We're driven to reduce this cognitive dissonance by justifying our beliefs or contesting those of others. Third, we go to great lengths to avoid loss or preserve the status quo; this is *loss aversion* (Thaler & Sunstein, 2009, p. 33).

Confirmation Bias. People tend to trust information that supports their beliefs and ignore or forget information that conflicts with or doesn't support them. A classic experiment illustrates the influence of prior beliefs on people's response to "objective data." Participants in the study are exposed to the results of two fake studies: One set of information supports the idea that capital punishment prevents violent crime, and the other contradicts it. When the data conflicts with their beliefs, they criticize the findings and methodology of the study. When it confirms their beliefs, they think the findings are convincing (Lord, Ross, & Lepper, 1979). These findings have been substantiated over many decades in ensuing studies (Kunda, 1990).

Confirmation bias interferes with a group's ability to come to a common understanding of the issues at hand. Individuals have their own views of what "the truth" is. This is why it's critical to include the following in your process design:

- stakeholders who represent diversity of all kinds, including ideological and intellectual diversity;
- unbiased education for all stakeholders about the issues at hand;
- the use of diverse small groups (maximum of five or six) in meetings so people can engage meaningfully and safely with one another (i.e., build bridging social capital); and
- ground rules to guide the conduct of the interactions and help people feel safe.

In small groups, ask people to (a) share how they came to believe what they believe and why it's important to them; (b) share the impact of what they're hearing in nonjudgmental, descriptive language; (c) set aside their beliefs and positions for the time being and focus on understanding; and (d) not go too long in the conversation without sensing into their bodies and being mindfully aware of their internal atmosphere.

Questions help people become aware of bias and choose to honestly consider information and points of view that challenge their beliefs. Avoid asking people to justify their beliefs—this provokes defensiveness. Instead, ask them to explain how their ideas would work in real life.

Make time and space for dissenters. Remember that socially bonded groups tend to reward conformity and unanimity and that solving complex problems requires building bridging social capital among people with multiple perspectives.

Use a variety of process tools other than discussion to help people engage in divergent and convergent thinking. For example, instead of having a freewheeling discussion about the issues at hand, brainstorm, categorize, and prioritize them. For dozens of process tools, I recommend *The Facilitator's Guide to Participatory Decision-Making*, 3rd Edition, by Sam Kaner or the resources available at Interaction Associates (www.interactionassociates.com).

Cognitive Dissonance. Holding conflicting ideas simultaneously challenges our need for certainty. It throws us into uncharted waters in which we feel adrift and possibly frightened. Unfortunately, in order to reduce our sense of dissonance and fear, we tend to rationalize our ideas and build a case against those of others. You can probably feel the constriction in your body when you move into a rigid stance of "I need to be right about this." This kind of stance elicits a combative response in others, is exhausting, and is counterproductive to the process.

As stated in Chapter 3, once we get emotionally hijacked, we go through "a refractory state during which time our thinking cannot incorporate information that does not fit, maintain, or justify the emotion we are feeling" (Ekman, 2007, p. 39). We can move through this refractory period and beyond ideas of right or wrong and true or untrue by first acknowledging the discomfort or fear we feel. Then, by sensing into our feet on the ground, our bottoms on the chairs, and our breaths moving in our bodies, we can make room for possibilities beyond right and wrong. It is in this space that seemingly disparate ideas can emerge into a new complex whole (for information on this, I recommend Peggy Holman's *Engaging Emergence* [2010]).

To help people constructively manage cognitive dissonance, include the following features in the design and conduct of the overall architecture:

- Schedule a reasonable amount of time to achieve the outcomes in each phase, and test your thinking with key stakeholders to see whether they deem the time allotments "reasonable." Maintain a human pace in meetings so people feel calm and more able to manage dissonance when it occurs.
- Educate participants about how they might be emotionally or cognitively hijacked in the process and how they can prevent and manage it when it happens.

Cognitive dissonance can also be prevented by explicitly paying attention to the discomfort people experience while holding conflicting ideas. Build on the tension among conflicting ideas to discover "new, superior ideas" by applying "integrative thinking"

(Martin, 2007). *Integrative thinking* includes considering elements of an issue that might initially seem less relevant; examining relationships among issues and causes of issues; looking carefully at how potential solutions fit together or affect one another; resisting the natural inclination to simplify things so we can feel certain and "get on with it"; and avoiding *either/or* thinking and embracing *both/and* thinking.

Normalize the tension by naming it and making a process observation and a process suggestion: "We have a number of ideas that, on the surface at least, seem contradictory. Let's take a moment of silence to individually consider what all these ideas might have in common and whether there's another perhaps larger idea that connects them in some way. What might be in the space between our points of view?" Or "This might seem a bit messy and uncomfortable at the moment. I suggest we just let this be messy a while longer and see what emerges from it. Let's do our best to hang in there with one another and this uncertainty. Are you all willing to do that?" Usually when anyone names the uncertainty, people recognize their feelings and they can calm down.

Loss Aversion. Similar to the negativity bias described previously, in which we notice threats to our safety more than we notice enhancements, we go to great lengths to avoid loss. Multiple studies substantiate that we humans feel the pain of loss more keenly than we do the enjoyment of gain (Kahneman, 2011). And the more meaningful the potential loss appears, the greater our aversion to it will be (Brafman & Brafman, 2008, p. 22).

Loss aversion inclines us to want to stay with the current situation or the status quo. As the saying goes, "Better the devil you know than the devil you don't." We find it difficult to give up what we already have for better options, especially when the losses *appear* larger than the expected gains (Bazerman, Baron, & Shonk, 2001, p. 28). Because of this, we tend to give more weight and attention to the present at the expense of future possibilities (p. 29). The challenge is how to help everyone understand how the benefits of a change outweigh the losses.

To help offset loss aversion, incorporate a specific step in which people do the following:

- bring loss aversion to conscious awareness (Have them ask themselves, "What am I working hard to protect or avoid? How meaningful or deleterious is this potential loss to me, really?");
- create a vision of the desired future state of your organization or community ("What do we want the future to be for ourselves and for the generations to come?");
- evaluate each potential solution or action against this vision ("Will it help us move toward or away from our vision?"); and
- ask over and over, "What's the win/win/win solution? What will benefit us, stakeholders, and our organization and communities as a whole?"

In addition, conduct a thorough cost/benefit analysis of any potential decision or action in all dimensions, not simply financial. Use the list of stakeholders to identify what each stakeholder or stakeholder group will lose or gain with each of the potential solutions before determining which solutions you want to proceed with. Imagine any potential unintended consequences that might eventuate for the organization and relevant communities as a whole.

Recording Interactions Visually

Visual recording is indispensable for tackling complex issues. Creating graphic displays of the various perspectives among stakeholders and relationships among the facts about an issue helps people see the issue in context.

Visual recording also enables a group to do what the brain longs to do: organize information into chunks or categories. For example, you can start an interaction by defining the problem—that is, by recording the various elements of it. When you look at the charts, you can decide whether all the salient aspects have been captured. Then you can identify what's causing the problem, generate and evaluate potential solutions, and agree on solutions you want to pursue. Having all this visually recorded in categories allows a group to go back and forth among the ideas to analyze and compare them. For example, while pointing at the relevant ideas on the wall, anyone can ask questions like "Will this solution take care of this problem without making this other issue worse?" and "How might we group some of these solutions into one project?"

If your group functions as many do, you might try talking about the whole situation at once, wandering among issues, causes, potential solutions, and how you might implement solutions. If the recorder writes separate comments on separate sticky notes or index cards, the group can more readily categorize their comments at the end of their discussion. (See Chapter 10 for more information on visual recording.)

Trying to talk about the whole situation at once without visual recording undermines the group's ability to understand and solve the problem because of the strain of trying to think about every-thing at once. This phenomenon, called "dual-task interference," has been studied in depth, primarily by psychologist Harold Pashler in the 1980s. Performance plummets when anyone, let alone a group, tries to do two *conscious* mental tasks simultaneously—for example, pressing one of two foot pedals when a high or low tone sounds while adding two single-digit numbers (Rock, 2009, p. 35).

Engaging People Virtually

Information and communication technology (ICT) can constructively complement complex problem-solving but rarely replaces the need for in-person gatherings that are actually or virtually face-to-face. Some advantages of ICT include being able to engage more people and to do so asynchronously. People can chime in whenever they want from wherever they are.

Unfortunately, contributing to a "conversation" via blogs, tweets, and online comments as occurs now aggravates cognitive hijacking and polarization as people communicate in short bursts and often anonymously. It's usually impossible to hold anyone accountable for insulting remarks or "facts" that aren't true. People broadcast their biases without the opportunity to listen to others with the benefit of being in relationship with them or the ability to observe body language, hear the tone of their voice, or look into their eyes. ICT can encourage the unfortunate dynamic of people talking *at* one another instead of *with* one another.

However, some platforms are emerging that might allow us to interact as effectively virtually as we do in person. I expect tapping the potential of new media platforms will involve another set of skills and practices—ones we can develop together.

Key Points

- To tackle complex issues, we need to carefully design process architecture so that people feel safe enough to engage with diverse stakeholders and complex issues with their whole selves, understand the complexity of the issues and the multiple perspectives about them, and delve into the content in constructive and productive ways without getting emotionally or cognitively hijacked.
- Designing process architecture involves
  - defining the process's purpose and outcomes in neutral and inclusive ways;
  - developing principles to guide how the process is designed and implemented;
  - making the process transparent by defining phases and outcomes and by displaying it graphically in process maps;
  - making sure everyone involved understands and owns the process;
  - clarifying the level of involvement for stakeholders and who will make which type of decisions, how, and when; and
  - involving as many stakeholders as possible in meaningful ways.
  - Process architecture is more effective and successful when it has clear sponsorship from a group of leaders who provide the money and time to conduct the process.
- Sponsors are more likely to succeed in tackling complex issues when they enlist the help of a stakeholder advisory group to help them plan and lead the process.

- We should build elements into the architecture that help prevent cognitive hijacking, including confirmation bias (ignoring evidence that contradicts one's beliefs or cherry-picking information that supports them), cognitive dissonance (reducing dissonance with *either/or* thinking), and loss aversion (going to great lengths to avoid loss or maintain the status quo).
- Visual recording is indispensable for tackling complex issues collaboratively.

Questions for Reflection

How does your organization or community tackle complex issues now? What is working? What isn't?

What do you think are the most important aspects of process architecture?

How might carefully designing process architecture enable your group to move forward productively?

Which type of cognitive hijacking is your group most prone to: confirmation bias, cognitive dissonance, or loss aversion? What might you do to prevent it?

Epilogue

The future is not a place we're being driven to; it's a place we have the opportunity to create through our interactions. We can and must consciously choose who we want to be, how we want to relate with one another, and what we want our world to be. The opportunity we have to create such a future is here, now. It's questionable how much longer it will remain so. Decisions are being made every day that open or close our opportunities to positively shape our organizations and democratic institutions.

There are some who say, "Why bother?" or discount those of us who continue to be hopeful for the good that might still be accomplished. Their cynicism enjoins us to believe that (a) most issues are too big, too complex, or simply intractable and (b) it's impossible to bridge the great divides among us.

We can't afford the comfort of cynicism or hunkering down in our foxholes, hoping that somehow things will work out by themselves. Our quality of life and perhaps even life itself is at stake.

Again, as Dag Hammarskjöld, second Secretary-General of the United Nations, said in 1958,

> I cannot belong to or join those who believe in our move-
> ment toward catastrophe. I believe in growth, a growth to
> which we have a responsibility to add our few fractions of
> an inch. [This] is not the facile faith of generations before
> us, who thought that everything was arranged for the best
> in the best of worlds. . . . It is in a sense a much harder
> belief—the belief and faith that the future will be all right
> because there will always be enough people to fight for a
> decent future. (Lipsey, 2010, p. 29)

Many underestimate the power of conversational processes to create that decent or desirable future. Can so much depend on how we meet and interact with one another? I reply: Who else do we have but one another to figure things out? All we have is you and me and all the other *you*s and *me*s on the planet to work together to figure things out.

Thus far, however, we've been trying to make difficult choices with poor tools: the reactivity of the older parts of the brain, destructive patterns of communication, and ineffective processes. We see where this leaves us. *How* we talk with one another is keeping us from effectively considering *what* we need to talk about: understanding and solving the difficult issues facing us.

We now have the opportunity to work with better tools provided by brain science, mindful awareness, and effective process. The eight practices in this book are a synthesis of these three bodies of knowl-edge as they relate to how we meet and interact with one another. They show us how it's possible to engage with diverse viewpoints and tackle tough problems at work and in our communities. These practices are making conscious choices, being compassionate, defining intentions, opening to change, engaging with people who are different from us, using six indispensable communication skills, creating collaboration in meetings, and tackling complex issues together.

The practices described in this book can help us develop a deeper and broader view of others, the world, and ourselves—as we are and as we could be. They can help us consciously choose how we want to work together to tackle the challenges before us. Regardless of whether you're working locally, regionally, nationally, or globally, we all need to learn to talk across that which divides us so that we can create a desirable future in our relationships with one another, with our institutions, and with our earth.

My father's words to me during my college years still reverberate in my mind: "I don't care what you believe in, as long as you believe in something." He might be surprised by what I chose to believe in: you and me and our collective ability to effectively talk about what matters and save the world.

Works Cited

Adams, Marilee. 2004. *Change Your Questions: Change Your Life*. San Francisco: Berrett-Koehler.

Baime, Michael. 2011. This is your brain on mindfulness. *Shambhala Sun*, July: 45–48.

Bazerman, Max H., Jonathan Baron, and Katie Shonk. 2001. Enlarging the societal pie—A cognitive perspective. *Negotiation, Organizations and Markets Research Papers. Harvard NOM Research Paper*. September.

Begley, Sharon. 2008. *Train Your Mind, Change Your Brain*. New York: Ballantine Books.

Benkler, Yochai. 2011. The unselfish gene. *Harvard Business Review*, July–August: 77–85.

Berkowitz, Gale. 2002. UCLA Study on friendship among women. *Melissa Kaplan's Chronic Neuroimmune Diseases*. http://www.anapsid.org/cnd/ (Accessed November, 15, 2015).

Block, Peter. 1987. *The Empowered Manager: Positive Political Skills at Work*. San Francisco, CA: Jossey-Bass.

Blow, Charles. 2013. The meaning of minority. *New York Times*, Dec. 12.

--------. 2013. A nation divided against itself. *New York Times*, June 19.

Bosson, Jennifer K., Amber B. Johnson, Kate Niederhoffer, & William B. Swann, Jr. 2006. Interpersonal chemistry through negativity: bonding by sharing negative attitudes about others. *Personal Relationships*, 13: 135–150.

Bourne, Heidi. Pain and suffering. http://www.heidibourne.com/2014/06/ (Accessed June 30, 2014).

Boyce, Barry. 2012. Taking the measure of mind. *Shambhala Sun*, March: 43–49.

--------. 2011. The healing power of mindfulness. *Shambhala Sun*, January: 42–50.

Brafman, Ori. & Rom Brafman. 2008. *Sway*. New York: Doubleday.

Brown, Juanita & David Isaacs. 2005. *The World Café: Shaping Our Futures Through Conversations That Matter*. San Francisco: Berrett-Koehler.

Charles, Susan Turk, Mara Mather, & Laura L. Carstensen. 2003. Aging and emotional memory: The forgettable nature of negative images for older adults. *Journal of Experimental Psychology*, 132: 310–324.

Cuddy, Amy J. C., Matthew Kohut, & John Neffinger. 2013. Connect, then lead. *Harvard Business Review*. July–August: 55–61.

Davidson, Richard J. with Sharon Begley. 2012. *The Emotional Life of Your Brain*. New York: Hudson Street Press.

De Llosa, Patty. 2011. The neurobiology of "we." *Parabola*, Summer: 68–75.

Delman, Russell. Mindfulness and beyond: Resting in intimacy and awareness. http://www.russelldelman.com/ (Accessed January, 2013)

Delman, Russell. Awareness . . . and the light shines in the darkness. http://www.russelldelman.com/ (Accessed November, 2007)

Destano, David. 2015. How mindfulness meditation builds compassion. *The Atlantic*, July 21 (Accessed Aug. 28, 2015).

Doidge, Norman. 2007. *The Brain That Changes Itself*. New York: Penguin Books.

_____. 2016. *The Brain's Way of Healing: Remarkable discoveries and recoveries from the frontiers of neuroplasticity*. New York, Penguin Books.

Egan, Timothy. 2006. *The Worst Hard Time*. New York: Houghton Mifflin.

Ekman, Paul. 2003. *Emotions Revealed*. New York: St. Martin's Press.

Ellinor, Linda & Glenna Gerard. 1998. *Dialogue: Rediscover the transforming power of conversation*. New York, John Wiley & Sons, Inc.

Farb, Norman A. A., Zindel V. Segal, & Adam K. Anderson. 2013. Mindfulness meditation training alters cortical representations of interoceptive intention. *Social, Cognitive, Affective Neuroscience* 8: 15–26.

Fiske, Susan. 2008. Look twice. http://greatergood.berkeley.edu/article/item/look_twice. June 1 (Accessed Nov. 24, 2015).

Fischer, Norman. 2012. *Training in Compassion*. Boston, MA: Shambhala Publications.

Gobodo-Madikizela, Pumla. 2003. *A Human Being Died That Night: A South African woman confronts the legacy of apartheid*. New York: Houghton Mifflin.

Goleman, Daniel. 2013. *Focus: The Hidden Drive of Excellence*. New York: Harper Collins.

--------. 2013. Rich people just care less. *The New York Times*, October 5.

--------. December, 2013. The focused leader: How executives direct their own—and their organization's—attention. *Harvard Business Review*, December: 51-60.

--------. 2006. *Social Intelligence: The new science of human relationships*. New York: Bantam Dell.

--------. 2003. *Destructive Emotions: How can we overcome them? A scientific dialogue with the Dalai Lama*. New York: Bantam Books.

--------. 1995. *Emotional Intelligence: Why it can matter more than IQ*. New York: Bantam Books.

--------. Goleman, Daniel. 1994. New kind of memory found to preserve moments of emotion. *New York Times*, October 25.

Haidt, Jonathan. 2012. *The Righteous Mind: Why Good People Are Divided by Politics and Religion*. New York: Random House.

Hanson, Rick. 2013. *Hardwiring Happiness: The new brain science of contentment, calm, and confidence*. New York: Harmony Books.

--------. 2009. *Buddha's Brain: The practical neuroscience of happiness, love, and wisdom*. Oakland: New Harbinger Publications.

Harris, Lasana T. & Susan T. Fiske. 2006. Dehumanizing the lowest of the low: Neuroimaging responses to extreme out-groups. *Psychological Science*, 17, 847–853.

Hasson, Uri. 2010. "I can make your brain look like mine." *Harvard Business Review*, December: 32–34.

Herk, Monica. September 22, 2015. Which skills are most important on the job and which skills are in short supply? *The Committee for Economic Development of The Conference Board.* https://www.ced.org/blog/entry/which-skills-are-most-important-on-the-job-and-which-skills-are-in-short-supply, September 22 (Accessed Oct. 23, 2015).

Holman, Peggy. 2010. *Engaging Emergence: Turning Upheaval into Opportunity.* San Francisco: Berrett-Koehler.

Holman, Peggy, Tom Devane, & Steven Cady. 2007. *The Change Handbook: The Definitive Resource on Today's Best Methods for Engaging Whole Systems.* San Francisco: Berrett-Koehler.

Iacoboni, Marco. 2009. *Mirroring People: The science of empathy and how we connect with others.* New York: Picador.

Isaacs, William. 1999. *Dialogue: The art of thinking together.* New York: Currency.

Kabat-Zinn, Jon. 2005. *Coming To Our Senses: Healing ourselves and the world through mindfulness.* New York: Hyperion.

Kahneman, Daniel. 2011. *Thinking Fast and Slow.* New York: Farrar, Straus and Giroux.

Kaner, Sam. 2014. *Facilitator's Guide to Participatory Decision-Making, 3rd* Edition. San Francisco: Jossey-Bass.

Kania, John & Mark Kramer. Winter, 2011. Collective impact. *Stanford Social Innovation Review*, Winter: 36–41.

Katie, Byron. 2002. *Loving What Is: Four questions that can change your life.* New York: Three Rivers Press.

Keltner, Dacher. 2010. The compassionate instinct. In *The Compassionate Instinct.* Dacher Keltner, Jason Marsh, and Jeremy Adam Smith, Eds., 8-15. New York: W. W. Norton.

Kim, W. Chan & Renée Mauborgne. 1997. Fair process: managing in the knowledge economy. *Harvard Business Review*, July-August, 65-75.

Killingsworth, Matthew A. & Daniel T. Gilbert. November, 2010. A wandering mind is an unhappy mind. *Science*, 330, 932.

Kornfield, Jack. 2008. *The Wise Heart: A guide to the universal teachings of Buddhist psychology*. New York: Bantam Books.

Kraus, Michael W. & Dacher Keltner. *Signs of Socioeconoomic Status: A Thin-Slicing Approach*. http://greatergood.berkeley.edu/dacherkeltner/docs/kraus.inpress.pdf (Accessed Nov. 19, 2015)

Kunda, Ziva. 1990. The case for motivated Reasoning. American Psychological Association: *Psychological Bulletin*, 108: 480–498.

Labarre, Polly. 2011. Do you have the will to lead? *Fast Company*, March.

Langer, Ellen J. 2009. *Counter Clockwise: Mindful health and the power of possibility*. New York: Ballantine Books.

--------. 2005. *On Becoming an Artist: Reinventing yourself through mindful creativity*. New York: Ballantine Books.

Lamott, Anne. 1994. *Bird by Bird: Some instructions on writing and life*. New York: Anchor Books.

Lewis, Thomas, Fari Amini, & Richard Lannon. 2000. *A General Theory of Love*. New York: Vintage Books.

Lieberman, Mathew D. 2013 *Social: Why our brains are wired to connect*. New York: Crown Publishers.

Lipsey, Roger. 2010. Desiring peace: a meditation on Dag Hammasrskjöld. *Parabola* 35, 29.

Logan, John R. March 24, 2011. The persistence of segregation in the metropolis: New Findings from the 2010 Census. *American Communities Project of Brown University* http://www.s4.brown.edu/us2010/Data/Report/report2.pdf (Accessed Nov. 23, 2015)

Lord, Charles G., Lee Ross, & Mark R. Lepper. 1979. Biased assimilation and attitude polarization: The effects of prior theories on subsequently considered evidence. *Journal of Personality and Social Psychology*, 37: 2,098–2,109.

Lukensmeyer, Carolyn J. 2013. *Bringing Citizen Voices to the Table: A guide for public managers*. San Francisco, CA: Jossey-Bass.

Martin, Roger. 2007. How successful leaders think. *Harvard Business Review, June: 60–67.*

Miller, Lisa. 2012. The money-empathy gap. *New York Magazine, July 1* (accessed November 19, 2015).

Nabatchi, Tina and Matt Leighninger. 2015. *Public Participation for 21st Century Democracy.* San Francisco, CA: Jossey-Bass.

Oliver, Rosamund. 2013. Being present when we care. In *The Healing Power of Meditation,* Andy Fraser, Ed., 66–78. Boston: Shambhala.

Porges, Stephen W. 2011. *The Polyvagal Theory: Neurophysiological foundations of emotions, attachment, communication, and self-regulation.* New York: W. W. Norton and Company.

Putnam, Robert D. 2000. *Bowling Alone: The collapse and revival of American community.* New York: Touchstone.

Putnam, Robert D., and Lewis Feldstein. 2003. *Better Together: Restoring the American Community.* New York: Simon and Schuster.

Ramachandran, V. S. 2011. *The Tell-Tale Brain: A neuroscientist's quest for what makes us human.* New York: W. W. Norton.

Ratey, John J. 2002. *A User's Guide to the Brain: Perception, attention, and the four theaters of the brain.* New York: Vintage Books.

Reardon, Sean F. & Kendra Bischoff. Growth in Residential Segregation of Families by Income, 1970-2009. US2010 Project http://www.s4.brown.edu/us2010/Data/Report/report111111.pdf (Accessed Nov. 23, 2015).

Rilke, Rainer Maria. 1934. *Letters to a Young Poet.* New York: W. W. Norton.

Rock, David. 2009. *Your Brain at Work.* New York: HarperCollins.

Rogers, Carl R. & F. J. Roethlisberger. 1991. Barriers and gateways to communication. *Harvard Business Review,* November-December: 105–111.

Rogers, Carl R. 1961. On Becoming A Person: A Therapist's View of Psychotherapy. Boston, MA: Houghton Mifflin.

Rome, David I. 2014. *Your Body Knows the Answer: Using your FELT SENSE to solve problems, effect change & liberate creativity.* Boston, MA: Shambhala.

Rosenthal, Robert & Lenore Jacobson. 1968. *Pygmalion in the Classroom*. New York: Holt, Rinehart, and Winston.

Ryan, Joan. 1998. The path of honest ignorance. *San Francisco Chronicle*, June 21.

Senge, Peter M. 1990. *The Fifth Discipline: The art & practice of the learning organization*. New York: Currency.

Shaw, George Bernard. 1916. *Pygmalion*. New York: Brentano.

Sibbet, David. 1994. *Graphic Guide to Facilitation: Principles and Practices*. San Francisco, CA: The Grove Consultants International.

Siegel, Daniel J. 2011. *Mindsight: The new science of personal transformation*. New York: Bantam Books.

--------. 2011. The neurobiology of "we." *Parabola*, Summer: 68–75

Siegel, Ronald D. *The neurobiology of mindfulness: Clinical applications*. http://www. nicabm.com/ (Accessed Oct. 18, 2011)

Smith, Huston. 1994. *The Illustrated World's Religions: A guide to our wisdom traditions*. San Francisco, CA: HarperCollins.

Smith, Jeremy Adam. Aug. 6, 2014. How to foster empathy for immigrants. http://greatergood.berkeley.edu/article/item/how_to_foster_empathy_immigrants (Accessed Aug. 28, 2015).

Stafford, William. 1998. *The Way It Is*. Minneapolis, MN: Graywolf Press.

Stephens, Greg J., Lauren J. Silbert, & Uri Hasson. 2010. Speaker-listener neural coupling underlies successful communication, *Proceedings of the National Academy of Science*, June 18: 1–6. (www.pnas.org/cgi/doi/10.1073/pnas.1008662107)

Sweeney, Michael. 2009. *Brain: The complete mind*. Washington, D.C.: The National Geographic Society.

Tan, Chade-Meng. 2012. *Search Inside Yourself: The Unexpected Path to Achieving Success, Happiness (and World Peace)*. New York: Harper Collins.

Taylor, Shelley E., Laura Cousino Klein, Brian P. Lewis, Tara L. Gruenewal, Regan A. R. Gurung, & John A. Updegraff, John A. 2000. Biobehavioral responses to stress in females: tend-and-befriend, not fight or flight. *Psychological Review*, 107: 411–429.

Thaler, Richard H. & Cass R. Sunstein, 2009. *Nudge: Improving Decisions about Health, Wealth and Happiness.* New York, Penguin Books.

Watts, Allan. http://www.karmatube.org/videos.php?id=5625 (Accessed Dec. 5, 2015).

Wilson, James Q. & George L. Kelling. 1982. Broken windows. *The Atlantic Monthly*, March.

About the Author

Mary V. Gelinas, Ed.D., is a managing director of Gelinas James, Inc., and co-director of the Cascadia Center for Leadership. She is also an associate of the Community Democracy Workshop, a national project of Philanthropy Northwest. As an expert in organization development, process design, and facilitation, she has served boards, leaders, and organizations in all sectors with strategies based in the behavioral and brain sciences. With her partner Roger James, Ed.D she has developed pioneering and transformative approaches to leading, creating change, planning, and solving complex problems. She lives in Arcata, California.

www.gelinasjames.com

Index